Conjure
Codex

A Compendium of

INVOCATION

EVOCATION

&

CONJURATION

Conjure Codex: A Compendium of Invocation, Evocation & Conjuration
Content Editor: Jake Stratton-Kent
Art Editor: Dis Albion
Layout Editor: Erzebet Carr
Volume 1, Issue 1
©2011 Hadean Press
Cover Art ©2011 Johnny Jakobsson
ISBN 978 1 907881 01 5
All Rights Reserved Worldwide.

No portion of this book may be reproduced by any means, physical or electronic or otherwise, without the written consent of the publisher.

"Old Wizard" © Jake Stratton-Kent
"The Paladins of Earth and Fire" © Nicholaj de Mattos Frisvold
"The Tree of the Grimoires" & "Language of the Birds" © Humberto Maggi
"Modern Grimoiric Evocation" © Michael Cecchetelli
"Infernal Conjure Craft" © Chad Barber
"Lessons from Ginen" © Drac Uber
"Nefarious Occult Dealings: Ghosts and Spirit Expeditions in the Graeco-Roman, Hoodoo and Vodou Magical Traditions" © Kim Huggens

"Ritual for Life" & "Dark Lord" © Mrs. V. Midian
"Hades", "Astaroth" & "Hekate" seals © S. Aldarnay
"Garden Goblin" © Erzebet Carr
"Exu mor", "Exu retinue", "Rainha" & "Rei Rainha" © Nicholaj de Mattos Frisvold
"Spirit Chest" © Mike Cecchetelli
"Botsina de-qardinuta" & "The aureate elixir of Astaroth " © Johnny Jakobsson
"Infernal Mojo" & "Wax Dolly" © Chad Barber
"Fet Guede" & "LaSirene Wanga" © Drac Uber

HADEAN PRESS
WWW.HADEANPRESS.COM

Conjure Codex

Edited by Jake Stratton-Kent
Dis Albion & Erzebet Carr

ILLUSTRATIONS

Ritual for Life   2
original photography by Mrs. V. Midian

Seal of Hades   5
original art by S. Aldarnay

Seal of Astaroth   9
original art by S. Aldarnay

Garden Goblin   10
original art by Erzebet Carr

Exu Retinue   16
Exu Mor   21
Rainha   28
Rei Rainha   33
original photography by Nicholaj de Mattos Frisvold

The Tree of Yggdrasil   35
from the 1908 edition of 'Sæmund's Edda', illustrated by W.G. Collingwood

Spirit House   55
original photography by Michael Cecchetelli

Botsina de-qardinuta   92
The aureate elixir of Astaroth   93
original paintings by Johnny Jakobsson
photographed by Max Kielland

Wax Dolly   116
Infernal Mojo   121
original art by Chad Barber

Fet Guede   126
La Sirene Wanga   127
original photography by Drac Uber

Untitled   135
original art by Audrey Melo

Necromancer's Altar, Detail   136
Necromancer's Altar   142
original photography by Dis Albion

Seal of Hekate   180
original art by S. Aldarnay

Dark Lord   181
original photography by Mrs. V. Midian

Table of Contents

9	**Editorial**
10	**Old Wizard** *Jake Stratton-Kent*
16	**The Paladins of Earth and Fire** *Nicholaj de Mattos Frisvold*
34	**The Tree of the Grimoires** *Humberto Maggi*
46	**Modern Grimoiric Evocation** *Michael Cecchetelli*
56	**The Comte de Gabalis** *Abbé N. de Montfaucon de Villars, English trans. anon.* *with an introduction by Jake Stratton-Kent*
88	**The Great and True Natural Secret of the Queen of the Hairy Flies** *trans. Brendan Hughes, with addenda by Jake Stratton-Kent*
94	**Language of the Birds** *Humberto Maggi*
108	**Infernal Conjure Craft** *Chad Barber*
126	**Lessons from Ginen** *Drac Uber*
136	**An Interview with England's Most Notorious Necromancer** *Jake Stratton-Kent talks about his practices and beliefs*
150	**Nefarious Occult Dealings: Necromancy, Ghosts and Spirit Expeditions in the Graeco-Roman, Hoodoo and Vodou Magical Traditions** *Kim Huggens*

Welcome to the
Conjure Codex

This is in many ways a new kind of occult journal. In the most important sense of all, it is new in that it presents us – issue by issue – with a vision of magical practice across the globe. Most particularly magic in the original and perennially relevant sense, of conjuring spirits to achieve magical purposes. This primeval focus was often obscured and ignored in the under-informed and over-opinionated occult revival of Western magic (1875-1975), of which traces still remain. With the *Conjure Codex* it could be said to return, if it were not that in reality it never went away.

The journal breaks new ground also in presenting us with inter-related material from a range of traditions, embracing ancient cultures, the grimoires, New World traditions and others; by publishing new translations and rare texts alongside accounts of work in these traditions, and elucidations of them. Certainly it would be better had this ground been well-trodden before. Sadly it has been long neglected or pushed to the borders by obsession with other, lesser matters. In reparation for this past neglect here is no over-appreciation of Aleister Crowley or other fledgling pioneers – those who sought to sweep the old approaches under the carpet in a welter of egoism and 'modern' improvements; who alleged they had superseded the ancestral traditions of several continents before they ever examined them properly.

Instead we bring you core material, some of it of enduring and extensive influence, such as the *Comte de Gabalis*, whose importance few have suspected in the modern era. So too we invite contributions including new translations and analyses of operative systems of spirit magic from around the globe.

Old Wizard

by Jake Stratton-Kent

My apologies in advance

for not including in this article any well-crafted paradigm of thought-forms and archetypes existing in the human mind, and for speaking so simplistically of spirits and manifestations. While I speak of spirits as if they possess a separate existence, it is not that I have failed to consider other theories. It is merely that such theories take up a lot of time and energy in the debating room that could be better spent in the Oratory.

Whether their existence is mental or not, Cerberus and Persephone existed for others long before I did, and will continue to do so after I have gone. Since they do not only exist for me, it is of little practical importance how they exist, if indeed the human mind is capable of answering such questions. In practice, the appropriate rites put us in touch with such entities, and I prefer to pursue excellence in the performance rather than the explanation. If this approach is not to your taste, consider acquainting yourselves with my perspective as an exercise in anthropology; since I am reasonably old and my methods are older, also an exercise in ancient history.

Without expecting any sympathy, I know from personal experience that older magicians are misunderstood. They are of course misunderstood by the non-spell-casting public, but also by younger magicians. It is not that older magicians aren't suitably well versed in arcane lore, and able to recite astonishingly long and unintelligible incantations from memory. Naturally we are but, nevertheless, as soon as certain details emerge we get that look known as a 'double take'. It is not – of course – the copulating with demons and the sacrificing of virgins. Everyone in our day and age understands that one does the former in order to be able to do the latter. What is likely to get us given that surprised and unsought for look is mention of such important but neglected matters as 'goetic gardening'.

Imagine if you will, that I am a magician of a certain age. It doesn't require any great feat of visualisation; my grey hairs should help you acquire the desired impression. It may also have reached your ears that I am versed in that most diabolical of texts: *The True Grimoire*. Abominated by Mathers, described by Waite as an undisguised handbook of goetic art, mysteriously omitted from the reading list of the A∴A∴ lest it corrupt the disciples of the Great Beast... You get the picture, and yes I am exceedingly well versed in it.

Among the items required for *The True Grimoire*'s ritual is what is known as an *aspergillus*. Essentially this is a bunch of herbs tied to a handle on a Wednesday under a waxing moon, and used for sprinkling holy water. Well, strange as it may seem, it doesn't require too many waxing moons to go by before the herbs dry out and shed their leaves everywhere. If allowed to, with time the aspergillus becomes more like some dried stalks on a stick. So naturally the old codger takes his magical knife into his magical garden and cuts some more magical herbs, tying them firmly to the same handle with a thread spun by virgins. (Incidentally, if no thread spun by virgins is available, a cord from a crucifix will suffice).

This being the case, of course the goetic conjurer needs a herb garden. Oddly enough the idea that gardening is integral to goetic magic often strikes young neophytes as a joke. They only realise I am deadly serious when I hand them a spade! The truth is that as time goes on the garden becomes more important magically than the great Circle of Art. So, far from being the result of advancing age, interest in gardening is a natural consequence of goetic practicalities.

The *True Grimoire* has a spirit whose role is herbal medicine, and with regular attention the spirit is likely to move into the herb patch. When, that is, he isn't hanging around the kitchen, another place much busier in goetic work than youthful conjurors generally anticipate. Herbal lore is actually a lot more useful in goetia than some stuff young magicians expect of older wizards, like fluent Hebrew. So yes, the spirit of herbal lore got that attention and we became good friends. He's a shy, mischievous, but a friendly and intelligent creature, disconcertingly resembling a goblin with a grin.

That is another thing which gets me funny looks from younger wizards. When I confess to dealing with the damned, the dead and the demonic, I get approving looks, slaps on the back and other generation-crossing expressions of camaraderie and mutual understanding. They expect me to traffic with devils, but a goblin in the garden? That, like the gardening, is likely to result in sideways glances to check if I am indulging in a leg-pull. Which I am not, although said goblin certainly has a sense of humour. When I asked for knowledge of herbal lore the spirit arranged for me to receive a large box of books on herbalism. Although the books cost me nothing the acquisition of herbal knowledge certainly involved more effort than waking up one day and miraculously knowing it all. However, the relationship with the spirit is more than adequate compensation.

It is no surprise to me that these details differ from what is written in books. From my point of view, approaches to goetia that remain – rather than begin – 'by the book' become stale and clichéd. Reliance on the book once some experience with it has been gained is neither satisfying nor convincing. Old wizards like myself, who hail from a time before magic became commercially driven, are prone to more experimental approaches – departing from the more instantly recognisable avenues. As time goes on it becomes apparent that some of these departures make sense of older traditions – and others not so old – whose relationship with goetia is at first less than obvious.

In these days of niche markets, modern occultism is prone to dividing the magic of the past into brands. Drawing links between magical approaches in different periods and cultures can draw suspicion where none is necessarily deserved. The idea that some old bloke might be right, and the mass produced manuals might be wrong can take a long time to arise. Such prejudice is especially likely when he insists on drawing parallels, say, between magical papyri and later grimoires which are considered different brands – even though the papyri were written in the same language as that in which the word goetia first occurred. Such fashion-driven suspicion is not soothed when I go on to compare both with New World magical traditions.

But let's not get ahead of ourselves. Did I not mention my interest in a certain abominable book? Known as the *Grimorium Verum* (*The True Grimoire*), doubtless it seems conventional enough at first glance. Those familiar with the grimoires may notice some departures from the genre here and there if they look closer. Where it resembles the others is in an apparently two dimensional view of the spirits. Though some signs of personality are not lacking, they are not exactly emphasised either. This is a generic feature of the grimoires, and another area where an old conjurer's chance remarks are likely to surprise those who have yet to get below the surface. Where *The True Grimoire* scores is that, when applied thoroughly, its process leads below the surface very quickly.

Need I point out that books are almost entirely composed of near two dimensional surfaces? Getting below the surface can take different routes. Whereas you get to know the characters in a novel by reading about them, reading a grimoire only acquaints you with the ritual. It is by performing the ritual you get to know the 'characters'. Assuming the ritual isn't the scaredy-cat one where the 'characters' are enclosed in a triangle and threatened with dire punishments for any attempt to get to know you better. Which the *Verum* ritual isn't – it is based not on divisive threats but on the much-maligned process known as the pact. The word *pact* means a mutually binding agreement, which, you may be surprised to hear, is also the meaning of the word conjure, the literal meaning of which is 'to swear together'. A fairly obvious parallel, for those who are not cynical about such things, is the marriage vow. The relationship is one of give and take, and involves getting to know one another, working together and mutually assisting one another.

Once you get to know a spirit, the two-dimensionality of its description in the grimoire rapidly fades, and its character or inner nature becomes apparent. At first this may appear to be coming from you, reading nuances into the text, but in time it becomes obvious that it is the nature of the spirit unveiling itself.

For example, a spirit whose supposed role is 'power over women' can be as helpful in getting over a bad relationship as in getting a frustrated conjurer laid, quite possibly more so. Assuming the conjurer is male, understanding the nature of the spirit may reveal what qualities women find attractive in men. By extension, if the conjurer is female they may enjoy the presence of this spirit on account of its possessing these qualities. On becoming familiar with the grimoire you may notice this same spirit being involved with processes that have no obvious relation to its stated power. This too is indicative of the fuller nature of the spirit, which reliance on the tabulated powers would not clarify.

So, with practice, spirits develop a well-rounded character, and an increased possibility of ongoing relationships with spirits rapidly develops from this. If this is reminiscent of Voodoo religion, that is all to the good.

Incidentally, another aspect of the processes of *The True Grimoire* (which provides another parallel with Voodoo ceremonial) is the potential for evoking more than one spirit in one ritual. The ritual where I first became acquainted with the spirit alluded to above was one of these. While not all of my rituals are productive of spectacularly striking visuals, this one certainly was. One of the spirits evoked looked very similar to his portrait in another grimoire, and I must confess that my mouth dried to desert-like aridity at the sight. However, although no such instruction appears in the text, I was able to spontaneously croak out the words 'come not in that form', whereupon the spirit took on another less frightening appearance. Several others appeared who had no portrait available, and it was extremely interesting to see that their shapes were indicative of their powers.

In one striking case this was a matter of posture and demeanour, rather than complex symbolism. The spirit exuded power and confidence, the self-possessed calm of a powerful athlete at rest. This was a good deal more impressive than the hideous features or waving tentacles of popular imagination. It was also very appropriate to his role of aiding male magicians in their love life. Similarly the grinning and green-skinned goblin, which looks so natural peeping out from the cover of a herb garden, has at very least a natural appearance for his role.

Another aspect of evocatory work, which draws together threads from the papyri and comparatively modern approaches, involves 'the assumption of god forms'. This is usually seen as a mental or astral technique, whereby the magician deliberately envelops themselves in a visualised shape. Such indeed it can be, but occasions exist where these forms appear quite spontaneously, and involve shapes the magician had not practiced. On one momentous occasion I was performing the ritual of the Headless One (the so-called Bornless Rite), as a preliminary to a multiple evocation. Completely spontaneously I found myself in the form of the god Set, with reddish skin, the Typhonian head and – most spectacularly of all – a forked tail lashing to and fro. This experience was way beyond my normal powers of visualisation, and occurred without any conscious effort. That it was a result of performing the ritual particularly well I do not doubt. Having identified myself successfully with the Headless One (who in some aspects of Graeco-Egyptian syncretism is a form of Typhon) I spontaneously took on one of his forms. While the Golden Dawn's 'assumption of god-forms' gives us a modern perspective, it would be ingenuous to imagine that the magicians of antiquity had no such experiences.

All of which brings me to a suitable place to bring my antique ramblings to a conclusion. Much as some modern pagans imagine that their magic derives from a Celtic twilight, if not a Neolithic matriarchal age, so modern ceremonial magicians imagine their practices are rooted in the teachings of Moses or his medieval successors. This fantasy is just as deserving of demolition by a sympathetic academic like Ronald Hutton as is the origin myth of modern pagan witchcraft. The truth is that ceremonial magic, and a good many of its adjuncts, has its origins not in ancient Judea but in the Graeco-Roman world. From an informed and impartial perspective this is hardly surprising; magic has been a long-standing part of our culture, much of which is built on the foundations of Imperial Rome and classical Greece. Give or take some local variations, the magic of the Roman period uniformly resembled that of the papyri, and the differences arising in the later grimoires are little more than a veneer suited to later religious fashion. There are – I optimistically presume – modern magicians who, while traditionally-minded, do not require their magic to be deceptively edited to the Judaeo-Christian model. They can save themselves a good deal of time by getting to the roots of their tradition and its practice, by focussing primarily on classical antiquity rather than the Kabbalah.

A detailed comparison of the papyri with the essential elements of the grimoires is beyond the space available. Nevertheless, a little investigation and thought will rapidly show that conjuring spirits at a crossroads has far more to do with the ancient cult of Hecate than with the Ten Sephiroth. When rituals in seventeenth century grimoires share the same outlines as rituals in second century papyri, except for the increase in use of Hebrew divine names, the main lines of continuity in the tradition should be apparent. There are lessons too in the remarkable facility with which elements of ritual magic can be integrated with African 'paganism' in the New World, and vice versa.

In my youth, which I remember vividly enough to be reasonably sure it actually happened, I supposed that ancient magicians had a better idea of what they were doing than we do. While I have come to appreciate the many benefits of modern science, and have some idea of the limitations of ancient belief, this supposition and its consequences have proven useful in my career as a magician. A wholehearted pursuit of ancient technique, without demanding modern explanations in advance of trying them, has served me well. Having become reasonably ancient myself, I have sought here to share the fruits of my labours with the younger generation, in the hope that they will be equally wholehearted. If I have encouraged younger wizards to peruse the Greek magical papyri, to compare the spirits of the grimoires with Voodoo gods, and to plant a herb garden, then my efforts will have been well served.

The Paladins of

A short exploration on the Cult of Exu and Spirit possession

"the devil has a bad reputation exactly because of his divinely appointed role as the one who affirms truth and oneness by negation."

Earth and Fire

Nicholaj de Mattos Frisvold

The iconography of *Kimbanda/Quimbanda* paints the king and queen of Inferno with wide strokes upon the canvas of night. Black and red dominates the cult as much as the stroke of midnight sets the seven kingdoms ablaze and announces the arrival of the denizens of the Underworld. With laughter and challenging counsel they take possession of their 'horses', or mediums, and partake for a moment of the pleasures of the earth, such as scents, foods, drinks and herbs. In these moments heaven, earth and hell meet for the possible benefit for humankind.

The diabolic iconography is in itself challenging and one can ask why these spirits chose to accept this format as their eidolon. The answer rests in the nature of challenge and the true essence of the Devil. Let us first address the nature of the challenge. Rumi said in one of his poems that: "the mother of idols is your own ego". Ego in this context refers to the *nafs ammara* or 'the compulsive ego'. This is the lower ego that pulls towards separation and by this isolates us in a state of *wham*, or delusional fantasy, where any form of self deception, arrogance and jealousy takes form. This is the challenge the Devil gives – and he gives this due to his self sacrifice. Al-Hallaj said about the 'self sacrifice of *Iblis*' that this was the role given to *Iblis* in order to effectuate the unfolding of the All-Possible. As such the Devil marks the boundaries for divine manifestation; he is the enabler and witness of the divine unity. In this way the Devil affirms the divine truth by telling what it is not as discussed at length by Al Arabi in his 'Meccan revelations', when he observes for instance that: "Through their opposites, things become distinct". This must not be seen from a dualist perspective, as *Iblis* does affirm the All Possible and thus marks the borders of negation of this possibility. It follows from this that the divine design is of such magnitude that the illusion of separation easily can enter. Constantly *Iblis* is in *tasawwuf* (popularly known as Sufism) an attribute of the 99 beautiful names of God, *al-Mudill,* meaning 'the misguider'. This role is intimately linked to temptation and challenge. *Iblis* presents to the world what god is not, so we can know what God is. Similar thoughts are found in *advaita vedanta*, which like *tasawwuf* is also monist in its outlook on the world and the divine design.

The same idea is replicated in the cult of *Exu*; the challenge is always about being a slave to one's passions and lower inclinations or their master. The Devil has a bad reputation exactly because of his divinely appointed role as the one who affirms truth and oneness by negation. It is from this angle I believe we must comprehend *Exu*, considering how willingly this spirit adopted the diabolic iconography for himself and his retinue. The Devil is misunderstood and thus there is reason to question why *Exu* chose to adopt this particular form and I believe this was done in order to continue the divine assignment as *al-Mudill*.

The similarities do not stop here. *Iblis* is described as fire, the king of djinns and like *Azaz'il* (or *Azazel*, the leader of the fallen angels in western esoteric traditions) he represents the fierceness and wrathfulness of God. We are speaking of fire, of Mars and of the south. *Exu* takes delight in chili peppers, high proof alcohol, tobacco and wormwood, which are all of the nature of Mars. Mars is traditionally said to be informed by the qualities in the *sephirah* known as *Din* or *Geburah*. We shall in passing just note the phonetic similarity between *Din* and Djinn.

The retinue of *Kimbanda* takes its redness from Mars and it takes its blackness, not only from the night and the grave, but also from Saturn and the soil, the earth itself. Bonatti in his *Book of Astronomy* tells us that Saturn also rules: "the substance of the dead which remains behind them", which echoes necromancy. This would support the common consensus that *Kimbanda* is a cult of necromantic potency. And it is here, through making the darkness, what is hidden from the sun, visible we find the domain of the *goes*, of the *pythias* and of the *manes*. We are speaking of spirits who dress 'the substance the dead left behind' – and they dress it with fire, horns and tridents. They do this in order to challenge you to become the best you can be.

The *modus operandi* for working this cult is largely by possession and ecstatic interaction with spirit. This can take various forms. You can receive messages, design, and creative inspirations from the beyond by lending out your body and mind to 'alien intelligences' so they can work through you in body, soul and mind, so to speak. We need to address the issue of spiritism at this point, because *Kimbanda* is intimately linked with *Umbanda*, and *Umbanda* is by definition of a spiritist inclination, but can we say so about *Kimbanda*?

The Character of Spiritism

Spiritism invites a set of complications in relation to necromancy. These complications are perhaps less evident in Brazil than anywhere else in the world due to the massive integration from many corners of the world conjoined with the native population. Spiritism came to Brazil in 1863, brought by homeopaths and doctors of a French origin. These doctors and healers settled in urbanized areas predominantly in the south and east of Brazil and through their work Spiritism became an immediate success. The anthropologist Roger Bastide suggests that Spiritism came as a response to a general spiritual need for salvation that had two main factions of attendance. On one side Spiritism attracted people feeling uprooted and lost in the world; Spiritism was as such a way of returning to a state of being rooted by communing with ancestors. The other fold was scientifically inclined people of the higher middle class that had a general interest in the field of parapsychology and the mysterious.

The Spiritist practice and the Spiritist doctrine must now be addressed, as the Spiritist practice is of a far more arcane pedigree than what the doctrine itself would dictate. The Spiritist doctrine owes much to modern Theosophy, or rather it was influenced by a similar zeitgeist, and took on a theosophical hue. The doctrine displays a similar pseudo-Christian[1] orientation as we find in H. P. Blavatsky's Theosophical Society. Essential for Spiritism is the dual law of metempsychosis and karma. This means that the human condition is a state of suffering, misery, loss and purification. All this is here in order to temper man into becoming "imperfect spirits of light who must suffer if they wish to regain the astral plane after death", in the words of Roger Bastide.

Allan Kardec, the founder of Spiritism, when describing the doctrine highlights amongst several tenants the following:

1. There are Spirits, all of whom are created simple and ignorant, but owning the power to gradually perfect themselves.
2. The natural method of this perfection process is reincarnation, through which the Spirit faces countless different situations, problems and obstacles, and needs to learn how to deal with them.
3. As part of Nature, Spirits can naturally communicate with living people, as well as interfere in their lives.

These 'laws' were presented in a Christian framework where Jesus Christ was seen as the moral summit of becoming; all spirits had a duty to become like Jesus Christ, not on theological grounds, but on moral. This reflects the moralist idea of karma, a clear distortion of the Brahminic idea of karma. Karma proper is not referring to any form of action, but ritual action, to act in conformity with destiny. This means simply that social status or caste gives one man different authority than it does for another. Today the idea of caste is looked upon with eyes of disgust, but originally the caste spoke about your destiny and gave a foundation for how to achieve fulfillment and happiness in this life. It was absolutely essential to stay in your station and understand all its implications in order to make good use of it. What the Spiritist doctrine tells us is that we all are destined to be Brahmins, so of course the idea of caste is abhorred because our perception of what it really entails has been falsified and deluded. This very human and material perception of karma is also infecting the idea of reincarnation and gives it a wholly profane moral content. The third point is the most agreeable, and it is here things get interesting in terms of Kimbanda. Here the Bantus felt at home, because this tied the ancestors in with nature – and it was possible to commune with them. This lingered true for them and thus in the 1890s the 'animism' of the blacks merged with Spiritism into a pejorative category, namely 'low Spiritism'. This subtle racism is sad, but it also affirms a distinction between the attitudes taken

---

[1] With 'pseudo-Christian' must be understood the presentation of a Christian doctrine that is not rooted or supported by tradition, as such it mimics tradition, but does not reflect traditional doctrine.

towards the mediumistic practice in Spiritism. Allan Kardec in his time made a great point of making a distinction between 'Spiritism' and 'Spiritualism'. He saw the latter as a doctrine opposing materialism, and could not support it since it disregarded the importance of matter. This is quite the opposite of traditional doctrine[2] that sees the unmanifest 'blackness', the world of ideas, as more real than the imperfect material manifestations.

From Spiritism was born in the 1920s *Umbanda* by the medium Zelio. What was different in this session was that Zelio was taken over by a *caboclo* (the spirit of a native Indian) referring to himself as Sete Encruzilhadas (Seven Crossroads). This spirit was very much elevated from the Spiritist perspective as its focus was on charity and 'demande', meaning the unbinding of works of magic. In spite of the morally good message it caused conflict and separation, because the cabolcos were viewed by the Spiritists to be of an 'inferior nature' and thus unsuitable as spirit guides. This perspective was of course informed by the naïve idea of progress being universally good in the sense of refining the primitive and crude and the white man being the dominator of progress. This conflict takes amazing proportions in 1942 when the First Congress of Brazilian Spiritists redefined Umbanda as an esoteric Hindu doctrine under the rulership of Saint Michael. While all this was happening the blacks and those exiled from Portugal and Spain ever since the 17th century managed to revive the initiatory secrets of the cult. At least, so says Freyre and Bastide. The *Umbandistas* on the other hand bickered between them that the African roots of *Umbanda* are from Himalaya, Ethiopia or anywhere in West Africa. Looking over the records we have from the 1920s to the 1950s, it appears to have been a complete confusion in all possible ways as to where to locate that particularly unruly strain of spirits that we might dub 'African portents of a Hindu doctrine from Egypt and Lemuria'. The truth is that the founders of *Umbanda* came both from Spiritism and 'macumba'[3]; for them the focus was on spirits of nature and the dead and they sought to fuse this into a workable cult. Here they used Kardec's idea that spirits of affinity, either of passion or intellect, would fuse into phalanxes. Hence the lines of *Umbanda* and *Kimbanda* were born.

Already in the 1940s Leal de Souza had defined that the chief of *Umbanda* was Jesus Christ syncretized with the Orixa Oxalá. His regime is quite interesting as in this first presentation of seven lines, replicating the powers of the seven planets, the seventh and last line was referred to as African and under the rulership of Saint Cyprian. Asian or 'oriental' spirits were in the third line under the rulership of St. John the Baptist. The early *Umbandistas* truly made an attempt of being good Catholics in the true sense of the word, being universal. There was room for everything in *Umbanda*. It was a great syncretistic effort that resulted in a separation where the materialist and moralist dogma of Kardec followed like a suffering ghost demanding separation. The problem continued with savage spirits, *caboclos* and spirits of African origin, namely *caticos*, and the latter class of spirits were assigned the infernal halls and made ambassadors of Hell. This was only natural given the Spiritist dogma of necessary elevation of all spirits towards the Christ principle. Some spirits were degraded and savage, *pagão*, or pagan (just here, in the terminology of the Christian conditioning is evident). They needed elevation and *Umbanda* was the answer.

---

[2] Traditional doctrine must be understood as rooted in true metaphysics and here we find amongst many Plato and Plotinus as portents and sustainers of traditional doctrine.

[3] A common reference to any form for magic, but especially 'black magic'.

"The truth is that the founders of umbanda came both from spiritism and 'macumba'; for them the focus was on spirits of nature and the dead and they sought to fuse this into a workable cult."

Let us now comment on the meeting point. As seen it was certainly not in the doctrine, but in the methodology. A typical séance focuses around the medium that is a passive channel for whatever is passing through (let's keep in mind that originally Spiritist doctrine indicates that any spirit in nature can enter) and a conductor of the séance. The conductor is responsible for maintaining order in the circle, to dispel malefic spirits and to structure the communication. Spiritists seek communion with our departed ones and seek to elevate them, but this idea of elevation towards the light infests how they see all spirits. The goal is a big ball of light, and let me say, I am not defying this idea of light, but I find the way it is understood to be dislocated from tradition and quite infantile. Light must be reached in the assigned station, this by and in itself generates union. This means that light must pulsate from the assigned station and waymark. The oneness is a complex of manifest possibility that belongs together as One. The séance itself is interesting as it involves the interaction between a passive and active principle and there is reason to believe that it was here, from the nature of the séance itself, that the Africans (especially of a Bantu origin) adopted Spiritism as a useful format for spirit congress, but their understanding of what happened was not bound by the Kardescist doctrine. In the face of Spiritism and *Umbanda* a return was actuated.

The Metamorphosis of Death and Fire

To establish the African origins of *Kimbanda* is close to impossible. This I believe is due to both *Umbanda* and *Kimbanda* being purely Brazilian – and with this I mean it became what it is due to a spiritual synthesis that honors the land itself. We have few records to point us in the right direction, but the practice that became known as *Kimbanda* during the establishment of *Umbanda* carries a triple impulse. Here we find remnants of European peasant practice, native practices and African practices. And curiously the 'black magic' banquet performed by 'proto *kimbandistas*' is somehow similar to the Spiritist séance. The difference is however that these 'old school' magicians were not working within a pseudo-Christian parameter, but a natural one. And yes, I say, 'magicians', because they seemed to be active actors in creating their own world and fate. In all this Christian focus it is interesting to note that in the 1940s people were very clear in this matter. *Umbanda* from its etymological root derived from the Angola term *ymbanda*, a name used in reference to the chief of the cult.

The phalanxes of *Umbanda* became Legions in *Kimbanda* in the 1940s, but before this matters were quite different. The origins of *Kimbanda* must be addressed in relation to slavery and its consequences. In many ways we can recognize a sociological similarity between the gradual shaping of *Kimbanda* and the birth of the *Petwo* nation of *Lwa* in Haitian Vodou. The first consequence of slavery is the separation of families, and considering the importance of ancestral lineage in all West African cults this gave a hard blow to continuity. Instead new ancestral foundations were created for the generations to come. In the sea of time memories were fused and blended with cultural diversity. People from diverse clans, families and nationalities met in these unique circumstances and from sympathy and similarity, Brazilian cults grew out from memory and land. For instance, as both Gilberto Freyre and Saint-Hilaire commented, 'the Indians had a preference towards the Africans' and for the slaveholders anyone of a mixed blood would automatically be considered as 'not-white'. Children from interracial marriages or liaisons also found themselves gravitating both by force and identity with African and Indians. An important meeting point was the *quilombos*. These were safe places around the country where runaway slaves and other outcasts could seek refuge. It was here the Slave protest and revolt started – and it was here we find *Kimbanda* in its more original form. The word *quilombo* gained rapidly a slightly different meaning in the sense of being any gathering of blacks. Like in a poem of Gregorio de Mattos where we read:

"All these *quilombos*
With peerless masters
Teaching by night
Calundus and fetishism

This much I know; in these dances
Satan's an active partner
Only that jovial master
Can teach such ecstasy"

Calundu is the name of an Angola spirit, which Bastide suggests possesses women during labor. This is indicative of a strong Bantu element present in the formative stages of *Kimbanda*. In the state *Minas Gerais*, where slaves were used in mining, we find more *quilombos* than anywhere else in Brazil. These *quilombos* were also referred to as *calundas*. The historian Aires da Mata Machado Filho holds the view that it is exactly here we find the survivals of what was once Bantu faith, as the priests were called *ngangas* and their cult focused largely on *Zambiapungo* (God) and *Cariacariapemba* (the spirit of fire, syncretized with the Devil). In these *calundas* they performed *engiras*, which is still in use today under the name *gira*, in reference to the festive gathering in celebration of spirit. The Bishop Dom João Nery described one of these gatherings that he seemed to have observed while hiding close by – or in participation. He describes a ceremony where two tables are worked. One of them dedicated to Sta. Barbara and the other to Sta. Mary. The presiding priest and the spirit taking possession of him are both referred to as *Tatá*. During possession the *Tatá* chews the embers of the coal used for the incense whereupon he is given wine and herbs. In this state initiations are performed, but also what the Bishop calls 'ceremony of faith'. At some point in the service the *Tatá* starts to beat the ground before the tables with a '*quimbandon*', which here means 'a whip'. The goal of the service is to enter into possession with a *santé*, meaning a saint, a spirit.

We also need to keep in mind that the Africans were not unfamiliar with Christianity before coming to Brazil. In fact in Angola and parts of upper Congo, at least, we find the syncretizing of nature spirits with saints already in the 16th Century. Certainly in the 16th and 17th Century the popular Catholicism was of a more 'magical' character. Prayers had power and it was possible to use the divine power for healing and hexing. The *mana* or *ase* that embedded potency and force in all things were easily recognized as the power behind prayers.

What we are left with is a cult that is focusing on the powers of the spirit of fire, the importance of receiving and transmitting *santé* with the prospect of teachings and healings. The ecstatic character of this cult along with its magical Catholicism, indigenous and African elements was as we have seen earlier difficult to fully unite with *Umbanda* in the early 20th Century. They were given a line under the rulership of Saint Cyprian and somehow the spirit of fire *Cariacariapemba* (at times also called *Bombongira* and several other epitaphs) was fused with a fiery Yoruba *Orisa*, namely *Èsú*. This is quite remarkable, as prior to the founding of *Umbanda* Yoruba cults did not feel much inclined towards the Bantu derived cults. I believe what happened was a perceived similarity between the Bantu fire spirit and *Èsú* led to a linguistic syncretism into Exu. Exu then become the master of *macumba* and the chief of the kingdoms at the left side of God. And in this manner the legions of night with its spiritual potencies, void of light and in need of elevation, were then incorporated into *Umbanda* under the name *Kimbanda*. Prior to this it seems that the reference to the practices typical for *Kimbanda* were looser. It could be *macumba, magia negra, calunda, catimbó*, juju and so forth.

So, even if these cults of fire and night were similar in some respects with Spiritism in the way of having a medium or mediums to channel spirits, they were quite different in doctrine. Not only this, in Spiritist séances the medium was considered a passive receptor and as someone particularly gifted. For the *calundeiros* the medium was an active role and the gift of mediumship was ideally passed on to everyone gathered in the *gira*. Let us now look more in depth at the phenomena of possession and altered states of consciousness.

THE POTENCY OF POSSESSION

Possession is derived from the Latin *potencia*, referring to a legal function of having the power to possess your belongings. It was only in 1580 that it was first used to refer to demonic besiegement of a person, hence the word's further association with losing one's mind and becoming insane. Interestingly most modern dictionaries describe possession as being 'controlled by one's passion or a supernatural force'. In any case, a possession indicates that you are not exercising your vulgar and common personality. There are other forces or potencies at work. I believe there is reason to consider that spirit possession is made possible by the holders of *potencia*, the angelic class of *potestates*. The *potestates* are the 'Powers' that inform the 'Arche' or Principalities (*principatūs*) in the third heaven, where we in conformity with the Zohar find *Gan Eden*, the paradisiacal state. We find these terms in several of the epistles of St. Paul, always presented as warnings.

The Powers themselves were established as a class of warrior angels that were assigned a twofold task. They would be the carriers of consciousness and history and its distributors to all of humankind, and also they would be the fierce defenders of the divine kingdom. The servants, the Principalities, had the responsibility of delegating the knowledge of the Powers to the humans and thus blessing the material world with angelic light. Herein enters the mystery of rebellion and the Fallen Angels.

These two classes of angels, being so intimately linked with matter and humans, were naturally those most subject to temptation and fall. This is not the place to venture into this intricate mystery. I am merely pointing out that there might be a relationship between the warrior angels, the *potestates* and the form of power held by the retinue of spirits in the cult of *Kimbanda*. They both share the element of fire, the angels partake of this in the form of heat but on earth this takes the form of peppers and gunpowder that ignites the serpent within, mirroring the serpent of the heavens.

This means that possession starts from within. The potential within the person needs to be activated in order to join with the extended natural force that is called upon. Possession in other words unlocks a cosmic potential within a person that carries a specific ray. At this crossroad we find a delicate nuance, namely the difference between exercising spirit and one's psyche. With the latter I refer to possession given in what is called *equê*, to pretend to be in a state of possession. This takes the form of playing out a given spiritual theme.

At times the exercise itself can have a profound psychological effect and lead to healing of wounds of the soul. Other times, the pretender is unlocking the potential for possession and the spirit inside and around meets like flashes of rainbows – and genuine possession happens. In this range of possession, from pretending to losing consciousness while a spirit is using your flesh there is a wide range of nuances. I want to mention three forms.

The first one is 'to have *Exu* on your shoulders', the second is what is known as a 'two headed possession' and the third is a full possession. The full possession can be quite impressive and one sign of a full possession is a soft pillar of wind that is rising for a moment from the medium, just before the spirit strikes down. At this point the medium will appear to be in an internal battle as one consciousness goes and another comes. It is always exhausting to be subject to a full possession. Upon regaining consciousness the body is often tender and painful and you are often confused yourself. It takes time to master these forms of possession and they are rare. More common is the two headed possession. In this state the medium is partly aware of what is going on. The spirit is not clouding the consciousness of the host totally. This is a perfectly fine state of possession and if the medium dares to let go of the control it can also spark a full-fledged possession. In order to facilitate possession the medium's body and energetic centers can be prepared with herbs and magical powders – and also *Exu* travels well on tobacco smoke and 'spiritus'. When *Exu* or *Pomba Gira* is taking possession of their horse they need much tobacco and much liquor to stay in the human vessel. If life force offerings are given they tend to wash their hands and faces in the blood – at times eating parts of the internal organs, especially heart and liver. It seems that alcohol, tobacco and blood fixates their presence.

The last form of possession is to have the spirit 'on your shoulders'. This is an interesting form of possession, to be under the influence where you are no longer thinking your own thoughts. This is a delicate state and it demands a different form of surrendering to spirit to give up your thoughts and feelings and not the body. By doing this a vinculum of air is formed for the spirit to travel in and influence the medium. In several cases of haunting and 'demonic possession' throughout all times, it often starts with the victim either feeling something eerie around or starting to have disturbing or depressive thoughts. This would suggest that it is important to recognize the potency in this form of possession. Since this state is delicate, there are two ways of securing a true dialogue. One is to use an oracle, commonly four shells that are used to affirm what is being communicated. The other is to have an assistant that is calling the spirits and thus drives the medium into, at times, amazingly deep trance states bordering or crossing the 'shamanic'. With this I mean that this state, of having *Exu* on your shoulders, is the premise for some of the most profound possessions possible. Here possession meets dream and is why I believe dream work is a very good way of instigating contact with the denizens of Hell.

Possession is accordingly an altered state of consciousness that varies from dreamlike and airy influences to full body possession.

There is one other question that also needs to be addressed in this crossroad of spiritism/ spiritualism/ *Umbanda* and possession. All these factions have in common that they claim to work with spirits that are already to some extent enlightened, assuming that they were once unenlightened. They always have a universally celestial connotation. The departed ones, in the same manner, were called from beyond the celestial veil. This contributes to explain why *Umbanda* since the late 50s and in particular with the impact of Lourenço Braga on *Umbanda* developed hierarchies of angels side by side with the pure hierarchies of *Orixas*. *Exu* on the other hand was something set aside. Here were no celestial aromas to be found, just the smell of sulphur and gunpowder. The relocation of this spirit to Hell does lead to some serious implications that disjoint *Kimbanda* from *Spiritism* and brings it to the realm of the *nigromancer*.

Figulus Exu

I was walking at the edge of the trail
Firmly I walked when the train passed by
I heard the anvil and the hammer sounding from Hell
The Devil himself sent Exu from Hell
(Ponto cantado)

As the above *ponto cantado* ('evocative hymn') shows; *Exu* is the Devil's own representative from Hell. What the songs attest to is a diabolic imagery that brings together themes ecclesiastical, African and European. It is an icon very much shaped and molded by the Catholic Church that takes shape. The identification between the Devil, or at least his ambassador on earth, and the *Orisa Èsú* has led to countless delirious attempts of explanations. This form of forgetfulness Brazilian culture underwent was what Bastide referred to as 'the metamorphosis of memory', where even the oral transmission of sacred lore got subject to reinterpretations, caused by dislocation from ancestry.

It was a reconstructive memory that entered, in particular from the early 1900s when the Kardecists that were seen as somewhat suspect were driven to develop *Umbanda*. Kardec Spiritists possessed Christian ideals for morality and purity and a modern theosophical idea of light and its transformation. The *caboclos* were problematic to accept as an enlightened spirit for the Spiritists, while for the early *Umbandistas* this was a connection to the ancestry of the land itself. From this ambiguity the *Umbandistas* of the lower social strata somehow accepted the Manichaean dualism of the Spiritist that morphed everything indigenous, African and diabolic into a misrepresentation of the *Orisa Èsú*. The *Umbandistas* adopted the same segmentation and thus the term *Kimbanda* was used in reference to all things dark, evil, void of light and African. No wonder that there were several *terreiros,* or temples, that cultivated a strong Afro-centrism and barred Caucasians to participate – after all the distinction was partly caused by the white man's arrogance and racism.

The Yoruba *Orisa Èsú* had nothing to do with *macumba* prior to the formative years of *Umbanda*. The diabolic imagery was there as was the reference to Crossroad deities. The route of syncretism is difficult to ascertain due to lack of documentation prior to 1910, so in extension of the theory of metamorphosis, we might assume that it was the shared similarities that led to the fusion. The *Orisa Èsú* is the spirit that brings our prayers to *Olodumare*, God. It is the cosmic linguist and the power of transformation. He is associated with the lava at the centre of the earth and reputed to cause confusion when people resist change or fail to embrace destiny. The first Yoruba dictionary, brought together by the Yoruba Christian convert and Anglican minister Samuel Johnson, who died in 1901, does place in the entry 'devil' the name '*Èsú*', which has become a common standard. A curious incident as Yoruba faith does not endorse the existence of the devil as such; the association between *Èsú* and the devil is motivated by Johnson's desire to present the 'pagan' Yoruba faith as a Christian theology. The consequence is that Yoruba monist faith turns into a Manichean religion, little different in theology from Christianity, while the metaphysics perhaps remain quite eloquent.

We should at this point mention that

the Yoruba and the Bantu did not blend in very well. The Yoruba with their sophisticated and elaborated theology tended to find the Bantu world view to be base and crude and obsessed with fire and death. So, there is reason to find the origin of the iconic form of *Exu* as conglomerate of Bantu perspectives on death, fire spirits and departed masters that retained their influence upon earth from beyond the grave. Similar thoughts are found in *catimbó* as well, which affirms historical records from the beginning of slavery that the native people and Africans shared a mutual sympathy for each other.

We shall not go too deep into the nature of *catimbó*, just remark on the similarities between the use of tobacco, alcohol, possession and the focus on departed masters. In *catimbó*, this is similar and in some instances fused with the cult of Jurema, who sees their masters both as departed masters and priests that continue to influence their cult but also as *encantados*. The latter is a spiritual category consisting of people we would say were fairy-taken, simply vanishing in nature. At times this is also used in *Kimbanda*, then under the name of *catiço*. The idea of a spiritual master upon death retaining influence in this cult seem to be identical to what we find in *Kimbanda*. As such, the figure of *Exu* itself is a composite of native and African spirits of fire and earth conjoined with departed Masters that in life were dedicated to the cultivation of land, fire and night.

Figura Pomba Gira

The people of Hell is those that will take away
Take away what is not good to beyond the Oceans
Exu, King of the Lyre is Lucifer
Maria Padilha
Queen Exu woman
(Ponto cantado)

Ashtaroth is the plural form of *Ashtoreth*, so already here this Canaanite goddess of fertility, consort of Baal, is in the European grimoire tradition that seeped into the hierarchies of *Kimbanda,* as legion. In the Solomonic tradition this deity of lust and ecstasy turned into a male youthful demon riding a dragon – actually the whole imagery is quite striking in comparison to the courtesan riding the seven headed dragon in the 12th Chapter of the *Book of Revelations*. Exodus 32 speaks of the manufacturing of the golden calf and comments that they 'Indulge in revelry'. In the Book of Judges and the Books of Samuel this pagan worship the Israelites apparently had an affinity towards was directed towards 'Ashtoreths'.

As in the grimoires, *Ashtaroth* is male and identified as a force similar to *Exu Rei das Sete Encruzilhadas* (King of the Seven Crossroads). What is interesting with this *Exu* King is that several *kimbanderios* comment on the fierce presence of his female counterpart, *Pomba Gira Rainha das Sete Encruzilhadas* as being more domineering and demanding than *Exu*. This might indicate that in *Pomba Gira* a specific theme is presented that connects her both to revelry, prophecy and necromancy. I am here having in mind how *Hecate* over time saw a metamorphosis from the domains of fertility to be a mistress of ghosts holding the key and torch to the crossroads. I want to underscore that we are here dealing with a theme and not senseless syncretism. But it is interesting that in domestic shrines she was placed at the front door of the house, revealing the same perception about the crossroad and the door being both gateways. If we add a torch to this image we are luring the spirits of winter and cold to find the flame and warmth.

Pomba Gira also ventured into *Candomblé*, which is the Brazilian form for *Orisa* veneration – and in particular the *Candomblé* directing themselves towards

"In accordance with the hierarchy light flashes through the nights and invigorates the masculine principle that then seeks to join and impregnate the red mysteries held by 'queen exu woman'."

Angola as their root. It is from Angola many Bantus came to Brazil and brought their spirits under the names *mpungos* and *inquicis/nkisis*. This heritage is evident in the songs of *Candomblé de Angola* where they are not adhering to *Orisa* per se, but to Bantu spirits. Over time the format tends to have been in many places subject to a heavy Yoruba influence on both theology and format of the cult. Here we find a spirit called *Aluvaiá*. It is a male spirit of fertility and fire that curiously enough seem to be linguistically of a *Tupi* (native) origin. *Aluvaiá* possesses several qualities that are either of a Bantu and Congo origin or derivatives of these linguistic roots, such as *mavambo, marambo, mavil, sigatana* and most interesting, *pambunguera* (or in its more distorted form *Bongbongira* which most likely led to the popular form of *Pomba Gira*).

This is interesting, as from the perspective of traditional metaphysics the trinity composed of *Exu Lucifer, Exu Mor/Belzebub* and *Ashtaroth* will then reveal the traditional three colours that often indicate the presence of traditional doctrine to be informing the cult somehow. We will then find that *Pomba Gira* represents the red mysteries, while *Exu Mor* properly syncretizes with *Ashtaroth*'s spouse, *Baal Zebub*. *Exu Mor* chose to adopt the image of the goat, black lord of fertility. This leaves the white mysteries to *Exu Lucifer*. In accordance with the hierarchy light flashes through the nights and invigorates the masculine principle that then seeks to join and impregnate the red mysteries held by 'Queen Exu woman'. The quality known as *mavambo* is so pertinent for the function *Exu* and *Pomba Gira* has assumed that this term at times is used to refer to the quality of these spirits of *Kimbanda* in general. Mavambo is the form of Aluvaiá that lives at the gates and in the roads, while the other qualities mentioned do carry deep resonances not only to fire, but of blood in various forms.

THE ART OF COMMUNION

What emerges from a critical deduction of possibilities is how *Kimbanda* has gone through a tremendous synthesis with land and a great variety of cultures. It is like *Exu* and *Pomba Gira* have been molded by the fires of oppression and the ashes of every imprint made by exiled 'criminals' (or generic; those condemned for any form of *malefica*) from southern Europe, Africans, Natives and by immigration in general. The triad presided over by a unifying principle (the *Maioral*) whispers to us that they serve a particular function in the world and appease a particular spiritual need and inclination. Seeing how these spiritual qualities have taken shape the cult is truly Brazilian, but at the same time it also speaks of how transition of cults, culture and beliefs can be subject to metamorphosis in other parts of the world, especially those where Catholic faith has informed the social constructs.

Kimbanda rises as a composite of arcane principles that oversees the interaction between humans and departed ones, or the revenants, a term used by *Ishtar* and *Ereshkigal* in the Epic of Gilgamesh when they speak of the returning of the dead from the Underworld. Accepting this term, that strictly speaking was used in reference to vengeful departed ones and also informed vampire legends, the dangerous reputation is made more understandable.

When we enter into communion with these spirits we find that many of them have stories to tell of how their vibrant spirit lingered in terrestrial proximity and was adopted into the fold *Kimbanda*. Here we find people from different social layers, they are *malandros* (wise guys and trickster types), doctors or clerics. These stories at times read as hagiographies speaking of the human struggle that does not lead to divine salvation, but a fiery enlightenment of the human condition. It seems plausible to suggest that when the Roman Catholic Church introduced the idea of *purgatorium* around 1160 that the spirits of *Kimbanda*, as well as the saints find their place here. Purgatory itself was a Catholic response to the pagan practice of caring for the dead and herein meets the Cult of Saints and the *nigromantic* arts.

The prayer for the dead was a complicated affair for the Church since its early and formative years. How serious the Church took the affairs of the dead is testified by the exhumation of Pope Formosus' corpse in 897, its trial, conviction and consequent burning. Theologians constantly observed care with the dead and in particular crossroads. The 5th Century clerics Césaire d'Arles and Martin de Braga stated in their sermons that no oaths should be taken and no torches lit in crossroads in order not to call attention from the dead ones. The connection between the dead and crossroads is testified for instance in the *Laralia*, the feast of Crossroads, dedicated to *Hecate* and the *lares* of the crossroads. The patriarch of the family would then hang masks and wooden dolls representing living family members in the trees asking the spirits of night and death to take these substitutes. This suggests a similar theme resurging with *Pomba Gira*, Queen of the Seven Crossroads.

Necromancy was a form of divination that invited a particular danger for the neophyte and unprepared: to be subject to *larvaetus*. This meant to be possessed by a *larvae*, a malevolent dead person, the 'astral husk' if you will. This would lead to states that today are considered as 'demonic possession', but in reality this was commonly possessions caused by restless dead and not malefic spirits. In *Kimbanda* these spirits are often known as *kiumbas*. This word is used as a definition that covers both the Roman idea of *larvae* as well as nocturnal elemental spirits that are drawn towards passions of any form, hence their reputation of inducing obsession in people. It is in this context of the larvae we are interested, as here we find a meeting ground between Kimbanda spirit work and Spiritism in essence, but not in explanation and perception, even though we are most likely speaking of the same spiritual substance.

Safed kabbalists, like Isaac Luria, believed that wise men of good character (great kabbalists) would operate under the influence of *maggids*, which are angelic teacher-guardians of one's consciousness. But in the process of *gilgul*, or the soul's metempsychosis, it could happen that a soul in the process of migration besieged a vacant husk and through this station was able to return and influence people. For instance the possession of King Saul in the First Book of Samuel is the description of a man obsessed, bitter and enraged; it is Mars afflicted. Luria also comments that this 'soul impregnation' is possible due to many souls sharing a common root. This root is based on the spiritual limbs of *Adam Kadmon*, 613 in all, which means that this is the number of possible souls/ghosts that can attend to partake in one given impregnation. Maybe this explains the metaphysical dimensions of angelic hierarchies as well as the legions of *Kimbanda*. In later years this phenomena has been given the name of *dybbuk*.

The besiegement of vacant husks, what the dead leaves behind, was a hot topic in early Spiritism. The turning tables and ouija boards developed could at times be controlled by malefic spirits or *larvaes*, ghostly pretenders. Several cases of haunting following experimentation with making spirit contact by clueless people are often caused by these 'zombie husks'. As the Roman proverb says: "A fool embraces another fool", and this we can apply to the visible and invisible world. In *Kimbanda* the techniques for dealing with these spirits are quite simple, and in fact, in most cases the *Exu* himself takes care of these matters. A whole line of *Exus* with the epitaph, '*das Almas*' (of the Souls) are the taskmasters of metempsychosis in *Kimbanda*.

Here at the necromantic nerve we find a way of spirit congress that is highly efficient and actually equally dangerous. I believe there is reason to trace this form of activity to the Orphic traditions surrounding Apollo and the role of the *pythia*, the priestess at Apollo's temple in Delphi. There is no reason to go deeply into this myth, only to point out some factors that maybe give a slightly different perspective on the *nigromantic* arts. Apollo was in charge of the temple activity for nine months. During these months the virgin prophetesses were entering oracular states of possession where prophecies were given. The name *pythia* would suggest that the oracle was stimulated by serpentine powers, perhaps similar to the red serpent energy of wild territories. However, during the three months of winter the temple was not in function, as this was the time given to Apollo's brother Dionysus, a deity slain and resurrected, which would exemplify the necromantic dynamic. The *Laralia* was also a feast executed during the winter and as such the winter solstice emerges as a period of time where the dead were more restless than usual. Winter is also the time of year when the nights are longer and the solstice is marked by the longest night upon earth. Throughout time it was not uncommon to spend time at the grave with the departed, to eat, drink and enjoy gambling – a custom the Church abolished successively between the 4th and 7th Century. Here we find a remnant of what in *Kimbanda* is at times referred to as a banquet for the dead or, 'the communion'. Now, it must be remarked that I have only come across a small handful of practitioners that knew about this format of spirit congress, while many others claim this is a practice pertaining to *catimbó*. In any case, it is a powerful tool akin to working with infernal spirits from the Solomonic tradition by discarding protecting circles and seals. Here states of frenzy, inspiration and prophecy can take place in a macabre delight that hives the practitioner into not only an altered state of consciousness, but into the other world. Some people refer to this as 'going to the kingdom'. In many ways it resembles the idea of '*igbodu*' in Ifá, the traditional faith of the Yoruba people, and the essence behind the secrets of the '*guevo*' in Haitian Vodou.

The communion is very much similar to what happened in the prayers of the dead in Antiquity as well as all over Europe in the same time. Remnants of this practice are found in the obligatory feeding of the guests of the departed at burials, but not much is being done for the departed itself. Our ancestors interacted with the kingdom of death in more direct and involved ways. Greek and Roman funerary rites attest to the use of herbs to ward off scavengers and also to assure the peaceful transition to the afterlife. The songs of lament would both praise and aid the soul in its transition and offerings would be placed at the grave. These were libations of honey, milk and wine, but also fruits and foods were left together with gifts of any form.

During the middle ages in Franco-Germanic lands the festivities at the graveyards in honour of the dead were considered sacrilegious. St. Ambrose already in the 4th Century spoke of the pagans who went to the graves of martyrs with their ale horns after dark to commune with the dead. The ecclesiastical prohibitions from the 4th and to the 8th Century testify to a constant struggle with these pagan banquets in honour of the dead. The ecclesiastical concern with festivities for the dead is rooted in the Church father Tertullian's text *On the Soul* (made available around 210) where he reasons that the return of the dead equals the appearance of evil demons from Hell. Lecouetux refers to a sermon from around 737 where it is explicitly stated that sacrifices are prohibited in the presence of corpses and upon tombs. He further suggests that the idea of return inherited in the funeral banquets was renewed every year. In Germanic countries this took place at the winter solstice, the Yule, which was substituted with the Dionysian mystery of the birth of Jesus Christ.

So, the communion with the retinue of *Kimbanda* should be done with songs, prayers, fires, drinks and tobacco. Their temple is the crossroad and gate to their kingdom. They are called to partake of a banquet together with the living, but this banquet is the banquet of the tavern. It is the ale horn that is raised and not so much the crystal glass of noble wine. In these occasions spirits are invited to influence and possess, to literally turn the mundane temple into the kingdom, something other. In these instances the Tatá presiding take on a controlling role where the spirits are kept in line, not by treats of fire and brimstone, but by mutual respect. I believe the forms of possession taking place at these nocturnal communions reflect what could have taken place at the banquets for the dead in the past. Oracles would be uttered, earthly delights would once again be consumed and most importantly the dynamic link between the living and the dead would be exercised.

Summa

Exu was baptized
And received his cross
In the phalanx of Dom Miguel
(Ponto cantado)

The ongoing multiple synthesis and metamorphosis is revealed in the preceding *ponto* that suggests that the *'maioral'* or chief of *Kimbanda* is not under the control of a satanic principle, but rather St. Michael, the Archangel. The idea found in *Kimbanda* of spirits going through an elevation from being pagan, to being baptized and then to being given a crown is simply only a reference to the consequences of praying over the dead as typified in the nature of Purgatory. The 'purging' process is one of elevating consciousness and becomimg stable and positive spiritual influences.

In this process the shared consciousness between man and spirit, or possession, is an integral and important part. Through this act ancestral memory runs forth and releases potential in blood and soul amongst the living.

Still, they retain a particular function in showing you truth by what it is not. As such they challenge your weaknesses and they tempt your obsessive and possessive sides in order to temper and tame them so you, like them, can be master of your own life in this human journey.

SELECTED BIBLIOGRAPHY:

Bastide, Roger (1960). *Les Religions Afro-Brésiliennes.* Presses Universitaires de France: Paris
Braga, Lourenço (1951). *Umbanda e Quimbanda.* Editor Borsoi: Rio de Janeiro
Frisvold, Nicholaj de Mattos (2006). *Kiumbanda – A Complete Grammar of the Art of Exu.* Chadezoad: Brazil
Frisvold, Nicholaj de Mattos (2009). *Arts of the Night.* Chadezoad: Brazil
Guénon, René (2001). *The Spiritist Fallacy.* Sophia Perennis: NY
Johnston, Sarah, I. (1999). *Restless Dead.* University of California Press: Berkely
Lecouteux, Claude (2009). *The Return of the Dead.* Inner Traditions: Vermont
Molina, N.A. (1954). *Na Gira dos Exu.* Editora Spiritualista: Rio de Janeiro
Prandi, Reginaldo (ed.) (2001). *Encantaria Brasileira.* Pallas: São Paulo

"In the process of self-understanding this is one of the most basic laws:

we must learn to see ourselves as we are seen by the Spirits of the Dead and by other Spirits."

Michael Bertiaux

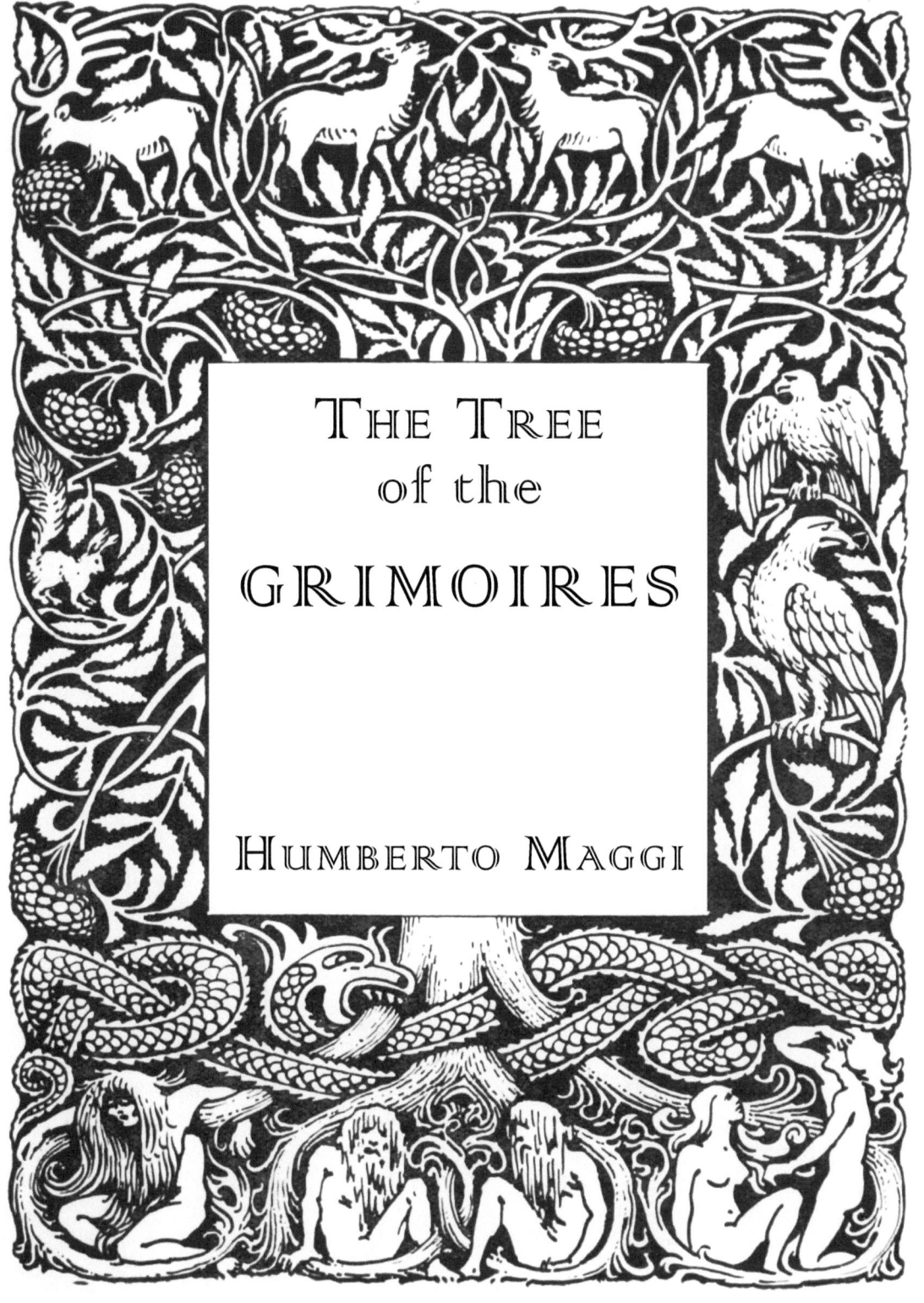

The Tree of the Grimoires

Humberto Maggi

It was in the year of 2008, during my research for the never-ending project on the life and works of Aleister Crowley – a history of the ideas behind his philosophy, poetry and magic – that I came to the seminal paper published by Aaron Leitch in the *Hermetic Virtues* e-magazine, named "Grimoire Shamanism". Aaron's exposition was thrilling, as it agreed with some conclusions I'd come to years before when reading Mircea Eliade's book on Shamanism.

Eliade's book is an amazing demonstration of scholarship and research, quoting from hundreds of ethnographic sources to establish what he believed to be the essential features of Shamanism. What became very evident for me then, going through all the information selected and thematically distributed in the book, was that almost every, if not all, magical phenomenon described in Western Tradition testimonies never deviated from the experiences reported by primitive shamans. Of course, from the testimonies of the Theurgists and the Neoplatonic mystics in late Antiquity through the Medieval and Renaissance magi up to the Golden Dawn adepts, the symbolism of the narratives varied considerably but, beneath the changing surface of different cultural moods, there are always found the same processes.

Meditative practices were not part of the magical training for western magicians until pioneers like Allan Bennett and Aleister Crowley opened the tradition to the Eastern wisdoms; previously the predominant techniques centred on the summoning or invocation of spirits. The centuries-long prohibition against the magicians under Graeco-Roman legislation and the persecution promoted by Judaeo-Christian faiths succeeded in large part in preventing magical lineages from developing. Thus we ended up with a core of magical practices founded upon Spirits and Books. Even when transcendence was the aim sought, Western magicians called upon the help and intervention of Angels and Gods to bring about the desired epiphany. The contact with these angelic or divine beings brought not only enlightenment, but was usually accompanied by the transmission of knowledge. The books of magic found themselves then at both extremes of the revelation process, being the providers of a method and also the fruit of revealed knowledge. The perfect example and one of the oldest of the known grimoires, *The Sworn Book of Honorius*, demonstrates this point perfectly, witnessing to being written with the help of the Angel Hocroel and containing detailed information both for the establishment of spiritual communications and for attaining the Beatific Vision.

Conversation with spirits and celestial visions were two of the fundamental features of primitive Shamanism, and not only the aims but also the methods and results used by primitive shamans are repeated with astonishing similarity in the grimoire tradition. Looking to some examples, we can check for a start the coinciding descriptions provided by ethnographic testimonies and the grimoire literature about the apparition of the spirits. The ethnographic data to follow comes from the aborigine's tradition studied by A. P. Elkin in his *Aboriginal Men of High Degree* and is quoted in chapter three of Eliade's work; the grimoire information comes from the *Heptameron* and Cellini's memories of the famous invocation at the Coliseum.

ELKIN	HEPTAMERON	CELLINI
However, some of them are evil spirits, some are like horses with men's heads, and some are spirits of evil men which resemble burning fires. You see your camp burning and the blood waters rising, and thunder, lighting and rain, the earth rocking, the hills moving, the waters whirling, and the trees which still stand, swaying about. Do not be frightened. If you do, you will break the web (or thread) on which the scenes are hung. You may see dead persons walking towards you, and you will hear their bones rattle. If you hear and see these things without fear, you will never be frightened of anything. These dead people will not show themselves to you again, because your miwi is now strong. You are now powerful because you have seen these dead people.	These things being duly performed, there will appear infinite visions, apparitions, phantasms, & etc., beating of drums, and the sound of all kinds of musical instruments; which is done by the spirits, that with the terror they might force some of the companions out of the circle, because they can effect nothing against the exorcist himself: after this you shall see an infinite company of archers, with a great multitude of horrible beasts, which will arrange themselves as if they would devour the companions; nevertheless, fear nothing.	Now the necromancer began to utter those awful invocations, calling by name on multitudes of demons who are captains of their legions, and these he summoned by the virtue and potency of God, the Uncreated, Living, and Eternal, in phrases of the Hebrew, and also of the Greek and Latin tongues; insomuch that in a short space of time the whole Coliseum was full of a hundredfold as many as had appeared upon the first occasion. Vincenzio Romoli, together with Agnolino, tended the fire and heaped on quantities of precious perfumes. At the advice of the necromancer, I again demanded to be reunited with Angelica. The sorcerer turned to me and said: "Hear you what they have replied; that in the space of one month you will be where she is?" Then once more he prayed me to stand firm by him, because the legions were a thousandfold more than he had summoned, and were the most dangerous of all the denizens of hell; and now that they had settled what I asked, it behoved us to be civil to them and dismiss them gently. On the other side, the boy, who was beneath the pentacle, shrieked out in terror that a million of the fiercest men were swarming round and threatening us. He said, moreover, that four huge giants had appeared, who were striving to force their way inside the circle.

First noting that this is far from being the only kind of result described in the grimoires as in the ethnographic data, we see that the three descriptions coincide in that the Spirits attend the ceremony in large numbers, with overwhelming manifestations and extremely aggressive behavior towards the magician and his assistants. We cannot prove whether the grimoire descriptions came from an ancient tradition with shamanic roots or if we are facing an archetypal experience; the point I want to emphasize is that, either way, the aboriginal shamans had been experimenting with the phenomenon for long ages before the grimoire writer and Cellini set their descriptions down. Nevertheless, more than the difference in time, the geographical distance between Australia and Europe in this case argues for the emergence of archetypal experiences: even if the writer of the *Heptameron* and the priest who conducted the ceremony at the Coliseum were heirs to a tradition much older than the presence of Christianity in Europe, this original tradition would be exempt from being influenced by the Australian one.

The aborigine's testimony also points to another important implication: it states that the aggressive and overwhelming manifestation of the Spirits was a kind of test of courage, which being successfully faced would not happen again. This raises the question of whether or not the *Heptameron* represents an incomplete system, and if it does, if the system is incomplete because (1) the transmission of the knowledge was imperfect, or (2) the writer on purpose omitted it or (3) the writer or his source never went beyond the first step of the process.

Cellini's description and the aborigine's account also points to an important feature of the spirit's conjuring: *the nature of the visions*. It is the priest who hears the answer of the spirits to Cellini's question and transmits it to him; it is the virgin boy who can see the giants and warns about their attempt to break the circle. In the same fashion, the aborigine instructs about avoiding fear as it will *"break the web (or thread) on which the scenes are hung"* – both cases indicate that the visions cannot be seen by everyone and that they require a determined concentration or state of mind. The *Heptameron* repeats the injunction to "not fear", although without mentioning a specific reason for this.

Another striking similarity between the European grimoires and the shamanic traditions refers to the form of the spirits, who very often take the shape of diverse kinds of animals. Eliade still in chapter three mentions that *"among the Siberians and the Altaians they can appear in the form of bears, wolves, stags, hares, all kinds of birds (especially the goose, eagle, owl, crow, etc)"*; it is instructive to compare this with the theriomorphic descriptions of the *Lemegeton*, which include bear, wolves, hart, and goose, crow, raven, dove and peacock. The list extends to lions, cat, toad, crocodile, horse, leopard, viper, bull, dog, ram and a dromedary.

The Spirits from the *Lemegeton* can assume human form, which is encouraged, and on the reverse they can transform men into animals, as does Andrealphus who can *"transforme a Man into ye likness of a Bird"*. A typical shamanic feature is precisely this same ability to transform oneself into an animal and back. According to Eliade (still in chapter three) *"from the most distant times almost all animals have been conceived either as psychopomps that accompany the soul into the beyond or as the dead person's new form"*. The relation of the theriomorphic shapes of the *Lemegeton*'s spirits with the souls of the dead points to the probable origin of the grimoire practices in ancient funerary rites, a matter fully described in Jake Stratton-Kent's work *Geosophia*.

Some of the *Lemegeton*'s spirits appear riding different kinds of animals, and following Eliade we note that *"in a considerable number of myths and legends all over the world the hero is carried into the beyond by an animal"* and *"it is always an animal that carries the neophyte into the bush (the underworld) on its back, or holds him in its jaws, or 'swallows' him to 'kill and resuscitate him', and so on."* Keeping in mind the initiatory character of being killed by the spirits in the Shamanic traditions throws another light on the description of one of the most feared denizens of the *Pseudomonarchia Daemonun*:

> *Andras* is a great marquesse, and is seene in an angels shape with a head like a blacke night raven, riding upon a blacke and a verie strong woolfe, flourishing with a sharpe sword in his hand, he can kill the maister, the servant, and all assistants, he is author of discords, and ruleth thirtie legions.

In the same fashion, Barbatos *"understandeth the singing of birds, the barking of dogs, the lowings of bullocks, and the voice of all living creatures"*, and Caym's power too *"giveth men the understanding of all birds, of the lowing of bullocks, and barking of dogs, and also of the sound and noise of waters"*. These are striking as clearly shamanic features, and if we follow the next quote from Eliade, it again establishes a connection with the rites for the dead:

> All over the world learning the language of animals, especially of birds, is equivalent to knowing the secrets of nature and hence to being able to prophesy. Bird language is usually learned by eating snake or some other reputedly magical animal. These animals can reveal the secrets of the future because they are thought to be receptacles for the souls of the dead or epiphanies of the gods. Learning their language, imitating their voice, is equivalent to ability to communicate with the beyond and the heavens.

The ability demonstrated by Barbatos to understand different kinds of animal sounds, which is probably mentioned to indicate also his ability to teach it to the magician, is described in a way very similar to what we see in a quote from Castagné made by Eliade, concerning the baqça from the Kirgiz-Tatar people, who *"barks like a dog, sniffs at the audience, lows like an ox, bellows, cries, bleats like a lamb, grunts like a pig, whinnies, coos, imitating with remarkable accuracy the cries of animals, the songs of birds, the sound of their flight, and so on, all of which greatly impress his audience"*. In its origins, then, Barbatos possibly was a spirit with the power to initiate a man, transforming him into a shaman, and/or was himself the spirit of a deceased shaman. Spirits of deceased shamans play a prominent role in shamanic initiations all around the globe.

Another shamanic feature attributed to the Spirits which appears to have survived or resurfaced in the *Lemegeton* is the differentiation between the *familiar* and other kinds of spirits. Allowing Eliade once again to introduce us to these categories:

> This appears even more clearly from an examination of the other categories of "spirits" that also play a role either in the shaman's initiation or in bringing on his ecstatic experiences. We said above that a relation of "familiarity" is established between the shaman and his "spirits". And in fact, in ethnological literature they are known as "familiars", "helping", "assistant", or "guardian" spirits. But we must distinguish carefully between familiar spirits proper and another and more powerful category of spirits known as tutelary spirits; so too, a distinction must be made between these last and the divine or semi-divine beings whom the shamans summon up during séances. A shaman is a man who has immediate, concrete experiences with gods and spirits; he sees them face to face, he talks with them, prays to them, implores them

> – but he does not "control" more than a limited number of them. Any god or spirit invoked during a shamanic séance is not by that fact one of the shaman's "familiars" or "helpers". The great gods are often invoked. [...] The shaman invokes them, and the gods, demigods, and spirits arrive – just as the Vedic divinities descend and attend the priest when he invokes them during the sacrifice. The shamans also have divinities peculiar to them, unknown to the rest of the people, and to whom they alone offer sacrifices. But all this pantheon is not at the shaman's disposition, as his familiar spirits are; and the divine or semi-divine beings who help him must not be classed among these familiar or helping or guardian spirits. [...] we must note that the majority of these familiar spirits have animal forms.

There are eight *Lemegeton* spirits who give familiars to magicians (Paimon, Purson, Morax, Malphas, Shax, Sabnach, Cimeries and Amy), and one who can deliver them from the service of other magicians (Gaap). This establishes the similarity with the shamanic feature of tutelary and familiar spirits, where some spirits are invoked on occasion while others stay with the magician in his daily life.

The kind of hierarchy displayed in the *Lemegeton*, although reflecting the ranks of the European nobility of the time, is reminiscent of the distinctions mentioned by Eliade about the gods, demigods and spirits invoked by the shaman, and also denotes the diminution of status that happened through time. This 'fall from grace' of gods and demigods into the spirit category, and the demonization of the spirits – principally the ones with a chthonic origin – together with the devaluation and posterior prohibition of the old chthonic and funereal rites, has its origins both in the Greek-Roman legislation and in the Jewish religion. Necromantic practices were familiar not just to the old Greeks and Jews but were also present in the Nordic cultures, for instance. As testimony of this see the parallel invocations of the ghosts of the prophet Tiresias by Odysseus, of the prophet Samuel by the Witch of Endor and of the prophetess Volva by the god Odin. It is remarkable that in the Greek culture at the time of Homer as in the North of Europe the invocation of a dead prophet's soul was not dealt with reproach, differently from what we see in the narrative of the Bible.

Jake Stratton-Kent has very well documented his thesis on the survival of archaic chthonic and necromantic rites in the magic of the grimoires, and this survival necessarily implies the breaking of a former coexistence of the chthonic and heavenly divinities and rites, a disruption of the previous complete cosmological view followed by the degradation and marginalization of the chthonic. Curiously, this is not a process unique to the history of Western magic, as some of its steps can be seen in other cultures, as remarked by Eliade in his chapter six:

> The most marked specialization, at least among certain people, is that of "black" and "white" shamans, although it is not always easy to define the distinction. M. A. Czaplicka mentions, for the Yakut, the class of *ajy ojuna*, who sacrifice to the gods, and the class of *abassy ojuna*, who have relations with the "evil spirits". But, as Harva observes, the *ajy ojuna* is not necessarily a shaman; he can also be a sacrificing priest. According to N. V. Pripuzov, the same Yakut shaman can invoke both the higher (celestial) spirits and those of the lower regions. Among the Tungus of Turukhansk the shamans are not differentiated into "black" and "white"; but they do not sacrifice to the celestial god, whose rites are always performed by day, whereas the shamanic rites take place at night.

The distinction is clearly marked among the Buryat, who speaks of "white" shamans (*sagani bö*) and "black" shamans (*karain bö*), the former having relations with the gods, the latter with the spirits. Their costumes differ, being white for the former and blue for the latter. Buryat mythology itself shows a marked dualism that has become celebrated: the innumerable class of demigods is divided into black Khans and white Khans, separated by a fierce enmity. The black Khans are served by the "black" shamans; these are not liked, though they have their use, since only they can fill the role of intermediaries to the black Khans. However, this situation is not primitive; according to the myths, the first shaman was "white", the "black" shaman appeared only later. We have seen, too, that it was the gods who sent the eagle to bestow shamanic gifts on the first human being it should meet on earth. This bipartition of shamans may well be a secondary and even rather late phenomenon, due either to Iranian influences or to a negative evaluation of the chthonic and "infernal" hierophanies, which in course of time came to designate "demonic" powers.

We must not forget that many of the divinities and powers of the earth and the underworld are not necessarily "evil" or "demonic". They generally represent autochthonous and even local hierophanies that have fallen in rank as the result of changes within the pantheon. Sometimes the bipartition of gods into celestial and chthonic-infernal is only a convenient classification without any pejorative implication for the latter. We have just seen a quite marked opposition between the white Khans and black Khans of the Buryat. The Yakut, too, know two great classes (*bis*) of gods: those "above" and those "below", the *tangara* (celestial) and the "subterranean", though there is no clear opposition between them; rather, it is a matter of classification and specialization among various religious forms and powers.

The dualism of the Zoroastrian religion, the Iranian influences mentioned above, seems to be also at the root of the radicalization of the monotheistic speech in Judaism and its later derivatives, but was not the only force in action moving the old necromantic and funeral rites towards marginalization and persecution. The typical roles of the shaman as psychopomp, intermediary between the living and the dead, between the people and the spirits and the gods, and healer, were one by one being absorbed by institutionalized structures in the developing societies, and the representatives of these structures obviously were at odds with the representatives of the old ways. That helps to explain why the persecution against the heirs to the old *goes* started in the Greek and Roman legislations prior to the Christianization of the Roman Empire.

As I mentioned, there are also strong similarities of *method* between the magic of the grimoires and these archaic techniques of ecstasy – as Eliade named them. The confrontation with the spirits seems to universally require some kind of preparation, in which elements like fasting and seclusion are frequently found in both systems. Both grimoire practitioners and shamans deal with such items as special clothes and special instruments, the use of odoriferous smokes or incenses, choice of appropriate place and even the use of blood: the *Key of Solomon* requires "*the blood of the bat, pigeon, and other animals*" and shamans during initiations and purifications are reported to use the blood of goats and pigs, amongst other animals. The general idea in all these cases is that preparations are needed to invoke spirits and to ascend to the heavens: first an initiatory preparation which makes the magician or the shaman apt and then purificatory preparations repeated every time a new attempt is made.

A good example of this can be seen in the following quotation, from Eliade's chapter four. It regards the initiation of the Carib shamans of Dutch Guiana, who "*cannot become a* pujai *without succeeding in seeing the spirits and establishing direct and lasting relations with them*". The study of this kind of ethnographic data is very useful for the study and practice of the magic of the grimoires because the latter comes to us in fragmentary form, in different versions of the same work, with abundant errors from copying and translating and without the benefits of the oral explanation given by the original writers, who very likely omitted secrets and details.

> Usually six youths are initiated at once. They live in complete isolation in a hut built especially for the purpose and covered with palm fronds. They are required to do a certain amount of manual work; they tend the master initiator's tobacco field and make a bench in the shape of an alligator from the trunk of a cedar and set it in front of their hut. On this bench they sit every evening to listen to the master or to wait for visions. In addition, each of them makes his own bells and a "magical staff" six feet long. Six girls, under the supervision of an old woman teacher, serve the candidates. They furnish the daily supply of tobacco juice, which the candidates are obliged to drink in large quantities, and every evening each of them rubs the entire body of one of the candidates with a red liquid; this is to make him handsome and worthy to enter the presence of the spirits.

Shamanism and European Ceremonial Magic share also many of their general goals, if we follow, for instance, Van James presentation of the term in his paper *Spirit and Art: and the Puzzles of Paradox*:

> The term *shaman*, once used to describe the sages and medicine people of the Tungus tribes of Siberia, is now generally applied to certain people and practices found in almost all indigenous cultures throughout the world. Three essential elements are found in most shamanic traditions: (1) Shamans voluntarily enter visionary states of consciousness, during which (2) they experience non-ordinary realms of existence where (3) they gain knowledge and power for themselves or for their communities. This journey into the supersensory, where the shaman is helped by spirit guides that appear most often in animal forms, usually leads to initiatory crisis, an experience of oneness with the fabric of the universe, and the ability to prophesy, heal, and control natural phenomena.

Knowledge, power and transcendence: these are the key notes we find throughout the entire grimoire genre. Even in the diaries of John Dee, in which Renaissance magic finds its summit, we see very clearly the preoccupations with "*the ability to prophesy, heal and control natural phenomena*". Which, I do not believe I err if I say, were the main goals of Dee.

The magician's search requires the attention of the denizens of the underworld and of the heavens, repeating the tripartite division also typical of Shamanism. Following that, everything in the grimoires speaks of Power and Grace, and the practitioner finds temptation to fall on both sides, something Aleister Crowley very correctly acknowledged in his essay *The Revival of Magick*:

> Very well; suppose we begin in a gross, selfish, avaricious way, and try to get the spirits to bring us gold. We call Hismael, the Spirit of Jupiter. Nothing happens. We learn that Hismael will not be commanded but by his proper Intelligence, Iophiel. So we call Iophiel. Equal recalcitrance on the part of Iophiel, who is only amenable to the orders of Sachiel, his Angel. Same story with Sachiel. We go to Tzadquiel the Archangel. Still no good; for Tzadquiel obeys none but El. We invoke El, the God. We must then become El; and having done so, having entered into that vast divine essence, we cannot bother any more as to whether we have any money. We have left all that behind.

But the grimoire tradition (from which Crowley derived the concept above) is tainted and incomplete, suffering from the influence of Christianity. If in the shamanistic traditions the magical universe is seen as a whole, and very often the road to the heavenly realms begins with a crossing of the underworld, in Christian cosmology the underworld is the abode of condemned souls and fallen angels, to whom the crimes and mistakes made in a moment receive an eternal punishment... The presence or manifestation of any spirit not accepted by the Church as an Angel is Magick, which in ecclesiastical language translates as Wicked. We can receive good visitations and even manifestations of God, but we cannot search for them. It was all right for Jesus to go to the underworld to free souls and then ascend to the sky, as any shaman worthy of the name would do, but this very old prerogative is not for anybody else anymore under the Church's rule.

This image from Van James' paper shows a Lapp shaman's drum, from early nineteenth-century northern Sweden, which demonstrates how near to the grimoire literature we can find surviving shamanic traditions. According to Van James, it *"depicts the traditional three worlds of (1) Middle Earth, the realm of human beings; (2) the Underworld, land of elemental spirits and souls of the dead; and (3) the Upperworld of gods and guardian spirits. The shaman first descends into the Underworld in a trance state induced by beating the drum and then ascends to the Upperworld pictured as a ride on a sleigh drawn by a reindeer and followed by a dog".*

The survival of the shamanic religion of the Lapps, or the Sami people, in Northern Europe up to the 18th century reminds us of the long and incomplete struggle of Christianity to eradicate all former religions and beliefs. That is why the survival of many shamanic ideas in the grimoires should not surprise us. Christianization of Europe did not finish until the conversion of Scandinavia, in the 12th century, and even then was far from being complete and absolute, as we can see in the following quotes from the always helpful Wikipedia, to be found under the *"Christianization of Europe"* and *"Christianization of Scandinavia"* entries:

> In 301 AD, the Kingdom of Armenia became the first country to establish Christianity as its state religion. Soon after, the Roman Empire officially adopted Christianity in AD 380. During the Early Middle Ages, most of Europe underwent Christianization, a process essentially complete with the Christianization of Scandinavia in the High Middle Ages. The emergence of the notion of "Europe" or "Western World" is intimately connected with the idea of "Christendom", especially since Christianity in the Middle East was marginalized by the rise of Islam from the 7th century, a constellation that led to the Crusades, which although unsuccessful militarily were

an important step in the emergence of a religious identity of Europe. At all times, traditions of folk religion existed largely independent from official denomination or dogmatic theology.

> The Christianization of Scandinavia took place between the 8th and the 12th century. The realms of Scandinavia proper, Denmark, Norway and Sweden, established their own Archdioceses, responsible directly to the Pope, in 1104, 1154 and 1164, respectively. The conversion to Christianity of the Scandinavian people would require more time, since it took additional efforts to establish a network of churches. The Samis remained unconverted until the 18th century.
>
> In fact, although the Scandinavians became nominally Christian, it took considerably longer for actual Christian beliefs to establish themselves among the people. The old indigenous traditions that had provided security and structure since time immemorial were challenged by ideas that were unfamiliar, such as original sin, the Incarnation, and the Trinity. Archaeological excavations of burial sites on the island of Lovön near modern-day Stockholm have shown that the actual Christianization of the people was very slow and took at least 150-200 years, and this was a very central location in the Swedish kingdom. 13th century runic inscriptions from the bustling merchant town of Bergen in Norway show little Christian influence, and one of them appeals to a Valkyrie. At this time, enough knowledge of Norse mythology remained to be preserved in sources such as the *Eddas* in Iceland.
>
> It may be a sign of the slowness of the conversion that many elements of the old faith, even several of the gods, remained part of Scandinavian folklore until modern times.

The resemblances and proximities between essential features of the grimoires and Shamanism are so many that we reach a point at which to keep reporting them becomes boring. The many striking resemblances, however, leave open the question as to whether they represent the resurgence of archetypical processes, the continuation of archaic traditions with roots in Prehistory, or *both*. If both, we lack sufficient evidence to discern when we have a *survival* and when we have a *resurgence*. As an example, let's look into these two images, one an example of Primitive Art, and the other a known image from the late *Grand Grimoire*:

It seems to me very improbable that the artist who illustrated the grimoire took his inspiration from the Native American Rock Art, from where the carved image comes. So, we could at first eliminate the possibility of the grimoire image representing a survival. Or not? It will depend on how we interpret the survival idea: the image of a man with horns and animal feet is a survival from Paleolithic times, which is the same as to say that it is a survival from shamanic practices, coming to us in this particular case mainly through Greek culture. The similarities of both images, separated in time by the Atlantic Ocean, makes the grimoire drawing a survival and a resurgence at the same time.

To strengthen in the mind of the reader the possibility that the grimoire literature represents the survival of the archaic themes we have been discussing, I present another example image taken also from Van James, which he presents as "*a figure at Le Gabillou, France, depicted with bison head and shoulders and human legs and feet, described as a Sorcerer or supernatural Animal Master*":

The resurgence of concepts, methods and results as distant in place as in time is a consequence of the fact that anywhere in the world, at any time, our species share the same neurological features. Van James mentions the three overlapping but discernible stages which neuropsychological research distinguishes in the trance experiences: (1) seeing geometric forms, (2) the forms are seen as images of objects: "*a crescent may be a bowl, a zigzag may be a snake, and a grid a ladder*", and (3) entered by way of a tunnel or vortex experience, after which animal, human and anthropo-zoomorphic figures like the *Lemegeton* Spirits appear. At this stage the subjects feel that "*they can fly and turn into animals or birds*". Van James goes on to quote Jean Clottes and J. D. Lewis-Williams, who notes that:

> These three stages are universal and wired into the human nervous system, though the meanings given to the geometrics of Stage One, the objects into which they are illusioned in Stage Two, and the hallucinations of Stage Three are all culture-specific... a San shaman may see an eland antelope; an Inuit will see a polar bear or a seal. But, allowing for such cultural diversity, we can be fairly sure that the three stages of altered consciousness provide a framework for an understanding of shamanic experiences.

The presence of anthropo-zoomorphic figures in all shamanic cultures in the world, since the Stone Age (when shamans already dressed as animals to talk with spirits with animal and human shapes), and in the grimoire tradition, together with the many points discussed already, strongly indicate the possibility of the later containing survival elements from the first. This does not necessarily condemn the resurgence hypothesis entirely. Both phenomena could have happened at different stages to help shape the grimoires as we inherit them. But what that means, in the end, is that grimoire magic is to a large extent a shamanic phenomenon, whether being in its origin a survival or not.

On the other hand, the culture-specific character of the these figures, as mentioned in the last quote above, gives a hint about the origin of the description of the spirits in the *Lemegeton*. Which kind of magician or shaman would be acquainted with such a vast bestiary, including lions, leopards and dromedaries side by side with bears and wolves? The presence of African and European animals in the text, of course, points to the late European culture of Mediterranean influence, the only one which was very used to all these beasts.

MODERN GRIMOIRIC EVOCATION

Mike Cecchetelli

"The spirits with whom we work exist in terms and forms as real as our own, and are more powerful than one who has not stood in their presence, visible and in all their glory, could ever hope to understand."

PREFACE

At present, we are experiencing a vast resurgence of interest in the Great and Ancient Traditions of Magick as presented in those manuscripts known as the grimoires. This is thanks, in large part, to the dedication and efforts of a handful of modern day adepts in bringing previously unknown works of this genre to light and, of equal importance, creating critical editions wherein the originals are finally restored by comparing the widely varying extant versions.

As a Magus of the Grimoiric Tradition, I am in a state of bliss. Each time a new volume in the Golden Hoard's Sourceworks Series is released, Joe Peterson offers a new definitive edition of one of our classics, or another practicing magus such as Jake Stratton-Kent casts new light on an old favorite, I am brought to a state of excitement similar to when I first achieved a visible manifestation in a ceremony of evocation.

This being the case, and in order to further this Grimoiric resurgence in my own way, I have dedicated myself, to the extent possible, to making this great tradition more accessible to the modern day student and practitioner. The supreme and ultimate act of Grimoiric Magick being Veritable Evocation, I endeavor here, in a work dedicated to that practice, to offer some measure of insight into the practice. This I do by introducing practical and effective techniques by which the ancient grimoires can be used by the modern magus. As a rule, I relate only workings which, for lack of a better term, work, and are proven out by my own experiences and those of my students. In my first work, *Crossed Keys*, I offered a definitive and corrected edition of the Black Dragon as well as the Enchiridion of Pope Leo III, both restored to their original glory, as they were before the passing of time and countless hands copying them imperfectly corrupted them. This, in and of itself, is of great value. Of even greater worth, though, is the secret I was permitted to reveal through my own journal entries and explanatory notes, which fully elucidate the Black Dragon's first part as a single, structured act of magickal initiation. I did this in order to show the reader how eminently practical and usable the Magick contained therein is, and how we as modern day practitioners can make use thereof. While innumerable skeptics initially chastised me for undertaking the translation of the Black Dragon, calling it hopelessly corrupted and impractical, I proved it was quite the opposite on both counts. Also that it could be used by the new millennium Magus to greater success than any Pentagram Ritual or Middle Pillar could ever aspire to.

It is in this spirit that the present instructional essay is offered, wherein I endeavor to help bring the art of Veritable Evocation back to its place of prominence as the supreme act of Magick. It is my intent to, at some point, pen an entire volume of instruction based thereon, But for now I hope that the present work is sufficient to ignite some measure of interest among my contemporaries. To that end, and taking into consideration those of you reading this who are more inclined to work with the "Angelic" beings as well as those whose path has drawn them to the "Demonic", I will herein present workings of evocation from both sides of the fence. While many modern mages have shunned the practices involving those spirits traditionally regarded as "Demons", foregoing them as too dangerous, unnecessary or sinful, I work as frequently and effectively with these entities as I do with their Angelic counterparts, having my feet planted in the deepest depths and my head ascending to the heavens.

My primary aspiration is to provide techniques and instruction which the modern Magus can, so long as he has a fundamental knowledge of Evocation and Grimoire Magick in general, implement and incorporate immediately. Therefore, rarely will you find more than a page or two of "Theory" in my works. Unlike many authors I will very rarely offer any futile attempt to explain why, how or by what authority the Magick I practice works, instead allowing the fact that *it works* to be all the explanation that is necessary. Therefore, before diving into the instruction for which you undoubtedly sought this work, I will offer but one brief segue into the realm of Magickal Theory, which I see as a cautionary admonition more so than an elucidation of my own beliefs.

That admonition, dear reader, is to never make the mistake of allowing yourself to accept the Crowleyan fallacy which is that the entities with whom we will work are merely part of your psyche, or are aspects of your being with which you must come to terms. The spirits with whom we work exist in terms and forms as real as our own, and are more powerful than one who has not stood in their presence, visible and in all their glory, could ever hope to understand.

Therefore, of paramount importance when undertaking operations from this or any other book of magickal instruction is that you understand your position in the grand scheme of things. Of even more importance is that you never, ever allow yourself to be lulled into a false sense of security or accept the belief that you are in charge and the spirits are at your command. Treat them with respect, regardless if they are termed angels, demons or gods, for in any of these cases they are powerful beyond your imagination and angering them with threats and curses you have no means of enforcing is foolhardy.

That said, I now proceed to the corpus of this short work.

The Angelic

The following is an evocation which I originally shared, in part, on my blog, Following that post, I received nearly two dozen emails requesting further details and instruction in this and other techniques of which I have made use from this corpus, which is a group of Papyrii presently available only in academic works and studies. The interest shown in this rite and the successes shared with me by those who have experimented therewith have led me to present it here in fuller detail.

Although this rite was derived from the corpus of a unique magickal lineage, it is suggested that the reader employ it in evocation of the more widely known angels with whom he is more familiar, as the scope of this project does not permit me to go into sufficient detail on the tradition of origin to make its use feasible.

Preparation

Let the Magus be purified inside and out on the day of the working, by fasting and having no intake of food on the day of the working, save for water to slake his thirst.

Let the day be of the planet most suitable for the intent of his rite, if indeed a specific change in the universe is desired. If the purpose of the rite be solely to achieve communion with and to learn from an Angel, let the Magus be cautioned that offerings must be made and proper respect shown in order to placate, for the Angels do not well appreciate being summoned from their repose to satisfy idle curiosity.

Before the rite is to begin, that is sixty minutes prior to its commencement, let the Magus take a purifying bath, cleansing himself thoroughly and reciting the traditional words, "*Asperges Me Adonai, Lavabis Me Et Super Nivem Dealbabor*" throughout.

Before entering the temple, the Magus should anoint himself using the Oil of Abramelin.

The Temple

The temple should be lit only by white candles, and should be fumigated by incense appropriate to the planet of the day, or, alternatively, the incense taught to be used as general offering. Sufficient incense is to be used that it will not burn out before the culmination of the rite, although it matters not whether it be of resin, cone, stick or powder.

A circle should be defined on the floor of the temple, unadorned and with naught but the Magus inside, not to protect him from the spirit for no such circle could bar the entry of such a one anyway, but to establish his place in the universe. The circle should ideally be of natron, whether natural or man made.

The Magus is to be clothed in perfectly clean garments, both white and new are preferred, but it matters not if it be a robe, pants and a shirt or what have you, save that they be clean and free of odors such as perfumes, detergents, etc.

Although no tools or material are necessary for the present work and the magus will do as well with naught but his hand, he may, if it suits his will, hold a wand or book which to him is holy and powerful.

Preliminaria

Let the ceremony be opened as follows:[1]

By the great name of the Father, and to his Glory!
And that of those who stand in his presence,
Athonas Siak Ksas Sabak Kaab Kaesas Ekoe
I call upon thee, O Angel of the Presence!
By Thy Great Names, Given Thee By God,
By Metatron, Draw for me your sword and banish the profane!
By Dynamis, Bend for me your bow against he that opposes me!
By Chasdiel, Cleanse for me the whole of this place!
By Jael, Cleanse for me the depths!
By Yahoel, Cleanse for me the East!
By Megameidan, Cleanse for me the North!
By Pa' aziel, Cleanse for me the South!!
By Na'ariel, Cleanse for me the West!
By Hadariel, Cleanse for me the heights!

At this point, having prepared the place of working for the work at hand, the Magus would be well to use the rite from The Stele of Jeu as a precursor and personal empowerment. I do, however, suggest that he not use the Crowleyan version known as Samekh or the Bornless Rite in this case, as it bears little resemblance to the original and carries with it associations and definitions of the "barbarous words" which Crowley attempted to assign through Gematria and which are as far from those which the originators of the rites intended as possible.

---

[1]. Note that this "Zoning" Rite, as Jason Miller aptly terms this type of working, is used in the place where other practitioners apply the LBRP or similar "Banishings". Unlike the latter, it is drawn directly from the ancient sources, as practiced in those times, and makes use of 9 of the names of the Archangel Metatron.

Evocation

Having thus cleansed the Temple of all undesired influences and powers, the Magus proceeds to the Evocation Proper. If the evocation be to the obsidian mirror, the bowl or crystal, let the evocation be thus spoken while he gazes into the appropriate medium. If the desired result be physical manifestation, let the Magus do the same while gazing with his third eye open over the whole of his circle, for an Angel has it within his power to appear in any quarter and is in no way limited to a particular area thereof.

I adjure you, Great _____
I adjure you by Orphamiel, The Great Finger of the Father!
I adjure you by the Throne of the Father;
I adjure you by Orpha, the entire body of God!
I adjure you by the Chariots of the Sun!
I adjure you by the entire host of angels on high!
I adjure you by the seven Cherubim who fan the face of the Father!
I adjure you by the great Name of God, who no one knows except the Camel!
I adjure you by the seven archangels!

I adjure you, by the 24 elders whose names are:
Achael, Banuel, Ganuel, Dedael, Eptiel, Zartiel Ethael, Thatiel, Iochiel, Kardiel, Labtiel, Merael, Nerael, Xiphael, Oupiel, Pirael, Rael, Seroael, Tauriel, Umnuel, Philopael, Cristuel, Psilaphael, and Olithiel Who sit upon 24 thrones with 24 Crowns upon their heads and 24 censers in their hands, that they may stretch out their right hands to me, each of them by name!
Send to me the 4 creatures, with 4 faces and 6 wings!
Alpha Leon Phone Aner,
Paramara, Zorothion Periton Akramata,
That they may stretch out their hands to me in the Name of the Father!

Send to me your 7 holy archangels,
Michael, Gabriel, Raphael, Suriel,
Zetekiel, Solothiel, and Anael[1]
That they may stretch out their hands to me!

Send unto me your 3 holy youths,
Ananias, Asarias, Misael,
Setrok, Misak, Abdenako
LAL, MOULAL, BOULAL,
Each of them, by Name!

Send unto me _____
Through the power of
Eloei Elemas Sabaoth,
Abaktani, Abnael Naflo,
AKRAMACHAMARI

Hear me, for I call to you this night!
Hear me and join me, by these holy names!
Hear me, great spirit _____!

Manifestation and Appearance

Know that under no circumstances is any Angel, Spirit or Demon obliged to attend you. If he or she chooses to do so, they will. If they choose not to, they will not. No cursing or threats, cajoling or coercion on thy part will change their will or bend it to yours. That being said, an evocation such as this, empowered and making use of the holy names to which the angels give respect, will <u>always</u> be heard, and in the Art of Magickal Evocation, persistence and patience are of equal virtue. To be discouraged or deem the whole of this art a fallacy after a failed attempt is to be turned with ease from a reward that dwarves temporal treasures.

Should the Spirit unto whom you have called manifest, whether in the physical form or in your chosen medium, it is incumbent upon you to immediately greet and receive

---

1. These are the names of the 7 Archangels as they appear in the MS, differing as they do from the traditionally accepted variation.

them warmly, and to make unto them offerings of the aforementioned incense and of other things as might please them. Know that these beings have duties and existences far beyond our comprehension, and that they do not appreciate to have their time wasted. Be succinct, polite and reverent, and above all, take any advice or counsel you are offered.

Throughout the corpus of the Western Magickal Tradition, even amongst practitioners of Grimoiric Magick, you will discover there are widely varying opinions on how spirits manifest, and what exactly constitutes appearance. Some will assure you that appearance of a spirit takes place within your mind and consciousness, their messages being delivered very clearly, albeit without them ever taking actual shape. Some will protest with equal vehemence that spirits can appear visibly, if called to do so in a physical medium such as a crystal, a mirror or bowl of liquid. Those that teach that spirits CAN take shape and appear before you as described in the Grimoires of the ancients are few in number, and constitute the minority among practicing Mages. I, however, make up part of an even smaller minority: those few who teach that all three of the above described theories are correct.

Spirits can and do communicate with us mentally, as described by those who are of the first class assure you. They can be called and evoked to commune with the Magus in this manner, and in many ways it is easier than the two latter. It is, however, also the easiest of the three for self delusion to take over and the Magus to believe he has achieved his result when, in fact, he has accomplished nothing.

Evocation to a medium wherein the spirit called can appear, such as an Obsidian Mirror, the smoke of incense, a crystal or bowl is somewhat more difficult to achieve as it requires that the Magus train himself to see that which he has been conditioned to ignore. Nevertheless, it yields a more potent result both magickally, for the Magus is able to experience in limited form the presence of such a being, as well as psychologically, in that the Magus will know with a greater degree of certainty that his work was successful, knowing that the manifestation and communication could not have taken place solely in his imagination.

Veritable Evocation, which is what I term the Evocation espoused in the Grimoires, is, as I have previously mentioned, the supreme act of magick in the tradition I teach. The reason for this is simply because once it is experienced, nothing else of which our human scope of comprehension can conceive could compare. It is a transcendent act, and one that elevates the Magus, albeit temporarily, to a level of which he has previously only imagined. To stand before an Angel, a Demon, even moreso a God, is something no hexagram ritual, star ruby or other working in his repertoire could prepare him for.

The Demonic

As promised above, I now offer a method of calling forth and working with a spirit known traditionally as a demon with which I and students of mine have had a great deal of success. The working is designed not to merely evoke, question and banish as many modern works on magick would advise, but rather to establish long-term relationships with the spirits we summon.

Those familiar with ATR's will recognize aspects of this working as reminiscent of the Spirit Housing methods used therein, and indeed this practice does play a role in the working. It does so, however, only after an act of evocation.

The ritual described on the following pages is of dual purpose then; it serves primarily to evoke the entity with whom we seek to establish a relationship, which in and of itself is as beneficial to the Magus in his development as was the rite provided in Section I, allowing the Magus to stand before a being far older and more powerful than he can imagine and commune therewith. Secondarily it facilitates the establishment of a relationship with that spirit which can (and will, if the Magus maintains mutual respect) be spiritually, intellectually and practically empowering.

It behooves us to first examine what is meant by the statement just made, to wit "if the Magus maintains mutual respect". As was shown in my work with The Black Dragon and its spirits, the concept of the Magus dominating or commanding a "demon" is fallacy. The idea of doing so in the name of, and hence by the authority of, a god to whom these beings owe no allegiance and give no respect, is even more so. The language of many of the ancient grimoires wherein this practice is prescribed was intended to give the work the cursory appearance of piety in the eyes of inquisitors, and was never intended to be taken as literal. Consider this modern analogy and think, for a moment, logically.

Imagine yourself walking down the street of Anytown, U.S., yourself being a regular Joe, perhaps better educated than most and of a more daring nature, but a citizen nonetheless and of no greater authority in society than any other. While walking towards your destination you observe a man running out of the local jewelry store, masked and armed and clearly of ill intent, perhaps having just harmed or even killed your fellow man in the interest of enriching himself at their expense. Now imagine yourself, an ordinary citizen, yelling loudly, "Stop in the name of the law!" How likely is it that this man is going to yield to your will, stop in his tracks, put down his weapon and acquiesce to wait for the police to arrive, simply because YOU have ordered him to do so in the name of "the law" for which he has already shown his contempt by his very actions? Is it not more likely that he will simply continue on his path, ignoring you as if he has not even heard your command? Is it not likely that, angered, or perhaps even threatened by your order, he might instead turn his weapon on you?

And thus it is in many cases where those who endeavor to work with "demons" report having been adversely or even maliciously affected by the spirits with whom they sought to work. Look now at our modernized analogy in context; a Spirit who was, in most cases, revered as a God or Goddess, loved by his people in the ancient world and who was, unto them, a benefactor. Or an "Angel", a being every bit as divine as those of the holy host, but who committed the unforgivable crime of teaching man something "god" did not wish him to know, or loving a woman. Millenia later, these ancient Gods as well as Fallen Angels are vilified – lumped together with all the other spirits and beings whose sole yet damnable crime is refusal to acknowledge the sovereignty of the Judeo-Christian God, and called evil, ugly, odiferous denizens of the abyss. Now, taking for example the "Fallen" Angel Semyaza, imagine you are he. Scorned, vilified and demonized, labeled as evil, your very name being used as a synonym for "Satan" or the source of all ills. Now imagine you hear a man calling to you, a man, who would not even know of the arts of Magick and Sorcery were it not for your supposed "defiance". The call you hear is "Semyaza! Ye master of the rebellious and wretched angels, fallen for the defiance of the lord thy god! I order thee in the name of that God, that thou appear and obey me lest I torture you endlessly!" Are you likely to attend him and obey as he says, or to at best ignore him and, at worst, seek to do him harm for his arrogance and insolence?

It should be noted that, while I defend such spirits as the aforementioned and maintain good, working and mutually respectful relationships with several, I am NOT inferring that our universe is not home to existences of pure evil, for it surely does. I AM stating that the majority of those whose names you will find in our classical grimoires, the bible, and in the corpus of both angelogy and demonology do not fall into that category and were assigned there by men more evil than they could ever be rightfully considered.

That being said, in my workings with such spirits and in those of my students, they are afforded all the respect and courtesy one would give a "holy angel", and have proven equally helpful and, at times, even more so, as they have none of the elitism about them and appreciate those who approach them respectfully. Therefore, if you are of the sort who seeks to follow in the footsteps of Solomon, subjugating and enslaving the horrible infernal demons to your will, go no further in this text. If, however, you are of an open mind and want to discover for yourself the truth of these spirits so maligned, proceed.

The Evocation I have chosen for inclusion in this work is that of Semyaza, the Great Angel and Watcher aforementioned, and one for whom I have great affection.

Preparation

1. Let the Magus be purified inside and out on the day of the working, by fasting and having no intake of food on the day of the working, save for water to slake his thirst.

2. If the Evocation be of a Spirit whose planetary nature is known, such as in the case of the ancient gods and goddesses, the rite is to be performed on the appropriate day. If the nature of the spirit is not known, let the day be of the planet most suitable for the intent of his rite.

3. Before the commencement of the rite, let the Magus bathe in the usual manner, washing with Hyssop Soap.

4. Before entering the temple, the Magus should anoint himself using the Oil of Abramelin.

The Temple

1. The temple should be lit only by white candles, and should be fumigated by incense appropriate to the planet of the day, or, alternatively, the incense taught to be used as general offering. Sufficient incense is to be used that it will not burn out before the culmination of the rite, although it matters not whether it be of resin, cone, stick or powder.

2. A circle should be defined on the floor of the temple, unadorned and with naught but the Magus inside, not to protect him from the spirit for no such circle could bar the entry of such a one anyway, but to establish his place in the universe. The circle should ideally be of natron, whether natural or manmade.

3. The Magus is to be clothed in perfectly clean garments, both white and new are preferred, but it matters not if it be a robe, pants and a shirt or what have you, save that they be clean and free of odors such as perfumes, detergents, etc.

4. Although no tools or material are necessary for the present work and the magus will do as well with naught but his hand, he may, if it suits his will, hold a wand or book which to him is holy and powerful. At no time should he hold or have near a dagger or blade!

Preliminaria:

Let the ceremony be opened as follows[2]:

Facing East – Stretch out right and left hands to the left, chant "A" (Alpha. As in Father)
Face North – Put forward your right fist, chant "E" (Epsilon. As in fret)
Face West – Extend both hands forward, chant "H" (Eta. As in the French *tete*)
Face South – Both hands holding the stomach, chant "I" (Iota. As in feed)
Face East – Touch the ends of the toes, chant "O" (Omicron. As in not)
Face East – Right hand on the heart, chant "Υ" (Upsilon. As in the French *rue*)
Face East – Looking to the sky with hands on the head, chant "Ω" (Omega. As in home)

Open, open four quarters of the cosmos,
For the lord of the inhabited world comes forth!
Archangels, decans and angels rejoice!
For Aion of Aion himself, the only and transcendent,
Invisible, goes through this place!
Open, door! Hear, bar! Fall into two parts, lock!
Cast up, Earth, for the lord, all things you contain,
For he is the storm sender and controller of the abyss,
The Master of Fire!

Let him now make the sign of the opening of the abyss, while speaking the Key 3x as follows:

Zazas, Zazas, Nasatanada Zazas

Let two candles of white, stood atop the Sigil of Semyaza[3] be ignited along with the offering incense, and let the Evocation be opened:

The Evocation

Great one Semyaza, Lord of the Watchers!
Teacher of Sorcery to Man and Lover of The Daughters of He!
Great Angel Semyaza, Hear me this night as I call on Thee!
Dweller in Orion, Father of Hiya and Hiwa, Hear My Call!
Semyaza! Who Made Man Partaker in the Mysteries of the Heavens!
Bestower of the Forbidden Truths and Teacher of the Magickal Arts,
Hear Me This Hour, For I Call To Thee Across Time and Space!
As Thou Leapt From the Cliff of Haradan, So Fly Now To Me!
As Though Gavest the Gift of Wisdom to Man, Give Thine Aid To Me!

Σεμιαζά   שמיחזה
The Sigil of Semjaza
In Greek   In Aramaic/ Hebrew

---

2. The opening ceremony is drawn from PGM and makes use of the 7 Greek Vowels which are seen as the 7 Keys to the Planetary Spheres, and calls on Aion, who transcends the whole of the Greek, Judeo-Christian and all other pantheons as the Source of Life and Creation.
3. The Sigil of Semyaza, bearing also his name in both Aramaic and Greek, is provided above.

Let the Magus chant the name of the Great Semyaza until the Lord of the Watchers makes himself known. As with all spirits, know that at no time is he obligated to attend and that it may take many such evocations to peak his interest sufficiently that he comes. This being the case, know also that for myself and four students with whom I have worked, <u>he has come</u>. Patience and perseverance in evocation, as in all things, are rewarded.

Once Semyaza has attended thee, he is to be welcomed warmly, with offerings of incense made to him. Let then the Magus, speaking always reverently and with great respect, announce his desire to set aside a permanent space in his altar or otherwise in his abode wherein Semyaza may be at home, and that it is his wish to partake in the wisdom and knowledge imparted by he unto man so long ago.

Should he accept your invitation, his dwelling is to be prepared according to his wishes and to his comfort. Examples of acceptable and pleasing homes wherein his spirit may "dwell", include a vessel such as a pot, cauldron-like if possible. At no time should the home be of bronze or iron as this is traditionally seen as an effort to imprison the occupant. Alternatively, a wooden chest such as that which is pictured below is also an excellent home, and is in fact what I presently use myself. On the home (the pot, the chest, or what have you) should be adorned with the sigil of Semyaza along with his names in both Aramaic and Ancient Greek, and it should be dressed thoroughly with Abramelin Oil before use. Once the home is established and filled according to the wishes of the spirit for whom it is built, the rite of evocation is to be performed again in full, calling down the spirit and making a formal presentation of their new home and inviting them to take possession of it.

Once the space has been offered and accepted by the spirit – any spirit – it is of great importance that the spirit unto whom it was given never be neglected. Offerings of incense and candles should be made as frequently as possible, but not less than once per month. Further, the onus falls on the Magus to develop the relationship, calling on the spirit and establishing rapport with him as one would a prospective lover whom he is courting. Ever should he be mindful that the spirit, whosoever he shall be, is an entity beyond the human scope of comprehension and must be given the respect one would give an elder relation.

A Chest Used By The Author As A Spirit House

Introducing...
The Comte de Gabalis

The Rosicrucians are a people I must bring you acquainted with. The best account I know of them is in a French book called Le Comte De Gabalis, with both its title and size being so like a novel, that many of the Fair Sex read it by mistake.
                                                                    Alexander Pope 1711

THE *COMTE DE GABALIS*, WHILE APPARENTLY A 'NOVEL' RATHER than a grimoire or magical text, has been a deeply influential text. It is recommended on the reading list of Crowley's magical order of the A∴A∴. Its influence on his own magical practice can be traced in his Magical Record where he mentions giving a sermon to the Elemental Spirits. The text may well have been one of the Golden Dawn's 'Elemental Prayers', employed in the Elemental Grade rituals. The idea of a sermon places the *Comte de Gabalis* in Crowley's thinking at the time.

Another aspect of *Gabalis* important to contextualise is its essentially positive view of spirits. The spirits in *Gabalis* are understood in strictly Paracelsian terms. The same terms describe them, and the obvious source of the author's ideas is Paracelsus' *Book on Nymphs, Sylphs, Pygmies and Salamanders*, whose concepts and ideas it reflects exactly. This differs markedly from the 'diabolism' of certain strands in the grimoires, including texts that are later (such as the *Grand Grimoire*). Thus it is important to delineate the confluence of opinion present in other strands of the tradition.

Since it was published in 1670, the influence of the *Comte de Gabalis* on magical literature including the grimoires has been immense and direct. A particularly salient example is the *Prayer of the Salamanders* in Discourse V. Incidentally this prayer originates in a fragment of Porphyry's work on the Chaldean Oracles. According to Michael Chase: "Hans Lewy thought it was a Chaldaean Oracle and opened his great book *Chaldaean Oracles and Theurgy* with a translation and discussion of it... ...Most scholars have not followed Lewy, and [it] is not included in most collections of the Chaldaean Oracles". The Comte, however, evidently agreed with Lewy.

From *Gabalis* this prayer found its way into various grimoires, most notably the *Grimorium Verum*, and – with three other elemental prayers – into the works of Eliphas Levi and onwards to the rituals of the Golden Dawn. While also an admirer of Paracelsus, Levi's view of elementals, and the ritual context in which these prayers are embedded, reflects Martinist influence. This context is as positive but less materialistic than the Paracelsian form. Implicit is a view of the Universe and its destiny that includes the redemption of all souls. This includes elementals and even fallen spirits; a doctrine attributed to Origen and known as 'Restitutionism'. The same idea, incidentally, is voiced by some spirits of the *Goetia of Solomon*, who expect to be restored to their former abodes. It was perhaps Weir who added the dismissals of these expectations.

So too, besides the printed *Bibliotheque bleue* grimoires, the influence of the *Comte de Gabalis* may be traceable in the manuscript grimoires. *Lansdowne 1203*, an important form of the *Key of Solomon*, patently views many grimoire spirits as elementals rather than accursed demons. It makes the Four Kings of the *Goetia of Solomon* the rulers of the Paracelsian elementals, rather than of evil spirits. This is further underlined by blaming the avarice of men rather than the malice of spirits for the dangers attending occult treasure hunting (see also my *True Grimoire* and *Geosophia*). There is no difficulty attributing such an influence to this branch of the Solomonic family. *Lansdowne 1203* is later than *Gabalis*, which was a virtual holy book of Rosicrucians of the time. Thus the owner of the manuscript may even have possessed a copy of the *Comte*. In any case, the influence of Paracelsus on the manuscript tradition is noncontroversial.

The motivations of the author of the *Comte* can only be guessed at. They were very likely polemical and revelatory, while nevertheless covert and disguised. While apparently a satirical novel there is no doubt whatsoever that the *Comte* represents very real doctrines and ideas. It is, in a sense, a master key to the Western occult tradition in a particularly important formative phase directly preceding our present era. As such it is deserving of close attention and scrutiny. It is indispensable to those researching and practicing grimoire magic; still more so to all seeking less negative and polarised views of spirits within general Western magical practice.

—Jake Stratton-Kent

Publisher's Note: The following is an anonymous English translation of the core of the book. Footnotes, subtext and commentaries have not been included.

The Comte de GABALIS

by the

ABBÉ N. DE MONTFAUCON DE VILLARS.

RENDERED OUT OF FRENCH INTO ENGLISH

DISCOURSE I

MAY THE SOUL OF THE COMTE DE GABALIS be now in the presence of God, for they have just written me that he has died of apoplexy. The Amateurs will not fail to say that this manner of death usually befalls those who deal incautiously with the secrets of the Sages, and that since the Blessed Raymond Lully so decreed in his testament, an avenging angel has never failed promptly to wring the necks of all who have indiscreetly revealed the Philosophic Mysteries.

But let them not condemn this learned man thus hastily, without having received an explanation of his conduct. He revealed all to me, it is true, but he did so only with the utmost cabalistic circumspection. It is necessary to pay his memory the tribute of stating that he was a great zealot for the Religion of his Fathers the Philosophers, and that he would rather have gone through fire than have profaned its sanctity by taking into his confidence any unworthy prince, or ambitious or immoral man, three types of persons excommunicated for all time by the Sages. Happily I am not a prince, I have but little ambition, and you will presently see that I have even a trifle more chastity than is requisite for a Philosopher.

He found me to be of a tractable, inquiring, and fearless disposition. A dash of melancholy is lacking in me, else I would make all, who are inclined to blame the Comte de GABALIS for having concealed nothing from me, confess that I was a not an unfit subject for the Occult Sciences. One cannot make great progress in them, it is true, without melancholy; but the little that I possess in no wise disheartened him. You have, he told me a hundred times, Saturn in an angle, in his own house, and retrograde; some day you cannot fail to be as melancholy as a Sage ought to be; for the wisest of all men, as we learn in the Cabala, had like you Jupiter in the Ascendant, nevertheless so powerful was the influence of his Saturn, though far weaker than yours, that one cannot find proof of his having laughed a single time in all his life.

The Amateurs must, therefore, find fault with my Saturn and not with the Comte de GABALIS, if I prefer to divulge their secrets rather than to practise them. If the stars do not do their duty the Comte is not to blame for it; and if I have not sufficient greatness of soul to strive to become the Master of Nature, overthrow the Elements, hold communion with Supreme Intelligences, command demons, become the father of giants, create new worlds, speak with God upon His formidable Throne, and compel the Cherubim who guards the gate of terrestrial Paradise to let me stroll now and then in its alleys, it is I, and I alone, who am to blame or to be pitied. One must not, on this account, insult the memory of that rare man by saying that he met his death because he taught me all these things. Since the fortunes of war are uncertain, is it not possible that the Comte may have been overcome in an encounter with some unruly hobgoblin? Peradventure while talking with God upon His flaming Throne, he could not keep his glance from straying to His face, now it is written that man may not behold God and live. Perhaps he merely pretended to die, as is the way of Philosophers, who feign death in one place, only to transplant themselves to another. Be that as it may, I cannot believe that the manner in which he entrusted his treasures to me merits punishment. This is what took place.

As common sense has always made me suspect the existence of much claptrap in all the so-called Occult Sciences, I have never been tempted to waste time in perusing books which treat of them, nevertheless it does not seem quite rational to condemn, without knowing why, all those who are addicted to these Sciences, persons often perfectly sane otherwise, and for the most part scholars, distinguished at the law and in society. Hence to avoid being unjust, and in order not to fatigue myself with tedious reading, I determined to pretend to all whom I could learn were interested in Occultism, that I was infatuated with it.

From the outset I had greater success than I had even dared hope. Since all these gentlemen, however mysterious and reserved they may pride themselves upon being, ask nothing better than to parade their theories and the new discoveries they pretend to have made in Nature, it was not long before I became the confidant of the most important among them, and I had always some one or another of them in my study, which I had purposely furnished forth with the works of their most fantastic authors. Without exception there was no foreign scholar upon whom I did not have an opinion, in short, as regards the Science in question, I soon found myself a personage of importance. I had as companions, princes, men of lofty rank, lawyers, beautiful ladies, (and ugly ones as well), doctors, prelates, monks, nuns, in fact people from every walk in life. Some were seeking Angels, others the Devil, some their guardian spirit, others evil spirits, some a panacea for every ill, others knowledge of the stars, some the secrets of Divinity, and almost all the Philosopher's Stone. They were to a man agreed that these mighty secrets, and especially the Philosopher's Stone, are hard to find and that few people possess them, but all entertained a sufficiently good opinion of themselves to fancy that they were of the number of the Elect.

Happily, the most advanced were at that time expecting with impatience the arrival of a German, a nobleman of high rank and a great Cabalist, whose lands lie toward the frontiers of Poland. He had written to the Children of the Philosophers at Paris, promising to pay them a visit when passing through France on his way to England. I was commissioned to answer this great man's letter. I sent him the map of my horoscope that he might judge whether I should aspire to the Supreme Wisdom. Fortunately my map and letter caused him to do me the honour of replying that I should be one of the first persons whom he would see in Paris, and that Heaven willing, it would not be his fault if I did not enter the Society of the Sages.

To my joy, I kept up a regular correspondence with the illustrious German. From time to time, I propounded to him weighty, and so far as in me lay, well reasoned problems concerning the Harmony of the World, the Numbers of Pythagoras, the Visions of St. John and the first Chapter of Genesis. The profundity of these subjects enraptured him, he wrote me unheard of wonders, and I soon recognised that I was dealing with a man of very vigorous and very vast imagination. I have three or four score of his letters written in so extraordinary a style that I could never bring myself to read anything else the moment I was alone in my study.

One day as I was marvelling at one of the most sublime of these letters, a very good looking man came in and bowing gravely to me, said in French but with a foreign accent, "Adore, oh my Son, adore the very good and the very great God of the Sages, and never allow yourself to become puffed up with pride because He sends one of the Children of Wisdom to initiate you into their Order, and to make you a sharer in the wonders of His Omnipotence."

The novelty of the salutation startled me, and for the first time in my life, I began to question whether people may not sometimes see apparitions; nevertheless, collecting myself as best I could, and looking at him as politely as my slight fear permitted, I said, "Who ever you may be whose greeting is not of this world, your visit does me great honour; but, before I adore the God of the Sages, may it please you to let me know to what Sages and to what God you refer, and if agreeable to you pray take this armchair and have the kindness to enlighten me as to this God, these Sages, this Order, and, before or after all this, as to the manner of being to whom I have the honour of speaking."

"You receive me very sagely sir," he replied with a smile, taking the proffered armchair; "You ask me to explain to you in the beginning certain things, which with your permission, I shall not touch upon to-day. The words of the compliment I have paid you the Sages address, at the outset, to those to whom they have determined to open their hearts and reveal their Mysteries. From your letters I adjudged you so advanced that this salutation would not be unknown to you, and that you would esteem it the most gratifying compliment the Comte de Gabalis could pay you."

"Ah Sir," I exclaimed, recollecting that I had a great role to play, "How shall I render myself worthy of such kindness? Is it possible that the greatest of all men is in my study, and that the renowned GABALIS honours me with a visit?"

"I am the least of the Sages, "he answered gravely, "and God, who dispenses the Light of his Wisdom together with its responsibilities in that measure which His Sovereignty deems best, has bestowed upon me but a very small portion of the Light, in comparison to that at which I marvel in my fellow Initiates. I expect you to equal them some day, if I dare judge from the map of your horoscope with which you have honoured me. But why Sir," he added mirthfully, "Are you doing your utmost to get into my bad graces by mistaking me at first sight for a phantom?"

"Ah, not for a phantom," I said, "But I confess, Sir, that I suddenly recalled that story of Cardan's. He says his father was one day visited in his study by seven unknown beings, clothed in different colours, who made rather strange statements to him as to their nature and occupation—"

"I am familiar with the incident to which you refer," interrupted the Comte, "They were Sylphs; I will tell you about them some day. They are a kind of etherial being, and now and then they come to consult the Sages about the books of Averroes which they do not understand very well. Cardan is a rattlepate to have published that in his 'Subtilties.' He found the reminiscence among his father's papers. His father was one of Us. Realising that his son was a born babbler, he did not wish to teach him anything of moment, and let him amuse himself with ordinary astrology whereof he knew only enough to forecast that his son would be hanged. So that rascal is to blame for your having insulted me by taking me for a Sylph?"

"Insulted you!" I exclaimed, "What have I done that I should be so unfortunate—?"

"I am not angry with you," he interposed, "You are under no obligation to know that all these Elementary Spirits are our disciples; that they are only too happy when we condescend to instruct them; and that the least of our Sages is more learned and more powerful than all those little fellows. We will speak of these matters, however, at another time; it is enough to-day that I have had the satisfaction of seeing you. Strive to render yourself worthy to receive the Cabalistic Light, my Son, the hour of your regeneration is at hand; it rests solely with you to become a new being. Pray ardently to Him, who alone has the power to create new hearts, that He may give you one capable of the great things which I am to teach you, and that He may inspire me to withhold from you none of our Mysteries."

Then he arose, kissed me solemnly, and without giving me a chance to reply said, "Adieu, my Son, I must see the members of our Order who are in Paris, afterward I shall give you my news. Meanwhile, WATCH, PRAY, HOPE AND BE SILENT."

With these words he left my study. On the way to the door I expressed my regret at the shortness of his visit, and at his cruelty in forsaking me so soon after he had shown me a Spark of his Light. But assuring me, with very great kindness, that I would lose nothing by waiting, he entered his coach and left me in a state of amazement which beggars description. I could believe neither my eyes nor my ears. "I am sure," I kept saying to myself "that this is a man of exalted rank, that he has inherited a yearly income of fifty thousand pounds; moreover he appears to be a person of great accomplishment; can it be that he has lost his head over these occult follies? He talked to me about those Sylphs in an exceedingly cavalier fashion. Is it not possible that he may be a sorcerer, and may I not have been altogether mistaken in believing, as I hitherto have, that sorcerers no longer exist? On the other hand, if he is a sorcerer, are they all as devout as he seems to be?"

I could not solve this riddle, nevertheless, I determined to see the matter through to the end, although I fully realised that I should have to put up with not a few sermons, and that the demon tormenting him was of a highly moral and pious character.

Discourse II

THE Comte wished me to pass the entire night in prayer, and the next morning at daybreak sent a note to say that he would be at my house at eight o'clock, and that, if agreeable to me, we would make an excursion together. I awaited him, he came, and after we had exchanged greetings, he said, "Let us go to some place where we may be alone, and where our interview cannot be interrupted."

I told him I thought Ruel a pleasant place and rather unfrequented. "Let us go there then," he replied. We got into the coach, and during the drive I kept studying my new Master. I have never in my life remarked in anyone so great a depth of contentment as was apparent in all that he said and did. His mind was more open and tranquil than it seemed possible for that of a sorcerer to be. His entire air was in nowise that of a man whose conscience reproaches him with black deeds; and I felt a marvellous impatience to have him enter upon the subject of our interview, for I could not comprehend how a man, seemingly so judicious and so perfect in every other way, could have let his mind become unbalanced by the visions to which I had perceived him to be subject on the preceding day. He discoursed divinely on political economy, and was enchanted to hear that I had read what Plato has written on this subject. "Someday you will have greater need of all that than you imagine," he said, "And if we come to an agreement to-day, it is not impossible that you may in time put these sage maxims into practice."

We were just entering Ruel and went to the garden; but the Comte disdained to admire its beauties and made straight for the labyrinth.

Perceiving that we were as much alone as he could desire, he raised his hands and eyes to Heaven and cried aloud, "I praise the Eternal Wisdom for inspiring me to conceal from you none of her Ineffable Truths. How happy you will be, my Son, if she is gracious enough to put into your soul the resolutions which these High Mysteries require of you. Soon you will learn to command all Nature, God alone will be your Master, and only the Sages your equals. The Supreme Intelligences will glory in obeying your desires, the demons will not dare to be found where you are, your voice will make them tremble in the depths of the abyss, and all the Invisible Peoples who dwell in the four Elements will deem themselves happy to be the ministers of your pleasure. I worship Thee, oh mighty God, because Thou hast crowned man with such great glory, and hast created him Sovereign Monarch of all the works of Thine hands. My Son," he added turning towards me, "do you feel within yourself that heroic ambition which is the infallible characteristic of the Children of Wisdom? Do you dare seek to serve God alone, and to master all that is not of God? Do you understand what it means to be a Man? And are you not weary of being a slave when you were born to [be] a Sovereign? And if you have these noble thoughts which the map of your horoscope does not permit me to doubt, consider seriously whether you will have the courage and strength to renounce everything which might prove an obstacle to your attaining that eminence for which you were born."

He paused and looked at me fixedly, as if either awaiting my reply or seeking to read my heart.

From the beginning of his discourse I had greatly hoped that we should soon enter upon the subject of our interview, but at these last words I gave up all anticipation of doing so. The word 'renounce' frightened me, and I no longer doubted he was about to propose that I should renounce either Baptism or Paradise. So not knowing how to get out of the difficult situation in which I found myself I said, "Renounce, Sir, is it necessary to renounce anything."

"It is absolutely necessary," he answered, "and truly, so vitally essential that it is the first thing required of one. I do not know whether you can make up your mind to it, but I know only too well that Wisdom never dwells in a body subject to sin, even as she never enters a soul prepossessed by error or malice. The Sages will never admit you to their Order if you do not from this moment renounce one thing which can never go hand in hand with Wisdom. It is necessary," he added in a whisper bending close to my ear, "It is necessary to renounce all sensual relationships with women."

I burst out laughing at this absurd proposal. "Sir," I exclaimed, "You have let me off easily. I was expecting you to propose some extraordinary renunciation, but since you merely desire me to renounce women, that was done long ago. I am chaste enough, thank God! Nevertheless Sir, since Solomon was more of a Sage than I may ever be, and since all his Wisdom could not prevent his becoming corrupted, pray tell me how you gentlemen manage to do without the other sex? And why would it be inconvenient if, in the Philosopher's Paradise, every Adam should have his Eve?"

"You are asking me something very important," he replied, as if reflecting whether or not he should answer my question. "Since I see, however, that you disengage yourself without difficulty from the society of the fair sex, I will tell you one of the reasons which have compelled the Sages to exact this condition from their disciples. Forthwith you will perceive in what ignorance all men live who are not of our number."

When you have been enrolled among the Children of the Philosophers, and when your eyes have been strengthened by the use of the very Holy Medicine, you will straightway discover that the Elements are inhabited by most perfect beings. Unhappy Adam's sin has deprived his unfortunate posterity of all knowledge of these beings and of all intercourse with them. The immense space which lies between Earth and Heaven has inhabitants far nobler than the birds and insects. These vast seas have far other hosts than those of the dolphins and whales; the depths of the earth are not for the moles alone; and the Element of Fire, nobler than the other three, was not created to remain useless and empty.

The air is full of an innumerable multitude of Peoples, whose faces are human, seemingly rather haughty, yet in reality tractable, great lovers of the sciences, cunning, obliging to the Sages, and enemies of fools and the ignorant. Their wives and daughters have a masculine beauty like that of the Amazons.

"Why, Sir," I ejaculated, "Do you mean to tell me that these hobgoblins are married?"

"Don't be upset by such a trifle, my Son," he rejoined, "Believe me, everything that I am telling you is sound and true. These are but the Elements of the ancient Cabala, and it only rests with you to verify my statements with your own eyes. Receive with a submissive spirit the Light which God sends you through my mediation. Forget all you may have heard on this subject in the schools of the ignorant, or later, when convinced by experience, you will have the sorrow of being compelled to own that you persisted stubbornly in the wrong."

"Hear me to the end and know that the seas and rivers are inhabited as well as the air. The ancient Sages called this race of people Undines or Nymphs. There are very few males among them but a great number of females; their beauty is extreme, and the daughters of men are not to be compared to them.

The earth is filled well-nigh to its centre with Gnomes, people of slight stature, who are the guardians of treasures, minerals and precious stones. They are ingenious, friends of man and easy to govern. They furnish the Children of the Sages with all the money they require, and as the price of their service ask naught save the glory of being commanded. The Gnomides, their wives, are small but very amiable, and their dress is exceedingly curious.

As for the Salamanders, flaming dwellers of the Region of Fire, they serve the Philosophers, but do not seek their company eagerly, and their daughters and wives rarely show themselves."

"They do right," I interrupted, "And I had rather have their room than their company."

"Why so?" inquired the Comte.

"Why so, Sir?" I replied, "Who would care to converse with such an ugly beast as a Salamander, male or female?"

"You are mistaken," he rejoined, "that is merely the idea which ignorant painters and sculptors have of them. The Salamander women are beautiful, more beautiful even than any of the others, since they are of a purer Element. I had not intended to speak about them, and was passing briefly over the description of these Peoples since you will see them yourself at your leisure, and with ease if you have the curiosity to do so. You will see their dresses, their food, their manners, their customs and their admirable laws. The beauty of their intellects will charm you even more than that of their bodies, yet one cannot help pitying these unfortunates when they tell one that their souls are mortal, and that they have no hope whatever of eternal enjoyment of the Supreme Being, of Whom they have knowledge and Whom they worship reverently. They will tell you that they are composed of the purest portions of the Element in which they dwell, and that they have in them no impurities whatever, since they are made of but one Element. Therefore they die only after several centuries; but what is time in comparison with eternity? They must return for ever into nothingness. This thought grieves them deeply, and we have utmost difficulty in consoling them.

Our Fathers the Philosophers, when speaking with God face to face, complained to Him of the unhappiness of these Peoples, and God, whose mercy is boundless, revealed to them that it was not impossible to find a remedy for this evil. He inspired them to the realization that just as man, by the alliance which he has contracted with God, has been made a participant in Divinity, so the Sylphs, Gnomes, Nymphs, and Salamanders, by the alliance which they have it in their power to contract with man, can become participants in immortality. Thus a Nymph or a Sylphid becomes immortal and capable of the Beatitude to which we aspire when she is so happy as to marry a Sage; and a Gnome or a Sylph ceases to be mortal the moment he espouses one of our daughters.

Thence sprang the error of the first centuries, of Tertullian, Justin Martyr, Lactantius, Cyprian, Clement of Alexandria, Athenagoras the Christian Philosopher, and of most writers of that period. They had learned that these Elementary Half-men sought the love of mortal maidens, and therefore imagined that the fall of the Angels had come about solely through their suffering themselves to be smitten with love for mortal women. Some Gnomes, desirous of becoming immortal, had sought to win the favour of our daughters by bringing them precious stones of which they are the natural guardians, and these authors believed, basing their conclusions upon the Book of Enoch which they did not understand, that these precious stones were snares laid by the enamoured Angels for the chastity of our women.

In the beginning these Sons of Heaven, being beloved by the daughters of men, engendered famous giants; and those indifferent Cabalists, Joseph and Philo, ([of which] almost all Jews are ignorant,) and subsequently all the authors I have just mentioned, as well as Origen and Macrobius, said that they were Angels, not knowing that they were Sylphs and other Elementary Peoples, who under the name of the Children of Elohim are distinguished from the Children of Men. Likewise that point which the Sage Augustine modestly refrained from deciding as to the pursuit of the African women of his time by so called Fauns or Satyrs; that also is cleared up by what I have just said concerning the desire to ally themselves with man which all Inhabitants of the Elements have, since such an alliance offers the only means whereby they may achieve the immortality to which they are not heirs.

Ah! Our Sages take care not to ascribe the fall of the first Angels to their love for women, nor do they accord the Devil such power over man as would enable them to attribute to him all the amorous intrigues of the Nymphs and Sylphs wherewith the writings of historians abound. There was never anything criminal in it at all. They were Sylphs who were striving to become immortal. Far from scandalizing the Philosophers, their innocent pursuits appeared so justifiable to us that we have, with one accord, resolved altogether to renounce women and to apply ourselves solely to the immortalisation of the Nymphs and Sylphids."

"Oh God!" I protested, "What do I hear? To what extent does the f—"

"Yes, my Son," the Comte interrupted, "Marvel at the extent of the philosophical felicity. Instead of women, whose feeble allurements fade in a few days and are succeeded by horrible wrinkles, the Sages possess beauties who never grow old and whom they have the glory of rendering immortal. Imagine the love and gratitude of these invisible mistresses and the ardour wherewith they strive to please the charitable Philosopher who applies himself to their immortalisation."

"Ah! Sir," I once more exclaimed, "I renounce—"

"Yes, my Son," he continued as before without giving me an opportunity to finish, "renounce all futile and insipid pleasures such as one finds in the society of women; the fairest of them all is horrible beside the most insignificant Sylphid. No revulsion ever follows our wise love making. Wretched ignoramuses! How greatly you are to be pitied for your inability to taste the pleasures of the Philosophers!"

"Wretched Comte de GABALIS!" I exclaimed with mingled wrath and compassion, "Will you let me tell you, once for all, that I renounce this insane Wisdom, that I find this visionary Philosophy absurd, that I abhor these abominable embracings of phantoms, and that I tremble for you lest one of your pretended Sylphids should suddenly carry you off to Hell in the midst of your transports, fearing that so good a man as you might at length perceive the madness of this chimerical ardour, and repent so great a crime."

"Oh! ho!" he answered, recoiling three steps and looking at me with wrathful eyes, "Woe to you intractable spirit that you are!"

His behaviour frightened me I confess, but what was infinitely worse, as he went away from me, I saw him take a paper from his pocket. I caught a glimpse of it from a distance and perceived it to be covered with characters which I could not quite make out. He read it attentively, seemed vexed, and kept muttering to himself. I believed that he was evoking spirits to compass my ruin, and I somewhat repented my rash zeal. "If I escape from this adventure," I kept saying to myself, "No more Cabalists for me!" I was keeping my eyes fixed upon him as on a judge about to condemn me to death, when I saw his countenance regain its serenity.

"It is hard for you to kick against the pricks," he said, smiling and rejoining me. "You are a chosen vessel, Heaven has destined you to be the greatest Cabalist of your time. Here is the map of your horoscope which cannot be at fault. If it does not come to pass now and through my mediation, it will at the good pleasure of your retrograde Saturn."

"Ah! If I am to become a Sage," said I, "It will never be save through the mediation of the Great GABALIS; but to be plain with you, I sadly fear that you will find it hard to bend me to this philosophic love making."

"Can it be," he replied, "that you are such a poor Natural Philosopher as not to be persuaded of the existence of these Peoples?"

"I hardly know," I answered, "But I think that I should always fancy them to be merely hobgoblins in disguise."

"And will you ever believe more implicitly in the nurse of your childhood than in your native reason, than in Plato, Pythagoras, Celsus, Psellus, Proclus, Porphyry, Iamblichus, Plotinus, Trismegistus, Nollius, Dornée, Fludd; than in Great Philip Aureolus, Theophrastus Bombast, Paracelsus of Hohenheim, and all the members of our Order!"

"I would believe you Sir," I responded, "As much and more than all of them; but, my dear Sir, could you not arrange with your Fellow Initiates that I should not be compelled to devote myself to these young ladies of the Elements?"

"Alas!" he answered, "You are undoubtedly a free agent, and one does not love unless one wishes to do so. Few Sages, however, have been able to resist their charms. Nevertheless, there have been some who have reserved themselves wholly for greater things, (as you will in time know), and who have not been willing to do the Nymphs this honour."

"Then I will be of their number," I replied, "As I should never be willing to waste time in the ceremonies which, I have heard a certain prelate say, one must practise in order to hold communion with such spirits."

"That prelate did not know what he was talking about," said the Comte, "For you will one day see that these are not spirits, and furthermore no Sage ever makes use either of ceremonies or of superstitious rites to get into touch with spirits, any more than he does in order to commune with the Peoples of whom we are speaking."

"The Cabalist acts solely according to the principles of Nature; and if strange words, symbols and circumlocutions are sometimes found in our books, they are only used to conceal the principles of Natural Philosophy from the ignorant. Admire the simplicity of Nature in all her marvellous works! And in this simplicity a harmony and concert so great, so exact, and so essential that it will compel you, in spite of yourself, to relinquish your idle fancies. What I am about to tell you, we teach those of our disciples whom we are not willing unreservedly to admit into the Sanctuary of Nature; yet whom we in no wise wish to deprive of the society of the Elementary Peoples because of the compassion which we have for these same Peoples."

"As you may perhaps already have grasped, the Salamanders are composed of the most subtle portions of the Sphere of Fire, fused together and organised by the action of the Universal Fire, of which I will discourse to you some day. It is called the Universal Fire because it is the inherent cause of every movement in Nature."

"Likewise the Sylphs are composed of the purest atoms of the Air, the Nymphs of the most subtle essences of the Water, and the Gnomes of the finest particles of the Earth. Adam was closely related to these perfect creatures, for being created out of all that was purest in the four Elements, he combined in himself the perfections of these four races of Peoples and was their natural King. As you will learn later, however, the moment his sin had precipitated him into the dregs of the Elements, the harmony was disturbed and there could no longer be any relation between him, gross and impure as he had become, and these pure and subtle beings. How remedy this evil? How restring the lute and recover that lost sovereignty? Oh Nature! Why art thou so little studied? Do you not understand, my Son, how easy Nature finds it to restore to man the estate which he has lost?"

"Alas! Sir," I answered, "I am very ignorant concerning all these facilities of Nature to which you refer."

"Nevertheless it is exceedingly easy to become well informed about them," he rejoined. "If we wish to recover empire over the Salamanders, we must purify and exalt the Element of Fire which is in us, and raise the pitch of that relaxed string. We have only to concentrate the Fire of the World in a globe of crystal, by means of concave mirrors; and this is the art which all the ancients religiously concealed, and which the divine Theophrastus discovered. A Solar Powder is formed in this globe, which being purified in itself and freed from any admixture of the other Elements, and being prepared according to the Art, becomes in a very short time supremely fitted to exalt the Fire which is in us, and to make us become, as it were, of an igneous nature. Thereafter the Inhabitants of the Sphere of Fire are our inferiors, and enraptured to see our mutual harmony re-established, and that we are again drawing near to them, they have as much friendship for us as for their own kindred, and all the respect which they owe to the image and lieutenant of their Creator. They pay us every attention they can bethink themselves of, through their desire to obtain from us the immortality which they do not possess."

"It is true that they live a very long time, since they are more subtle than the people of the other Elements; hence they are in no hurry to exact immortality from the Sages. If the aversion you have evinced should prove lasting, my Son, you might be able to adapt yourself to a Salamander, perhaps it would never speak to you of that which you so greatly fear. It would not be thus with the Sylphs, Gnomes, and Nymphs. As they live for less time, they have more to do with us, so their familiarity is easier to obtain."

"One has only to seal a goblet full of compressed Air, Water, or Earth and to leave it exposed to the Sun for a month. Then separate the Elements scientifically, which is particularly easy to do with Water and Earth. It is marvellous what a magnet for attracting Nymphs, Sylphs, and Gnomes, each one of these purified Elements is. After taking the smallest possible quantity every day for some months, one sees in the air the flying Commonwealth of the Sylphs, the Nymphs come in crowds to the shores, the Guardians of the Treasures parade their riches. Thus, without symbols, without ceremonies, without barbaric words, one becomes ruler over these Peoples. They exact no worship whatever from the Sage, whose superiority to themselves they fully recognise. Thus venerable Nature teaches her children to repair the elements by means of the Elements. Thus harmony is re-established. Thus man recovers his natural empire, and can do all things in the Elements without the Devil, and without Black Art. Thus you see my Son, the Sages are more innocent than you imagined. Have you no answer to make me?"

"I marvel at you, Sir," said I, "And I am beginning to fear lest you should make me into a distiller."

"Ah! God forbid, my child," he exclaimed, "Your horoscope does not destine you for such nonsense as that. On the contrary, I forbid you to trifle away your time over it. I have told you that the Sages only teach such things to those whom they have no wish to admit to their company. You will have all these, and infinitely more glorious and more desirable advantages, through Philosophic Procedures which are quite different in character. I have only described these methods to make you see the innocence of this Philosophy and to allay your panic terrors."

"Thanks be to God, Sir," I answered, "I no longer have so much fear as I had this afternoon. And although I have not yet made up my mind to this arrangement with the Salamanders which you propose, I cannot help being curious to learn how you have discovered that the Nymphs and Sylphs die."

"Verily," he replied, "They tell us so, and moreover we actually see them die."

"How is it possible you can see them die," I questioned, "when your alliance renders them immortal?

"That would be a point well made," said he, "if the number of Sages equalled the number of these Peoples; besides, there are many among them who prefer to die rather than run the risk of becoming immortal, and of being as unhappy as they see the demons to be. It is the Devil who inspires these sentiments in them, for he leaves no stone unturned to prevent these poor creatures from becoming immortal through alliance with us. So that I regard this aversion of yours, my Son, as a very pernicious temptation and a most uncharitable impulse,

and you ought so to regard it. Furthermore, as to the death of the Nymphs and Sylphs, of which you speak; who compelled the Oracle of Apollo to say, as Porphyry reports, that all those who used to speak through the Oracles were mortal like himself? And what, think you, was the significance of that cry, which was heard throughout the coasts of Italy, and which struck such terror into the hearts of all who chanced to be upon the sea? 'THE GREAT PAN IS DEAD.' It was the People of the Air who were announcing to the People of the Waters that the chief and oldest of the Sylphs had just died."

"It seems to me," I remarked," that at the time that cry was heard the world was worshipping Pan and the Nymphs. Were then these gentlemen, whose fellowship you extol to me, the false gods of the Pagans?"

"That is true, my Son," he answered. "The Sages are far from believing that the Devil ever had power to make himself worshipped. He is too wretched and too weak ever to have had such pleasure and authority. But he has had power to persuade these Hosts of the Elements to show themselves to men, and to cause temples to be erected in their honour; and by virtue of the natural dominion which each one of these Peoples has over the Element in which it dwells, they kept troubling the air and the sea, shaking the earth and scattering the fire of heaven at their own good pleasure. Thus they had little difficulty in causing themselves to be mistaken for divinities so long as the Sovereign Being neglected the salvation of the nations. Yet the Devil did not derive from his mischief all the advantage he had hoped. For from that time it chanced that as Pan, the Nymphs, and other Elementary Peoples had found a means of exchanging this traffic in worship for a traffic in love, (you must needs remember that, among the ancients, Pan was held to be the king of the so-called incubus gods who ardently courted maidens), many of the Pagans escaped from the Devil, and will not burn in Hell."

"I do not understand you, Sir," I replied.

"You take pains not to understand me," he continued mirthfully and in a mocking tone. "This is beyond your comprehension and would likewise be beyond that of all your doctors, for they have no idea.as to what glorious Natural Philosophy is. Here is the great mystery of all that part of Philosophy which has to do with the Elements, and which, if you have any self esteem, will surely remove the very unphilosophic repugnance which you have been evincing all day long."

"Know then, my Son, and be in no hurry to divulge this great Arcane to any unworthy ignoramus—know, that even as the Sylphs acquire an immortal soul through the alliance which they contract with men who are predestined: so men who have no right whatever to eternal glory, those unfortunates for whom immortality is but a fatal advantage, for whom the Messiah was not sent."

"You gentlemen of the Cabala are Jansenists then?" I interposed.

"We do not know what Jansenism is my child," he answered brusquely, "and we scorn to inform ourselves as to wherein consist the differences in the various sects and religions wherewith the ignorant are infatuated. We ourselves hold to the ancient religion of our Fathers the Philosophers, concerning which I must one day instruct you. But to resume the thread of our discourse, those men whose melancholy immortality would be but an eternal misfortune, those unhappy children whom the Sovereign Father has neglected, have still the resource of becoming mortal by allying themselves with the Elementary Peoples. Thus you see the Sages run no hazard as to Eternity; if predestined they have the pleasure on quitting the prison of this body, of leading to Heaven the Sylphid or Nymph whom they have immortalised. On the other hand, if not predestined, marriage with the Sylphid renders their soul mortal and delivers them from the horror of the second death. Thus the Devil beheld all those Pagans who had allied themselves with Nymphs escaping his clutches. Thus the Sages, or the friends of the Sages, to whom God inspires us to communicate any one of the four Elementary Secrets, which I have well nigh taught you, may be set free from the peril of damnation."

"Truth to tell," I exclaimed, not daring to put him into a bad humour again, and deeming it expedient to postpone fully telling him my sentiments until he should have revealed to me all the secrets of his Cabala which, from this sample, I judged to be exceedingly odd and recreative; " truth to tell, you carry wisdom to very great lengths, and you were right in saying that this would be beyond the comprehension of all our doctors. I even believe that it would be beyond the comprehension of all our magistrates as well, and that if they could discover who these people are who escape the Devil by this method, as ignorance is ever unjust, they would take sides with the Devil against these fugitives and would use them ill."

"For that reason," said the Comte, "I have enjoined secrecy upon you, and I solemnly adjure you to maintain it. Your Judges are strange folk! They condemn a most innocent action as being the basest of crimes. What barbarism it was to condemn those two priests, whom the Prince de la Mirande knew, to be burned, each of whom had had his Sylphid for the space of forty years. What inhumanity it was to condemn to death Jeanne Hervillier, who had laboured to immortalise a Gnome for thirty six years. And what ignorance on the part of Bodin to call her a sorceress, and to make her amorous intrigues a justification of the popular misconception regarding the so called sorcerers, In a book as extravagant as his Republic is rational."

"But it is late, and I am unmindful of the fact that you have not yet dined."

"You are speaking for yourself, Sir," said I, "for my part I could listen to you until to morrow without inconvenience."

"Ah! as for myself," he rejoined, smiling and walking towards the gate, "evidently you do not in the least know what Philosophy is. The Sages only eat for pleasure and never from necessity."

"I had quite the opposite idea of Sageness," I replied, I supposed that the Sage should only eat to satisfy necessity."

"You are mistaken," said the Comte, "How long do you think we Sages can go without eating?"

"How should I know?" said I, Moses and Elias fasted forty days, no doubt you Sages fast for some days less."

"What a mighty endeavour that would be!" he answered, "The most learned man who ever lived, the divine, the almost to be worshipped Paracelsus affirms that he has seen many Sages who have fasted for twenty years without eating anything whatsoever. He himself, before being acknowledged Monarch of the Empire of Wisdom, whose sceptre we have justly accorded him, was pleased to essay living for several years by taking only one half scruple of Solar Quintessence. And if you wish to have the pleasure of making any one live without eating, you have only to prepare the earth as I have indicated that it may be prepared for the purpose of securing the partnership of the Gnomes. This Earth applied to the navel, and renewed when it is too dry, makes it possible for one to dispense with eating and drinking without the slightest inconvenience whatever, even as the veracious Paracelsus relates that he himself demonstrated during six months."

"But the use of the Catholic Cabalistic Medicine liberates us in the very best way from the importunate necessities to which Nature subjects the ignorant. We eat only when it pleases us to do so, and every superfluity of food vanishes by unconscious transpiration, we are never ashamed of being men. Then he fell silent, perceiving that we were within hearing of our servants, and we went to the village to take a slender repast, as is the custom of the Heroes of Philosophy".

DISCOURSE III

AFTER DINNER WE RETURNED TO THE labyrinth. I was pensive and my pity for the Comte's madness, which I fully realised would be hard to cure, prevented my being as much amused at all that he had told me as I should have been, could I have had any hope of restoring him to reason. I kept searching antiquity for some counter arguments which he would be unable to refute for, on my adducing the opinions of the church, he had declared that he cared for naught save the ancient religion of his Fathers the Philosophers; and to seek to convince a Cabalist by reason would be a long winded undertaking, besides I was not anxious to get into a dispute with a man whose motives I did not as yet altogether understand.

It crossed my mind that what he had said concerning the false gods, for whom he had substituted the Sylphs and other Elementary Peoples, might be refuted by the Pagan Oracles whom Scripture everywhere calls devils, and not Sylphs. But not knowing whether the Comte might not in the tenets of his Cabala attribute the answer of the Oracles to some natural cause, I believed that it would be to the point to make him explain what he thought about them.

He gave me an opportunity to broach the subject when, before entering the labyrinth, he turned towards the garden. "This is very fine," he said, "and these statues are rather effective."

"The Cardinal who had them brought here," I replied, "had a fancy little worthy of his great genius. He believed the majority of these figures to have given forth Oracles in bygone days, and paid exceedingly dear for them on that account."

"That is a failing of many people," the Comte rejoined. "Every day ignorance causes a very criminal kind of idolatry to be committed, since people preserve with such great care and consider so precious those very idols which they believe the Devil formerly employed to make himself worshipped. O God, will people never in this world know that Thou hast precipitated Thine enemies beneath Thy footstool from the birth of time, and that Thou dost hold the demons prisoners under the earth in the vortex of darkness? This unpraiseworthy desire to collect these counterfeit instruments of the demons might become innocent, my Son, if people would let themselves be persuaded that the angels of darkness have never been allowed to speak through the Oracles."

"I do not believe," I interrupted, "that it would be easy to establish that hypothesis amongst the antiquarians, but possibly it might be amongst the free thinkers. For not long ago it was decided by the leading minds of the day, in a conference called for the purpose, that all these pretended Oracles were either a fraud due to the avarice of the Gentile priests, or but a political trick of the Sovereigns."

"Was this conference held and this question thus decided by the members of the Muhammedan Embassy sent to your King?"

"No Sir," I answered.

"Then of what religion are these gentlemen," he retorted "since they set at naught the Holy Scriptures which make mention in so many instances of so many different Oracles, especially of the Pythian Oracles who made their abode and gave forth their replies in places destined for the multiplication of the image of God?"

"I mentioned all those ventriloquists," I answered, "and I reminded the company that King Saul had banished them from his kingdom where, notwithstanding, he found one of them on the evening of the day before his death, whose voice had the wondrous power of raising Samuel from the dead in answer to his prayer, and to his ruin. But these learned men did not alter their decision that there never had been any Oracles."

"If the Scripture made no impression upon them," said the Comte, "you should have convinced them by all antiquity, wherein it would have been easy to point out a thousand marvellous proofs. There were so many virgins pregnant with the destiny of mortals, who brought forth the good and bad fortunes of those who consulted them. What do you allege as to Chrysostom, Origen and Oecumenius, who make mention of those divine men whom the Greeks called 'Engastrimyths,' whose prophetic abdomens articulated such famous Oracles? And if your gentlemen did not care for the Scriptures and the Fathers, you should have reminded them of those miraculous maidens of whom the Greek Pausanias speaks, who changed themselves into doves and in that form delivered the celebrated Oracles of the Doves of Dodona. Or else you might have said, to the glory of your nation, that there were of old in Gaul illustrious maidens who transformed their entire appearance at the will of those who consulted them and who, in addition to the famous Oracles which they delivered, had a wonderful power over the waters and a salutary authority over the most incurable diseases."

"They would have treated all these fine proofs as apocryphal," said I.

"Does their antiquity render them suspect?" he rejoined. "If so, you had only to adduce the Oracles which are still delivered every day."

"And in what part of the world?" said I.

"In Paris," he replied.

"In Paris!" I exclaimed.

"In Paris," he repeated, "'Art thou a master of Israel and knowest not these things?' Do not people daily consult Aquatic Oracles in glasses of water or in basins, and Aerial Oracles in mirrors and on the hands of virgins? Do they not recover lost beads and pilfered watches? Do they not learn news from distant countries in this way, and see the absent?"

"Eh, Sir, what are you saying?" said I.

"I am recounting that which I am positive happens every day," he answered, "and it would not be difficult to find a thousand eyewitnesses of it."

"I cannot believe that Sir," I returned. "The magistrates would make an example of such culprits and people would not permit idolatry—"

"Ah! how hasty you are!" interrupted the Comte. "There is not so much evil in all this as you might suppose, and Providence will not permit the total destruction of that remnant of Philosophy which has escaped the lamentable shipwreck Truth has sustained. If there yet remains among the people any vestige of the dread power of the Divine Names, are you of the opinion that it should be blotted out and that they should lose the respect and recognition due to the great name AGLA, which works all these wonders, even when invoked by the ignorant and sinful and which, spoken by a Cabalist, would perform many other miracles. If you had wished to convince your gentlemen of the truth of the Oracles, you had only to exalt your imagination and your faith, and turning towards the East cry aloud 'AG'—"

"Sir," I interposed, "I was careful not to advance that kind of argument to such proper folk as those with whom I was debating. They would have taken me for a fanatic for, depend upon it, they have no faith whatever in that sort of thing, and even if I had known the Cabalistic Procedure to which you refer, it would not have succeeded when pronounced by me; I have even less faith than they."

"Well, well," said the Comte, "If you lack faith we shall supply it. If you had reason to believe, however, that your gentlemen would not credit that which they can see any day in Paris, you might have cited a story of rather recent date. That Oracle, which Celius Rhodeginius says he himself witnessed, delivered towards the end of the last century by that extraordinary woman who spoke and predicted the future by means of the same organ as did the Eurycles of Plutarch."

"I should not have cared to cite Rhodeginius," I answered, "it would have seemed pedantic to do so, moreover they would certainly have told me that the woman was beyond question a demoniac."

"They would have said that very monachally," he replied.

"Sir," I ventured to say, "notwithstanding the Cabalistic aversion to monks which I perceive you to entertain, I cannot help siding with them on this occasion. I believe that there would not be so much harm in absolutely denying that Oracles ever existed as there is in saying it was not the Devil who spoke through them because, in short, the Fathers and the theologians—"

"Because, in short," he interrupted, "do not the theologians agree that the learned Sambethe, the most ancient of the Sibyls was the daughter of Noah?"

"Eh! what has that to do with it?" I retorted.

"Does not Plutarch say," he rejoined, "that the most ancient of the Sibyls was the first to deliver Oracles at Delphi? Therefore the Spirit which Sambethe harboured in her breast was not a devil nor was her Apollo a false god, for idolatry did not begin until long after the division of languages, and it would be far from the truth to attribute to the Father of Lies the sacred books of the Sibyls, and all the proofs of the true religion which the Fathers have drawn from them. And then, too, my Son," he laughingly continued, "it is not for you to annul the marriage of David and the Sibyl which was made by a celebrated cardinal, nor to accuse that learned personage of having placed side by side a great prophet and a wretched demoniac. Since either David strengthens the testimony of the Sibyl or the Sibyl weakens the authority of David."

"Sir," I exclaimed, "I entreat you again to become serious."

"Willingly," said he, "provided you will not accuse me of being too much so. Is it your opinion that the Devil is sometimes divided against himself and against his own interests?"

"Why not?" said I.

"Why not!" said he, "Because that which Tertullian has so felicitously and so grandly termed 'the Reason of God' does not find it fitting. Satan is never divided against himself. It therefore follows either, that the Devil has never spoken through the Oracles, or that he has never spoken through them against his own interests; and therefore if the Oracles have spoken against the interests of the Devil, it was not the Devil who was speaking through the Oracles."

"But," said I, 'has not God been able to compel the Devil to bear witness to the truth and to speak against himself?"

"But," he answered, "What if God has not compelled him to do so?"

"Ah, in that case," I replied, "you are more in the right than the monks."

"Let us look into this matter then," he continued, "and that I may proceed invincibly and in good faith, I do not care to introduce the evidence concerning Oracles cited by the Fathers of the Church, although I am aware of the veneration you entertain for those great men. Their religion and the interest they took in the matter might have prejudiced them, and seeing Truth to be rather poor and naked in their own time, their love of her might have caused them to borrow from Falsehood's self some robe and ornament for Truth's adornment. They were men and consequently capable of bearing false witness, according to the maxim of the Poet of the Synagogue. I shall therefore take a man who cannot be suspected of such a motive, a Pagan, and a Pagan of a very different kind to Lucretius, or Lucian, or the Epicureans. A Pagan thoroughly imbued with the belief that there are gods and devils without number, immeasurably superstitious, a mighty magician, or supposedly so, and consequently a great partisan of devils namely Porphyry. Here are word for word some Oracles which he reports.

ORACLE.

Above the Celestial Fire there is an Incorruptible Flame, ever sparkling, Source of Life, Fountain of all Beings, and Principle of all Things. This Flame produces all, and nothing perishes save that which it consumes.

It reveals itself by virtue of itself This Fire cannot he contained in any place; it is without form and without substance, it girdles the Heavens and from it there proceeds a tiny spark which: makes the whole fire of the Sun, Moon and Stars. This is what I know of God. Seek not to know more, for this passes thy comprehension howsoever wise thou mayest be. Nevertheless, know that the unjust and wicked man cannot hide himself from God, nor can craft nor excuse disguise aught from His piercing eyes. All is full of God, God is everywhere.

"You will admit, my Son, that this Oracle is not too greatly influenced by his devil."

"At least," I answered "the Devil in this instance rather departs from his character."

"Here is another," said he, "that preaches still better."

ORACLE.

There is in God an immense depth of Flame. The heart must not, however, fear to touch this adorable Fire nor to be touched by it. It will in no wise he consumed by this gentle Flame, whose tranquil and peaceful warmth causes the union, harmony and duration of the world. Nothing exists save by this Fire, which is God himself It is uncreate, it is without mother, it is omniscient and unteachable: it is unchanging in purposes, and its Name is Ineffable. This is God; as for us who are His messengers, WE ARE BUT A LITTLE PART OF GOD.

"Well! What say you to that?"

"I should say of both," I replied, "that God can force the Father of Lies to bear witness to the truth."

"Here is another," rejoined the. Comte, "which will remove that scruple."

ORACLE.

Alas Tripods! Weep and make funeral oration for your Apollo. HE IS MORTAL, HE IS ABOUT TO DIE, HE EXPIRES; because the Light of the Celestial Flame extinguishes him.

"You see, my child, that whoever this may be who speaks through these Oracles, and who so admirably explains to the Pagans the Essence, Unity, Immensity and Eternity of God, he owns that he is mortal and but a spark of God. Therefore it cannot be the Devil who is speaking, since he is immortal, and God would not compel him to say that he is not. It is therefore proven that Satan is not divided against himself. Is it a way to make himself worshipped to say that there is but one God? The Oracle says that he is mortal, since when is the Devil become so humble as to deprive himself of even his natural qualities? Therefore you see, my Son, that if the principle of Him who is called par excellence the God of the Sciences exists, it cannot have been the Devil who spoke through the Oracles."

"But if it was not the Devil," said I, "either lying from gaiety of heart when he speaks of himself as mortal, or telling the truth under compulsion when he speaks of God, then to what will your Cabala ascribe all the Oracles which you maintain to have been actually delivered? Is it to an exhalation of the earth, as Aristotle, Cicero and Plutarch say?"

"Ah! not to that my child," said the Comte. "Thanks to the Sacred Cabala my imagination has not led me astray to that extent."

"What do you mean?" I inquired, "Do you consider that opinion so exceedingly visionary? Nevertheless its partisans are men of good sense."

"Not in this instance," he replied, "and it is impossible to attribute to an exhalation all that happened in the Oracles. For example, that man in Tacitus, who appeared in a dream to the priests of a temple of Hercules in Armenia, and commanded them to make ready for him hunters equipped for the chase. Up to this point exhalation might account for it: but when those horses returned in the evening jaded, and their quivers emptied of shafts; and when the next day exactly the same number of dead beasts were found as there had been arrows in the quivers, you will perceive that exhalation could not have produced this effect, much less the Devil. For to believe that the Devil has been permitted to divert himself by chasing the hind and hare, is to have an irrational and uncabalistic idea of the misery of the enemy of God." "Then," said I, "to what cause does the Sacred Cabala ascribe all this?"

"Wait," he answered "before I reveal this mystery to you I must overcome any prejudice you might have because of this hypothetical exhalation. For, if I remember aright, you cited Aristotle, Plutarch and Cicero with emphasis. You might likewise have cited Iamblichus, who very great genius though he was, laboured for a time under this delusion, but speedily relinquished it when he had examined the matter at close range in the Book of the Mysteries.

Peter of Aponus, Pomponatius, Levinius, Sirenius, and Lucilius Vanino were also overjoyed to find this subterfuge in some of the ancient writers. All these pseudo-geniuses who, when they treat of divine things, say rather what pleases them than what they know to be true, are unwilling to admit that there is anything superhuman in the Oracles, lest they should acknowledge the existence of something superior to man." They fear lest men should make of the Oracles a ladder wherewith to mount to God, Whom they dread to acknowledge as manifesting through gradations of His spiritual creatures, and they prefer to manufacture a ladder to descend into nothingness. Instead of mounting towards heaven they delve into the earth, and instead of seeking in Beings superior to man the cause of those transports which lift him above himself and restore to him a kind of divinity, they weakly ascribe to impotent exhalations this power to penetrate the future, discover hidden things, and attain to the supreme secrets of the Divine Essence."

"Such is the misery of man when possessed by the spirit of contradiction and the disposition to think differently to others. Instead of achieving his ends he becomes involved and fettered. These intellectual libertines do not wish to make man subject to substances less material than himself, and yet they make him subject to an exhalation: and disregarding the absence of any connection whatever between this chimerical vapour and the soul of man, between this emanation and future events, between this frivolous cause and these miraculous effects, the mere singularity of their theories is to them sufficient evidence of their reasonableness. They are content to deny the existence of spirits and to assume the role of free thinkers."

"Then, Sir, is singularity exceeding displeasing to you?" I asked.

"Ah! my Son," said he, "'tis the bane of commonsense and the stumbling block of the greatest minds. Aristotle, great logician though he was, could not avoid the snare into which the passion for singularity leads those whom it unbalances as violently as it did him. He could not, I say, avoid becoming entangled and contradicting himself. In his book on 'The Generation of Animals' and in his 'Ethics,' he says that the spirit and understanding of man come to him from without, and cannot be transmitted from father to son. And from the spirituality of the operations of man's soul he concludes it to be of a different nature to that composite material which it animates, the grossness of which only serves to becloud speculation and is far from contributing to its production. Blind Aristotle! Since you maintain that the matter of which we are composed cannot be the source of our spiritual thoughts, how can you expect a weak exhalation to be the source of sublime thought and of those soaring flights of spirit achieved by those who gave forth the Pythian Oracles? See, my child, how forcibly this genius contradicts himself, and how his craving for singularity leads him astray."

"You reason very logically, Sir," said I, enchanted to perceive that he was talking excellent sense, and hoping that his madness would not prove incurable, "God willing—"

"Plutarch, so sound in other respects," he said, interrupting me, "moves me to pity in his dialogue concerning the 'Cessation of the Oracles.' Convincing objections are raised which he in no wise refutes. Why does he not answer what is said to him, namely, that if it is the exhalation which causes these transports, all those who approach the prophetic Tripod would be seized with enthusiasm and not merely a single maiden who moreover must be virgin. But how can this vapour articulate cries through the abdomen? Besides this exhalation is a natural cause which must necessarily produce its effect regularly and at all times. Why is this maiden agitated only when consulted? And, what is more important, why has the earth ceased to breathe forth these divine vapours? Is it less earth now than then? Is it subject to other influences? Has it other seas and other rivers? Who then has stopped earth's pores or changed its nature?"

"I wonder that Pomponatius, Lucilius and the other Libertines should borrow this idea from Plutarch and cast aside his explanation. He spoke more judiciously than Cicero and Aristotle, for he was a man of great good sense and, not knowing what conclusion to draw from all these Oracles, after tedious irresolution, he decided that this exhalation, which he believed issued from the earth, was a most divine spirit. Thus he ascribed to divinity the extraordinary agitations and illuminations of the Priestesses of Apollo. 'This divinatory vapour is a breath and a most divine and most holy spirit,' said he."

"Pomponatius, Lucilius and modern atheists do not adapt themselves readily to fashions of speech which imply divinity. 'These exhalations', say they, 'were of the nature of those vapours which infect splenetics who speak languages they do not understand.' Fernelius refutes these impieties rather well, by proving that bile which is a peccant humour cannot cause that diversity of tongues which is one of the most marvellous effects under consideration and an artificial expression of thought. Nevertheless, he decided erroneously in subscribing to Psellus, and to all those who have not penetrated far enough into our Holy Philosophy for, like them, not knowing where to locate the causes of these surprising effects, he imitated the women and monks and attributed them to the Devil."

"Then to whom should one attribute them?" said I, "I have long awaited this Cabalistic secret."

"Plutarch has very well indicated it," he said, "and he would have been wise had he let matters rest there. Since this irregular method of expressing one's opinion by means of an unseemly organ was neither solemn enough nor sufficiently worthy of the majesty of the gods, says that Pagan, and since the sayings of the Oracles surpassed the powers of the soul of man, they have rendered great service to Philosophy, for they have established the existence of mortal beings between the gods and man to whom one can ascribe all that surpasses human weakness yet falls short of divine greatness."

"This is the opinion held in every ancient philosophy. The Platonists and the Pythagoreans took it from the Egyptians, and the latter from Joseph the Saviour, and from the Hebrews who dwelt in Egypt before the crossing of the Red Sea. The Hebrews used to call these beings who are between the Angels and man Sadaim, and the Greeks, transposing the letters and adding but one syllable, called them Daimonas. Among the ancient Philosophers these demons were held to be an Aerial Race, ruling over the Elements, mortal, engendering, and unknown in this century to those who rarely seek Truth in her ancient dwelling place, which is to say, in the. Cabala and in the theology of the Hebrews, who possessed the special art of holding communion with that Aerial People and of conversing with all these Inhabitants of the Air."

"Now, Sir, I think you have returned again to your Sylphs."

"Yes, my Son," he went on, "the Teraphim of the Jews was but the ceremony which had to be observed for that communion: and that Jew Micah, who complains in the Book of Judges that his gods have been taken from him, only laments the loss of the little image through which the Sylphs used to converse with him. The gods which Rachel stole from her father were also Teraphim. Neither Micah nor Laban are reproved for idolatry, and Jacob would have taken care not to live for fourteen years with an idolater, nor to marry his daughter. It was only a commerce with Sylphs; and tradition tells us that the Synagogue considered such commerce permissible, and that the image belonging to David's wife was but the Teraphim by virtue of which she conversed with the Elementary Peoples: for you can well imagine that the Prophet after God's own heart would not have tolerated idolatry in his household."

"These Elementary Nations, so long as God neglected the salvation of the world in punishment for the first sin, used to take pleasure in explaining to men through the Oracles what they knew of God, in teaching them how to live morally, and in giving them most wise and most profitable counsels, such as are seen in great number in Plutarch and in all historians. As soon as God took pity on mankind and was willing Himself to become their Teacher, these little Masters withdrew. Hence the silence of the Oracles."

"Then the upshot of your entire discourse, Sir," I remarked, "is that there certainly were Oracles, and that the Sylphs delivered them, and even to-day deliver them in goblets or in mirrors."

"The Sylphs or Salamanders, the Gnomes or Undines," corrected the Comte.

"If that be so," I replied, "all your Elementary Peoples are very dishonest folk."

"Why do you say that?" said he.

"Why? Could anything be more knavish," I pursued, "than all these responses with double meanings which they always give?"

"Always?" he replied. "Ah! not always. Did the Sylphid speak very obscurely who appeared to that Roman in Asia and predicted to him that he would one day return to Rome with the dignity of Proconsul? And does not Tacitus say that the event occurred exactly as predicted? That inscription and those statues famous in the history of Spain which warned unfortunate King Rodriguez that his indiscretion and incontinence would be punished by men dressed and armed exactly as they were, and that those black men would take possession of Spain and rule there for many a year. Could anything have been more explicit, and was not the prophecy verified by the event in that selfsame year? For did not the Moors come to dethrone that effeminate king? You know the story, and you must admit that the Devil, who since the reign of the Messiah does not dispose of empires, could not have been the author of this Oracle: and that it was undoubtedly some great Cabalist who had it from one of the most learned Salamanders. Since the Salamanders love chastity exceedingly, they willingly make known to us the misfortunes which must befall mankind for lack of that virtue."

"But, Sir," said I to him, "do you consider that heteroclitic organ which they made use of for the preaching of their ethics very chaste and altogether in keeping with Cabalistic modesty?"

"Ah!" said the Comte, smiling, "Your imagination is shocked, and you fail to perceive the physical reason which causes the flaming Salamander naturally to delight in the most igneous places and to be attracted by—"

"I understand, I understand," I interrupted, "Do not take the trouble to explain further."

"As for the obscurity of some Oracles which you dub knavery," he went on seriously, "are not shadows the usual cloak of Truth? Is not God pleased to hide Himself in their sombre veil? And is not Holy Writ, that perpetual Oracle which He has left to His children, enveloped in an adorable obscurity which confounds and bewilders the proud even as its Light guides the humble?"

"If this be your only difficulty, my Son, I advise you not to postpone entering into communion with the Elementary Peoples. You will find them very sincere folk, learned, benevolent and God-fearing. I am of opinion that you should begin with the Salamanders, for you have Mars in mid-heaven in your horoscope, which signifies that there is a great deal of fire in all your actions. And as for marriage, I rather think that you should choose a Sylphid. You would be happier with her than with any of the others, for you have Jupiter in the ascendant with Venus in sextile. Now Jupiter presides over the Air and the Peoples of the Air. You must, however, consult your own heart in this matter for, as you will one day see, a Sage governs himself by the interior stars, and the stars of the exterior heaven but serve to give him a more certain knowledge of the aspects of the stars of that interior heaven which is in every creature. Thus it rests with you to tell me what your inclination is, that we may proceed to your alliance with those Elementary Peoples which are most pleasing to you."

"Sir," I replied, "in my opinion this affair demands a little consultation."

"I esteem you for that answer," said he, laying his hand on my shoulder. "Consult maturely as to this affair, and above all, with him who is called in an eminent degree the Angel of the Grand Council. Go, and devote yourself to prayer, and I shall be at your house at two o'clock to-morrow afternoon."

We came back to Paris, and on the way I led him once more to discourse against atheists and libertines. I have never heard arguments so well supported by reason, nor such sublime and subtle ideas advanced for the existence of God, and against the blindness of those who go through life without wholly surrendering themselves to a serious and continual worship of Him to whom we owe the gift and preservation of our being. I was surprised at the character of this man, and I could not comprehend how it was possible for him to be at once so strong, and so weak, so admirable, yet so ridiculous.

DISCOURSE IV

I AWAITED THE COMTE DE GABALIS AT MY house, as we had arranged at parting. He came at the appointed hour and accosting me with a smiling air said, "Ah well, my Son, which of the Invisible Peoples does God give you most inclination for, and would you prefer an alliance with Salamanders, Gnomes, Nymphs, or Sylphids?"

"I have not yet quite made up my mind to this marriage, Sir," I replied.

"What deters you?" he inquired.

"To be frank with you, Sir," said I, "I cannot conquer my imagination, which always represents these pretended hosts of the Elements as so many imps of Satan."

"Dissipate, O Lord!" cried he, "O God of Light! Dissipate the darkness in which ignorance and a perverse education have enveloped the mind of this chosen one, whom Thou hast made me know that Thou dost destine for such great things! And you, my Son, close not the door against Truth which is willing to enter in unto you. Be non-resistant. Nay, you need not be so, for it is most injurious to Truth to prepare the way for her. She knows how to break through gates of iron and how to enter where she pleases despite all resistance of falsehood. What have you to oppose to her? Would you say that God has not power to create in the Elements real beings such as I have described?"

"I have not looked into the matter," said I, "to ascertain whether the thing itself be impossible, whether a single Element can furnish blood, flesh and bones; whether temperament can exist without admixture, and action without opposing force; but assuming that God has been able thus to create, what sound proof is there that He has done so?"

"Let me convince you of it at once, without further temporising. I am going to summon the Sylphs of Cardan; and you shall hear from their own lips what they are, and what I have taught you about them."

"By no means, Sir," I exclaimed hastily. "Postpone such proof, I beg of you, until I am persuaded that these folk are not the enemies of God; for until then I would rather die than wrong my conscience by—"

"Behold the ignorance and false piety of these unhappy times," interrupted the Comte wrathfully. "Why do they not expunge the greatest of the Anchorites from the Calendar of the Saints? Why do they not burn his statues? It is a thousand pities people do not insult his venerable ashes and cast them to the winds, as they would those of the poor wretches who are accused of having had dealings with devils! Did he bethink himself to exorcise the Sylphs? And did he not treat them as men? What have you to say to that, scrupulous Sir, you and all your miserable doctors? And is it your opinion that the Sylph who discoursed concerning his nature to this Patriarch was an imp of Satan? Did this incomparable man confer with a hobgoblin concerning the Gospel? And will you accuse him of having profaned the adorable Mysteries by conversing concerning them with a phantom enemy of God? In that case Athanasius and Jerome are most unworthy of the great name accorded them by your learned men, for they have written eloquent eulogies of a man who treated devils thus humanely."

"If they had taken this Sylph for a devil they would either have concealed the adventure or have altered the sense of the sermon, or of that very pathetic apostrophe, which the Anchorite—more zealous and more credulous than you—made to the city of Alexandria. Now if they thought him a being who had, as he affirmed, a share in the redemption as well as we ourselves, and if they considered this apparition an extraordinary favour bestowed by God upon the Saint whose life they wrote, are you rational in thinking yourself better informed than Athanasius and Jerome, and a greater Saint than the divine Antony? What would you have said to that admirable man had you been one of the ten thousand hermits to whom he recounted the conversation he had just been having with the Sylph? Wiser and more enlightened than all those terrestrial Angels, you would doubtless have demonstrated to the Holy Abbot that his entire adventure was but pure illusion, and you would have dissuaded his disciple Athanasius from making known to all the world a story so little in keeping with religion, philosophy, and common sense. Is not this true?"

"It is true," said I, "that I should have thought best either to say nothing whatever about it or to tell more."

"Athanasius and Jerome," replied he, "were careful not to tell more, for that was all they knew, and even though they had known all, which is impossible if one is not of our number, they would not rashly have divulged the secrets of the Sages."

"But why not? Did not the Sylph propose to St. Antony what you are to-day proposing to me?" "What?" said the Comte laughing, "Marriage? Ah! would that have been quite fitting?"

"Probably the good man would not have accepted the offer," I ventured.

"No, certainly not," said the Comte, "for it would have been tempting God to marry at that age and to ask Him for children."

"What! " I exclaimed. "Do people marry Sylphs for the purpose of having children?"

"Indeed! " said he, "Is it ever permissible to marry for any other purpose?"

"I did not imagine," said I, "that they aspired to the planting of family trees. I had supposed their sole object to be the immortalisation of the Sylphids."

"Ah! you are mistaken," quoth he. "The charity of the Philosophers causes them to have as their ultimate aim the immortality of the Sylphids: but Nature makes them desire to see them fruitful. Whenever you wish you shall see these philosophic families in the Air. Happy world, if there had been no other families and if there had been no children of sin!"

"What do you mean by children of sin?" I inquired.

"They are, my Son," he explained, "all children who are born in the ordinary way, children conceived by the will of the flesh and not by the will of God, children of wrath and malediction; in a word, children of man and woman. You are longing to interrupt me. I see exactly what you would like to say. Yes, my child, know that it was never the will of the Lord that men and women should have children in the way in which they do. The design of the Most Wise Craftsman was far nobler. He would have had the world peopled in a different manner than we see it. If wretched Adam had not grossly disobeyed God's command not to touch Eve, and had he contented himself with all the other fruits in the garden of pleasure, with the beauties of the Nymphs and Sylphids, the world would not have had the shame of seeing itself filled with men so imperfect that they seem monsters when compared with the children of the Philosophers."

"Apparently, Sir," said I, "you believe Adam's crime to have been other than that of eating the apple."

"Why, my Son," he replied, "are you one of those who are so simple-minded as to take the story of the apple literally? Ah! know that the Holy Language makes use of these innocent metaphors to prevent us from having improper ideas of an action which has caused all the misfortunes of the human race. Thus when Solomon said, 'I will go up unto the palm tree and gather the fruit thereof,' he had another appetite than that for eating dates. This language consecrated by the Angels, and in which they chant hymns to the living God, has no terms to express what it implies figuratively by the words apple and date. But the Sage easily deciphers these chaste figures of speech. When he sees that the taste and mouth of Eve were not punished, and that she was delivered with pain, he knows that it was not the tasting which was criminal. And discovering what the first sin was, by reason of the care which the first sinners took to hide certain parts of their bodies with leaves, he concludes that God did not will men to multiply in this vile way. O Adam! thou shouldst only have begotten men like unto thyself, or have engendered none save heroes or giants."

"Eh! What expedient had he," I asked, "for either of these marvellous generations?"

"Obeying God," he replied, "and touching only the Nymphs, Gnomids, Sylphids or Salamanders: Thus there would have been none save heroes born, and the Universe would have been peopled with marvellous men filled with strength and wisdom. God has been pleased to enable us to conjecture the difference between that innocent world and the guilty one we behold to-day by now and then permitting us to see children born in the manner He designed."

"Then, Sir, have these children of the Elements occasionally been seen? If so, a Master of Arts from the Sorbonne, who was citing St. Augustin, St. Jerome, and Gregory of Nazianzus the other day, was mistaken in believing that no issue can spring from the love of spirits for women, or from the relationship men can have with certain demons he called Hyphialtes."

"Lactantius has reasoned better," the Comte replied, "and cautious Thomas Aquinas has learnedly determined not only that these intimacies, may be fruitful, but also that the children thus born are of a far nobler and more heroic nature. In fact, when it pleases you, you shall read of the lofty deeds of those mighty and famous men whom Moses says were born in this manner. We have their records in our possession in the Book of the Wars of the Lord, cited in the twenty-first chapter of the Book of Numbers. Meantime just think what the world would be if all its inhabitants were like Zoroaster."

"What!" said I, "Zoroaster whom people say was the inventor of necromancy?"

"The same of whom the ignorant have written that calumny," said the Comte. "He had the honour of being the son of the Salamander Oromasis and of Vesta, Noah's wife. He lived for twelve hundred years, the sagest monarch in the world, and then was carried away to the Region of the Salamanders by his father Oromasis."

"I do not doubt that Zoroaster is with the Salamander Oromasis in the Region of Fire," said I, "but I should not like to put such an affront upon Noah as you have been guilty of."

"The affront is not so great as you might think," replied the Comte; "all your patriarchs considered it a great honour to be the reputed fathers of those children whom the Sons of God were pleased to have by their wives, but as yet this is too much for you. Let us return to Oromasis. He was beloved by Vesta, Noah's wife. This Vesta after her death became the tutelary genius of Rome, and the Sacred Fire, which she desired the virgins to preserve with so much care, was in honour of the Salamander, her lover. Besides Zoroaster, there sprang from their love a daughter of rare beauty and wisdom, the divine Egeria, from whom Numa Pompilius received all his laws. She compelled Numa, whom she loved, to build a temple to Vesta, her mother, where the Sacred Fire should be maintained in honour of her father Oromasis. This is the truth concerning the fable about the Nymph Egeria which Roman poets and historians have related."

"William Postel, least ignorant of all those who have studied the Cabala in ordinary books, was aware that Vesta was Noah's wife, but he did not know that Egeria was Vesta's daughter, and not having read the secret books of the ancient Cabala, a copy of which the Prince de Mirande bought so dearly, he confused things and believed that Egeria was merely the good genius of Noah's wife."

"In those books we learn that Egeria was conceived upon the waters when Noah was wandering upon the avenging floods which inundated the Universe. Women were at that time reduced to the small number who were saved in the Cabalistic Ark, built by that second father of mankind."

"This illustrious man, mourning over the frightful chastisement wherewith the Lord was punishing the crimes caused by Adam's love for Eve, and seeing that Adam had ruined his posterity by preferring her to the daughters of the Elements and by taking her from that Salamander or Sylph who would have gained her affection—Noah, I say, profited by the fatal example of Adam and was content that his wife Vesta should yield herself to the Salamander Oromasis, Prince of Fiery Beings; and persuaded his three sons likewise to surrender their three wives to the Princes of the three other Elements. The Universe was, in a short time, re-peopled with heroic men, so learned, so handsome, so admirable, that their posterity dazzled by their virtues has mistaken them for divinities. One of Noah's children, rebelling against his father's counsel, could not resist the attractions of his wife any more than Adam could withstand the charms of his Eve. But just as Adam's sin blackened the souls of all his descendants, so Ham's lack of complaisance for the Sylphs branded all his black posterity; whence comes the horrible complexion of the Ethiopians, say our Cabalists, and of all those hideous peoples who have been commanded to dwell in the torrid zone as punishment for the profane ardour of their father."

"These are very singular fancies, Sir," said I, marvelling at the man's ravings, "and your Cabala is of wonderful service in illuminating antiquity."

"Of wonderful service," he rejoined gravely, "and without it Scripture, history, fable and Nature are obscure and unintelligible. You believe, for example, that the injury Ham did his father was what it seems literally to be; as a matter of fact, it was something quite different. Noah went forth from the Ark, and perceiving that his wife Vesta had but grown more beautiful through her love for Oromasis, fell passionately in love with her again. Ham fearing that his father was about to re-people the earth with progeny as black as his own Ethiopians, seized his 'opportunity one day when the old man was full of wine, and mercilessly maltreated him. You laugh?"

"I laugh at Ham's indiscreet zeal," said I.

"Rather," replied he, "admire the kindness of the Salamander Oromasis, whom jealousy did not prevent from taking pity upon the disgrace of his rival. He taught his son Zoroaster, otherwise known as Japhet, the Name of Omnipotent God which expresses His eternal fecundity. Japhet pronounced the Redoubtable Name JABAMIAH six times alternately with his brother Shem, walking backward towards the patriarch, and they completely restored the old man. This story, misunderstood, caused the Greeks to say that the oldest of the Gods was maltreated by one of his children; but this is the truth of the matter. Hence you can see how much more humane are the ethics of the Children of Fire than our own, and even more so than those of the Peoples of the Air or the Water; for their jealousy is cruel, as the divine Paracelsus shows us in an incident he recounts, and which was witnessed by the entire town of Stauffenberg. A certain Philosopher, with whom a Nymph was engaged in an intrigue of immortality, was so disloyal as to love a woman. As he sat at dinner with his new paramour and some friends, there appeared in the air the most beautiful leg in the world. The invisible sweetheart greatly desired to show herself to the friends of her faithless lover, that they might judge how wrong he was in preferring a woman to her. Afterward the indignant Nymph killed him on the spot."

"Ah Sir," I exclaimed, "this is quite enough to disgust me with these tender sweethearts."

"I confess," he rejoined, "that their tenderness is apt to be somewhat violent. But if exasperated women have been known to murder their perjured lovers, we must not wonder that these beautiful and faithful mistresses fly into a passion when they are betrayed, and all the more so since they only require men to abstain from women whose imperfections they cannot tolerate, and give us leave to love as many of their number as we please. They prefer the interest and immortality of their companions to their personal satisfaction, and they are very glad to have the Sages give to their Republic as many immortal children as possible."

"But after all, Sir," I asked. "how does it happen that there are so few examples of all that you tell me?"

"There are a great number, my child," he answered, "but they are neither heeded nor credited, in fact, they are not properly interpreted for lack of knowledge of our principles. People attribute to demons all that they should ascribe to the Elementary Peoples. A little Gnome was beloved by the celebrated Magdalen of the Cross, Abbess of a Monastery at Cordova in Spain. Their alliance began when she was twelve years of age; and they continued their relationship for the space of thirty years. An ignorant confessor persuaded Magdalen that her lover was a hobgoblin, and compelled her to ask absolution of Pope Paul III. It could not possibly have been a demon, however, for all Europe knew, and Cassiodorus Renius was kind enough to transmit to posterity, the daily miracles wrought through the intercession of this holy maiden, and which obviously would never have come to pass if her relationship with the Gnome had been as diabolical as the venerable Dictator imagined. This same Doctor, if I mistake not, would impertinently have said that the Sylph who immortalised himself with the youthful Gertrude, nun of the Monastery of Nazareth in the diocese of Cologne, was some devil or other."

"And so he was, no doubt," I said.

"Ah, my Son," pursued the Comte mirthfully, "If that were the case the Devil is not the least unfortunate if he has power to carry on an intrigue with a girl of thirteen, and to write her such billets doux as were found in her casket. Rest assured, my child, that. the Devil, in the region of death, has sadder employment and that more in keeping with the hatred which the God of Purity bears him; but thus do people wilfully close their eves to the truth. We find, for instance, in Titus Livy, that Romulus was the son of Mars. The sceptics say that this is a fable, the theologians that he was the son of an incubus devil, the wags that Mademoiselle Sylvia had lost her gloves and sought to cover her confusion by saying that a god had stolen them from her."

"Now we who are acquainted with Nature, and whom God has called out of darkness into His wonderful Light, know that this so-called Mars was a Salamander in whose sight the young Sylvia found favour, and who made her the mother of the great Romulus, that hero who, after having founded his superb city, was carried away by his father in a fiery chariot as Zoroaster was by Oromasis. Another Salamander was the father of Servius Tullius. Titus Livy, deceived by c the resemblance, says that he was the God of Fire. And the ignorant have passed the same judgment upon him as upon the father of Romulus. The renowned Hercule and the invincible Alexander were sons of the greatest of the Sylphs. Not knowing this, the historians said that Jupiter was their father. They spoke the truth for, as you have learned, these Sylphs, Nymphs and Salamanders set themselves up for divinities. The historians, believing them to be so, called all those who were born of them 'Children of the Gods.'"

"Such was the divine Plato, the most divine Apollonius of Tyana, Hercules, Achilles, Sarpedon, the pious Æneas, and the celebrated Melchizedek. For do you know who the father of Melchizedek was?"

"No, indeed," said I, "St. Paul himself did not know."

"Rather say that he did not tell," returned the Comte, "and that he was not permitted to reveal the Cabalistic Mysteries. He well knew that Melchizedek's father was a Sylph, and that the King of Salem was conceived in the Ark by the wife of Shem. That Pontiff's method of sacrificing was the same as that which his cousin Egeria taught King Numa, as well as the worship of a Supreme Deity without image or statue, for which reason the Romans, becoming idolaters at a later period, burned the Holy Books of Numa which Egeria had dictated. The first God of the Romans was the true God, their sacrifice a true sacrifice. They offered up bread and wine to the Supreme Ruler of the Universe: but all that became perverted in course of time. In acknowledgment of this first worship, however, God gave the Empire of the World to this city which had owned His supremacy. The same sacrifice which Melchizedek—"

"Sir," I interposed, "Pray let us drop Melchizedek, the Sylph that begat him, his cousin Egeria, and the sacrifice of bread and wine. These proofs seem to be rather remote. I should be greatly obliged if you would tell me some more recent news. For when someone asked a certain Doctor what had become of the companions of that species of Satyr which appeared to St. Antony and which you call a Sylph, I heard him say that all these folk are dead nowadays. So it may be that the Elementary Peoples have perished since you own they are mortal and we hear no tidings of them."

"I pray God," exclaimed the Comte with emotion, "I pray God, who is ignorant of nothing, to be pleased to ignore that ignoramus who decides so presumptuously that of which he is ignorant. May God confound him and all his tribe! Where has he learned that the Elements are abandoned and that all those wonderful Peoples are annihilated? If he would take the trouble to read history a little, and not ascribe to the Devil, as the old wives do, everything which goes beyond the bounds of the chimerical theory which has been con-structed about Nature, he would find in all ages and in all places proofs of what I have told you."

"What would your Doctor say to this authentic account of a recent occurrence in

Spain? A beautiful Sylphid was beloved by a Spaniard, lived with him for three years, presented him with three fine children and" then died. Shall one say that she was a devil? A clever answer that! According to what Natural Philosophy can the Devil organise for himself a woman's body, conceive, bear children and suckle them? What proof is there in Scripture of the extravagant power which your theologians are forced in this instance to accord the Devil? And with what probable reason can their feeble Natural Philosophy supply them? The Jesuit Delrio in good faith naïvely recounts several of these adventures, and without taking the trouble to give physical explanations, extricates himself by saying that those Sylphids were demons. How true it is that your greatest doctors very often know no more than silly women!"

"How true it is that God loves to withdraw into His cloud-enveloped throne, and deepening the darkness which encompasses His Most Awful Majesty, He dwells in an inaccessible Light, and reveals His Truths only to the humble in heart. Learn to be humble, my Son, if you would penetrate that sacred night which environs Truth. Learn from the Sages to concede the devils no power in Nature since the fatal stone has shut them up in the depths of the abyss. Learn of the Philosophers to seek always for natural causes in all extraordinary events; and when natural causes are lacking have recourse to God and to His holy Angels, and never to evil spirits who can no longer do aught but suffer, else you would often be guilty of unintentional blasphemy and would ascribe to the Devil the honour of the most wonderful works of Nature."

"If you should be told, for example, that the divine Apollonius of Tyana was immaculately conceived, and that one of the noblest Salamanders descended to immortalise himself with his mother, you would call that Salamander a demon and you would give the Devil, the glory of fathering one of the greatest men who ever sprang from our Philosophic marriages."

"But, Sir," I remarked, "this same Apollonius is reputed amongst us to be a great sorcerer, and they have nothing better to say of him."

"Behold," exclaimed the Comte, "one of the most wonderful effects of ignorance and bad education! Because one hears one's nurse tell stories about sorcerers, every extraordinary occurrence can have only the Devil for author. The greatest doctors may strive in vain, they are not believed unless they echo the nurses. Apollonius was not born of man; he understood the language of birds; he was seen on the same day in different parts of the world. He vanished in the presence of the Emperor Domitian who wished to do him harm; he raised a girl from the dead by means of Onomancy. He announced at Ephesus, in an assembly gathered from all parts of Asia, that at that very hour they were killing the tyrant at Rome. A judgment of this man is the point at issue. The nurses say that he was a sorcerer. St. Jerome and St. Justin Martyr say that he was merely a Philosopher. Jerome, Justin and our Cabalists are to be adjudged visionaries, and silly women are to carry the day. Ah! Let the ignorant perish in their ignorance, but do you, my child, save yourself from shipwreck."

"When you read that the celebrated Merlin was immaculately conceived by a nun, daughter of a king of Great Britain, and that he foretold the future more clearly than Tyresias, do not say with the masses that he was the son of an incubus devil, because there never have been any; nor that he prophesied through the assistance of devils, since according to the Holy Cabala devil is the most ignorant of all beings. Rather say with the Sages that the English Princess was consoled in her retirement by a Sylph who took pity on her, that he diverted her with his attentions, that he knew how to please her, and that Merlin, their son, was brought up by the Sylph in all knowledge, and learned from him to perform the many wonders which English history relates of him."

"No longer cast aspersion upon the Comtes de Cleves by saying that the Devil is their father, and have a better opinion of the Sylph who, so the story goes, came to Cleves in a miraculous boat drawn by a swan harnessed with a silver chain. After having several children by the heiress of Cleves, this Sylph re-embarked on his aerial boat one day at high noon, in full view of everyone. What has he done to your doctors that constrains them to pronounce him a devil?"

"Have you so little regard for the honour of the House of Lusignan as to give your Comtes de Poitiers a diabolical genealogy? What will you say of their celebrated mother?"

"I verily believe, Sir," I declared, "that you are about to tell me the fairy tale of Melusina."

"Ah!" he replied, "If you deny the story of Melusina I am inclined to think you prejudiced. But in order to deny it you must burn the books of the great Paracelsus who affirms in five or six different places that nothing is more certain than the fact that this same Melusina was a Nymph. And you must give the lie to your historians who say that since her death or, to speak more accurately, since she disappeared from the sight of her husband, whenever her descendants are threatened with misfortune, or a King of France is to die in some extraordinary way, she never fails to appear in mourning upon the great tower of the Château of Lusignan which she had built. If you persist in maintaining that she was an evil spirit, you will pick a quarrel with all those who are descended from this Nymph, or who are related to her house."

"Do you think, Sir," said I, "that these noblemen prefer to trace their origin to the Sylphs?"

"They would undoubtedly prefer to do so," he rejoined, "if they knew that which I am now teaching you, and they would consider these extraordinary births a great honour. If they had any Cabalistic Light they would know that such births are more conformable with the method whereby God, in the beginning, intended mankind to multiply. Children born in this way are happier, more valiant, wiser, more renowned and more blest of God. Is it not more glorious for these illustrious men to be descended from beings so perfect, wise and powerful than from some foul hobgoblin or infamous Asmodeus?"

"Sir," said I, "our theologians are far from saying that the Devil is the father of all those men who are born without one's knowing who is responsible for them. They recognise the fact that the Devil is a spirit and therefore cannot engender."

"Gregory of Nice," replied the Comte, "does not say that, for he holds that demons multiply among themselves as men do."

"We are not of his opinion," I answered, "but it happens, our doctors say, that—"

"Ah!" the Comte interrupted, "do not tell me what they say or you will be talking very obscene and indecent foolishness as they do. What abominable evasion they have been guilty of! The way in which they have all, with one accord, embraced this revolting idea is amazing. And what pleasure they have taken in posting hobgoblins in ambush to take advantage of the unoccupied lower nature of the recluse, and so hasten into the world those miraculous men whose illustrious memory they blacken by so base an origin. Do they call this philosophising? Is it worthy of God to say that He has such complaisance for the Devil as to countenance these abominations, granting them the grace of fecundity which He has denied to great Saints, and rewarding such obscenity by creating for these embryos of iniquity, souls more heroic than for those formed in the chastity of legitimate marriage?"

"If I dared to break in upon your declamation, Sir," said I, "I would own, in order to pacify you, that it were .greatly to be desired that our doctors had hit upon some solution less offensive to such pure ears as yours. Indeed, they have been obliged altogether to deny the facts upon which the question is founded."

"A rare expedient! " he rejoined. "How is it possible to deny manifest truths? Put yourself in the place of an ermine-furred theologian and suppose the blessed Danhuzerus comes to you as the Oracle of his religion—"

At this point a lackey came to say that a certain young nobleman had come to visit me.

"I do not care to have him see me" remarked the Comte.

"I ask your pardon, Sir," said I, "but as you can readily judge from this nobleman's name, I cannot say that I am not at home to anyone; therefore may I trouble you to go into this closet?"

"It is not worth while," said he, "I am about to make myself invisible."

"Ah! Sir," I exclaimed. "A truce to deviltry, I beg of you, I am not prepared to jest about it." "What ignorance," said the Comte, smiling and shrugging his shoulders, "not to know that to become invisible one has only to place before oneself the opposite of the light! "He went into my closet and the young nobleman entered at almost the same moment. I now ask his pardon for not speaking to him of my adventure.

DISCOURSE V

WHEN THE ILLUSTRIOUS PERSONAGE HAD taken his departure, on my return from accompanying him to the door, I found the Comte de Gabalis in my study.

"It is a great pity," said he, "that the nobleman who has just left you is one day to become one of the seventy-two Princes of the Sanhedrin of the New Law, else he would be a great subject for our Holy Cabala. His mind is profound, pure, broad, lofty and fearless. Here is the geomantic figure which I cast for him while you were talking together. I have never seen happier aspens nor those denoting a finer soul. Just look at this 'Mother'—what magnanimity it gives him; and this 'Daughter' will procure him the purple. Bad luck to her and to destiny since they deprive Philosophy of a subject who might perhaps surpass you. But where were we when he came in?"

"You were speaking, Sir," said I, "of a Saint whom I have never seen in the Roman Calendar. I think you called him Danhuzerus."

"Ah! I remember," he replied, "I was bidding you put yourself in the place of one of your doctors and suppose that the Blessed Danhuzerus had just laid bare to you his conscience and said, 'Sir, the fame of your learning has brought me from beyond the mountains. I have a slight scruple which is troubling me. A Nymph holds her court in a mountain in Italy: and a thousand Nymphs almost as beautiful as their Queen attend upon her. The handsomest and most learned and most worthy men resort thither from all the habitable globe. They love these Nymphs and are beloved by them; they lead the most delightful life in the world; the Nymphs whom they love bear them very fine children; they worship the living God, injure no one and hope for immortality. I was one day walking upon this mountain and found favour in the eyes of the Queen of the Nymphs, who appeared to me and showed me her charming court. The Sages perceiving that she loved me, reverenced me almost as their Prince. They exhorted me to yield to the Nymph's sighs and beauty. She told me of her martyrdom, and left unsaid nothing which might touch my heart, and in short convinced me that she would die if I did not love her, and that if I loved her she would be indebted to me for her immortality. The arguments of those learned men prevailed over my principles, even as the charms of the Nymph won my heart. I love her and she has borne me children of great promise, but in the midst of my felicity I am sometimes troubled by the recollection that the Church of Rome might not approve of all this. I have come to consult you, Sir, about this Nymph, those Sages, these children and the state of my conscience.' Well, Mr. Doctor, what answer would you make to my Lord Danhuzerus?"

"I should say to him," I answered, "With all due respect to you, Lord Danhuzerus, you are letting your imagination run away with you, or else your vision is an enchantment, your children and your mistress are hobgoblins, your Sages are fools, and I must say that your conscience is thoroughly cauterized."

"By such an answer, my Son, you might achieve a doctor's hood, but you would not merit admission to our Order," rejoined the Comte with a deep sigh. "Such is the barbarous tendency of all your doctors nowa-days. A poor Sylph would never dare show himself lest he be straightway mistaken for a hobgoblin; a Nymph cannot labour to become immortal without passing for an impure phantom; and a Salamander would not dare appear for fear of being taken for the Devil himself, while the pure flames of which he is composed would be thought the hell fire which ever attends upon the Prince of Darkness. To dissipate these Most injurious suspicions they vainly make the sign of the cross on appearing, bow the knee at Divine Names, and even pronounce them with reverence. All these precautions are futile. They cannot succeed in changing their reputation for being enemies of the God whom they worship more devoutly than do those who flee from them."

"But seriously, Sir," said I, "do you really believe these Sylphs to be such extraordinarily devout folk?"

"Most devout," he answered, "and most zealous for Divinity. The superlatively excellent discourses upon the Divine Essence which they deliver to us, and their wonderful prayers edify us greatly."

"Have they prayers as well? " said I. "I should very much like to hear one of their making."

"It is easy to gratify you," he rejoined, "and that I may not quote anything of questionable authority, and that you may be unable to suspect me of having fabricated it, listen to the prayer which the Salamander who gave answers in the Temple of Delphi was pleased to teach the Pagans, and which is recorded by Porphyry. It contains a sublime theology from which you will perceive that if mankind did not worship the true God, it was through no fault of these Sage Beings.

PRAYER OF THE SALAMANDERS.

Immortal, Eternal, Inejble and Sacred Father of all things, Thou who art borne upon the ceaselessly-rolling chariot of the ever-turning worlds. Thou Ruler of the Etherial Countries where the Throne of Thy power is raised, from the summit whereof Thy formidable eyes discover all things, and Thine excellent and holy ears hear all things. Hearken unto Thy children whom Thou hast loved from the birth of time; for Thy golden, mighty, and eternal Majesty shines above the world and above the firmament of the Stars. Thou art exalted above them, O radiant Fire! There Thou kindlest Thyself and maintainest Thyself by Thine own Splendour, and there go forth from Thine Eternal Essence inexhaustible streams of Light which nourish Thine Infinite Spirit. Thine Infinite Spirit produces all things and causes the inexhaustible treasure of matter, which can never fail in that generation which forever environs it, because .of the forms without number wherewith it is pregnant and wherewith Thou in the beginning didst fill it. From this Thy Spirit, likewise, are born those Holy Kings who stand about Thy Throne, and who compose Thy court, O Universal Father! O Thou Unique God! O Father of mortal and immortal Saints! Thou hast in particular created Powers which are marvellously like unto Thine Eternal Thought, and unto Thine Adorable Essence. Thou hast set them higher than the Angels who announce to the world Thy Will. Lastly Thou hast created in the Elements a third rank of Sovereigns. Our continual exercise is to praise Thee and to worship Thy Will. We burn with desire to possess Thee, O Father, O Mother, who art tenderest of Mothers, O wonderful exemplar of the sentiments and tenderness of Mothers, O Son, the flower of all Sons, O Form of all Forms, Thou Soul, Spirit, Harmony and Number of all things!

"What say you to this prayer of the Salamanders? Is it not exceedingly learned, lofty and devout?"

"And exceedingly obscure as well," I answered. "I once heard it paraphrased by a preacher who proved thereby that the Devil, in addition to his other vices, is above all else a great hypocrite."

"Alas!" exclaimed the Comte, "Poor Elementary Peoples! What resource is left you? You tell marvellous things concerning the Nature of God, the Father, Son, and Holy Ghost, the Assisting Intelligences, Angels and Heavens. "You make wonderful prayers and teach them to man; yet after all you are nothing but hypocritical hobgoblins!"

"Sir," I hastily observed, "it makes me uncomfortable to have you thus apostrophise these Peoples." "Nay, my Son," he replied, "do not fear lest I summon them, but rather lest your faintheartedness should in the future prevent you from having any realisation beyond that of amazement that you see fewer examples of their alliance with men than you could wish for. Alas! Where is the woman whose imagination has not been beclouded by your doaors, and who does not look with horror upon this relationship, and who would not tremble at the appearance of a Sylph?. Where is the man with least pretension to being good who does not flee the sight of them? Do we find, save very rarely, a man of worth who would care to be on familiar terms with them? Only profligates, misers, ambitious men or knaves court this honour to which, however, PRAISE GOD, they shall never attain; 'for the fear of the Lord is the beginning of Wisdom.'"

"Then what is to become of all these flying Nations," I inquired, "now that honest folk are so prejudiced against them?"

"Ah!" said he, "The arm of God is in no wise shortened, and the Devil does not derive all the advantage he anticipated from the ignorance and error which he has spread to their detriment; for in addition to the fact that the Philosophers, of whom there are a great number, do their utmost to remedy it by absolutely renouncing women, God has given all these Peoples permission to make use of every innocent artifice of which they can bethink themselves in order to converse with men without their knowledge."

"What do I hear, Sir?" I exclaimed.

"You hear nothing but the truth," he replied. "But I have a much greater secret to communicate to you. Know, my Son, that many a man believes himself to be the son of a man, who is really the son of a Sylph. Did I not tell you the other day that the Sylphs and other Lords of the Elements are overjoyed that we are willing to instruct them in the Cabala? Were it not for us their great enemy the Devil would alarm them exceedingly, and they would have difficulty in immortalising themselves without the knowledge of the maidens."

"I cannot sufficiently wonder at the profound ignorance in which we live," I remarked. "It is currently believed that the Powers of the Air sometimes help lovers to attain their desires. Apparently the contrary is true; the Powers of the Air require the assistance of men in their love affairs."

"Quite so, my Son," the Comte went on, "the Sage lends assistance to these poor people who, were it not for him, would be too wretched and too weak to resist the Devil. But when a Sylph has learned from us to pronounce Cabalistically the potent Name NEHMAHMIHAH, and to combine it in mantric form with the delicious name Eliael, all powers of darkness take flight and the Sylph peacefully enjoys the society of his loved one."

"When these gentlemen are immortalised, they labour earnestly and live most piously that they may not lose their recently-acquired right to the possession of the Supreme Good. They therefore desire the person to whom they are allied to live with exemplary innocence, as is apparent in that celebrated adventure of a young Lord of Bavaria. He was inconsolable at the death of his wife, whom he loved passionately. A certain Sylphid was advised by one of our Sages to assume the likeness of the wife. She had confidence in the Sage and presented herself to the sorrowing young man, saying that God had raised her from the dead to console him in his extreme affliction. They lived together many years and had several beautiful children. The young nobleman, however, was not a good enough man to retain the gentle Sylphid; he used to blaspheme and use had language. She often warned him, but seeing that her remonstrances were unavailing she disappeared one day, and left him nothing but her petticoats and the regret of having been unwilling to follow her pious counsel. Thus you see, my Son, that Sylphs sometimes have reason to disappear. You see too that neither the Devil nor the fantastic caprices of your theologians can prevent the People of the Elements from working with success for their immortality when they are helped by one of our Sages."

"But honestly, Sir," I asked, "are you persuaded that the Devil is so great an enemy of these seducers of young girls?"

"A mortal enemy," said the Comte, "especially of the Nymphs, Sylphs and Salamanders. As for the Gnomes, he does not hate them nearly so much because, as I believe you have already learned, the Gnomes, frightened by the howlings of the Devils which they hear in the centre of the earth, prefer to remain mortal rather than run the risk of being thus tormented should they acquire immortality. Thence it comes to pass that these Gnomes and the demons, their neighbours, have a good deal to do with one another. The latter persuade the Gnomes, who are naturally most friendly to man, that it is doing him a very great service and delivering him from great danger, to compel him to renounce his immortality. In exchange, they promise the man whom they can persuade to this renunciation that they will provide him with all the money he asks for, will avert the dangers which might threaten his life during a given period, or will grant any other condition pleasing to him who makes this wretched covenant. Thus the Devil, wicked fellow that he is, through the mediation of a Gnome, causes the soul of such a man to become mortal and deprives it of the right to eternal life."

"Then, Sir," cried I, "in your opinion those covenants, of which demonographers cite so many examples, are not made with the Devil at all?"

"No, assuredly not," replied the Comte, "Has not the Prince of the World been driven out? Is he not confined? Is he not bound? Is he not the terra damnata et maledicta which is left at the bottom of the retort of the Supreme and Archetype Distiller? Can he ascend into the Region of Light and spread there his concentrated darkness? He can do nothing against man. He can only inspire the Gnomes, his neighbours, to come and make these propositions to those among mankind whom he most fears may be saved, to the end that their souls may die with their bodies."

"Then," said I, "according to you these souls do die?"

"They die, my child," he answered.

"And are not those who enter into such covenants damned?"

"They cannot be damned," said he, "for their souls die with their bodies."

"Then they are let off easily, and' they are very lightly punished for so heinous a crime as that of renouncing the saving grace of their Baptism, and the Death of Our Lord."

"Do you call it being lightly punished," said the Comte, "to return into the black abyss of nonexistence? Know that it is a greater punishment than that of being damned, and that there is still a remnant of mercy in the justice which God exercises towards the sinners in Hell: it is a great grace not to let them be consumed by the fire which burns them. Nonexistence is a greater evil than Hell. This is what the Sages preach to the Gnomes when they assemble them to make them understand the wrong they do themselves in preferring death to immortality and nonexistence to the hope of a blessed eternity, which they would have the right to possess if they would only ally themselves to men without exacting from them such criminal renunciation. Some yield to our persuasions and we marry them to our daughters."

"Then, Sir, do you evangelise the Subterranean Peoples?" I inquired.

"Why not?" he replied. "We are instructors to them as well as to the Peoples of the Fire, Air and Water; and Philosophic charity is extended without distinction to all these children of God. As they are more subtile and more enlightened than the generality of mankind, they are more tractable and amenable to discipline, and listen to the divine truths with a reverence which charms us."

"It must be charming indeed," I exclaimed mirthfully, "to see a Cabalist in the pulpit holding forth to these gentlemen!"

"You shall have that pleasure, my Son, whenever you wish," said the Comte, "and if you so desire I will assemble them this very evening and will preach to them at midnight."

"At midnight," I protested, "I have been told that that is the hour of the Sabbat."

The Comte began to laugh. "You remind me," he said, "of all the imbecilities related by the demonographers in that chapter on their imaginary Sabbat. You are not going to tell me that you also believe in it, that would indeed be a joke!"

"Oh!" I retorted, "as for those tales of the Sabbat, I assure you I do not believe one of them."

"That is right, my Son," said he, "for I repeat that the Devil has not power thus to amuse himself at the expense of mankind, nor to enter into covenants with men, still less to make himself worshipped as the Inquisitors believe. What has given rise to the popular rumour is that the Sages, as I have just told you, assemble the Inhabitants of the Elements to preach their Mysteries and Ethics to them. And as it usually happens that some Gnome turns from his gross error, comprehends the horrors of non-existence and consents to become immortalised, they bestow upon him one of our daughters; he is married and the nuptials are celebrated with all the rejoicing called for by the recent conquest. There are dances and those shouts of joy which Aristotle says were heard in certain isles where, nevertheless, no living being was visible. The mighty Orpheus was the first to convoke these Subterranean Peoples. At his first lecture SABAZIUS, the most ancient of the Gnomes, was immortalised; and from that SABAZIUS was derived the name of this Assembly wherein the Sages were wont to address a speech to him as long as he lived, as is apparent in the Hymns of the divine Orpheus."

"The ignorant have confounded things, and have made them the occasion of a thousand impertinent tales, and of defaming an Assembly which we convene solely to the glory of the Supreme Being."

"I should never have imagined the Sabbat to be a devotional assembly," said I.

"And yet it is a most holy and Cabalistic one;" he rejoined, "a fact of which it would not be easy to persuade the world. But such is the deplorable blindness of this unjust age; people are carried away by popular rumour and do not in the least wish to be undeceived. Sages speak in vain, fools are more readily believed than they. In vain does a Philosopher bring to light the falsity of the chimeras people have fabricated, and present manifest proofs to the contrary. No matter what his experience, nor how sound his argument and reasoning, let but a man with a doctor's hood come along and write them down as false,--experience and demonstration count for naught and it is henceforward beyond the power of Truth to re-establish her empire. People would rather believe in a doctor's hood than in their own eyes. There has been in your native France a memorable proof of this popular mania. The famous. Cabalist Zedechias, in the reign of your Pépin, took it into his head to convince the world that the Elements are inhabited by these Peoples whose nature I have just described to you. The expedient of which he bethought himself was to advise the Sylphs to show themselves in the Air to everybody; they did so sumptuously. These beings were seen in the Air in human form, sometimes in battle array marching in good order, halting under arms, or encamped beneath magnificent tents. Sometimes on wonderfully constructed aerial ships, whose flying squadrons roved at the will of the Zephyrs. What happened? Do you suppose that ignorant age would so much as reason as to the nature of these marvellous spectacles? The people straightway believed that sorcerers had taken possession of the Air for the purpose of raising tempests and bringing hail upon their crops. The learned theologians and jurists were soon of the same opinion as the masses. The Emperors believed it as well; and this ridiculous chimera went so far that the wise Charlemagne, and after him Louis the Débonnaire, imposed grievous penalties upon all these supposed Tyrants of the Air. You may see an account of this in the first chapter of the Capitularies of these two Emperors."

"The Sylphs seeing the populace, the pedants and even the crowned heads thus alarmed against them, determined to dissipate the bad opinion people had of their innocent fleet by carrying off men from every locality and showing them their beautiful women, their Republic and their manner of government, and then setting them down again on earth in divers parts of the world. They carried out their plan. The people who saw these men as they were descending came running from every direction, convinced beforehand that they were sorcerers who had separated from their companions in order to come and scatter poisons on the fruit and in the springs. Carried away by the frenzy with which such fancies inspired them, they hurried these innocents off to the torture. The great number of them who were put to death by fire and water throughout the kingdom is incredible."

"One day, among other instances, it chanced at Lyons that three men and a woman were seen descending from these aerial ships. The entire city gathered about them, crying out that they were magicians and were sent by Grimaldus, Duke of Beneventum, Charlemagne's enemy, to destroy the French harvests. In vain the four innocents sought to vindicate themselves by saying that they were their own country-folk, and had been carried away a short time since by miraculous men who had shown them unheard-of marvels, and had desired them to give an account of what they had seen. The frenzied populace paid no heed to their defence, and were on the point of casting them into the fire when the worthy Agobard, Bishop of Lyons, who having been a monk in that city had acquired considerable authority there, came running at the noise, and having heard the accusations of the people and the defence of the accused, gravely pronounced that both one and the other were false. That it was not true that these men had fallen from the sky, and that what they said they had seen there was impossible."

"The people believed what their good father Agobard said rather than their own eyes, were pacified, set at liberty the four Ambassadors of the Sylphs, and received with wonder the book which Agobard wrote to confirm the judgment which he had pronounced. Thus the testimony of these four witnesses was rendered vain."

"Nevertheless, as they escaped with their lives they were free to recount what they had seen, which was not altogether fruitless for, as you will recall, the age of Charlemagne was prolific of heroic men. This would indicate that the woman who had been in the home of the Sylphs found credence among the ladies of that period and that, by the grace of God, many Sylphs were immortalised. Many Sylphids also became immortal through the account of their beauty which these three men gave; which compelled the people of those times to apply themselves somewhat to Philosophy; and thence are derived all the stories of the fairies which you find in the love legends of the age of Charlemagne and of those which followed. All these so-called fairies were only Sylphids and Nymphs. Did you ever read those histories of heroes and fairies?"

"No Sir," said I.

"I am sorry to hear it," he replied, "for they would have given you some idea of the state to which the Sages are one day determined to reduce the world. Those heroic men, those love affairs with Nymphs, those voyages to terrestrial paradise, those palaces and enchanted woods and all the charming adventures that happen in them, give but a faint idea of the life led by the Sages and of what the world will be when they shall have brought about the Reign of Wisdom. Then we shall see only heroes born; the least of our children will have the strength of Zoroaster, Apollonius or Melchizedek; and most of them will be as accomplished as the children Adam would have had by Eve had he not sinned with her."

"Did you not tell me, Sir," I interposed, "that God did not wish Adam and Eve to have children, that Adam was to think only of Sylphids, and Eve only of some Sylph or Salamander?"

"It is true," said the Comte, "that they ought not to have had children in the way in which they did."

"Then Sir," I continued, "your Cabala empowers man and woman to create children otherwise than by the usual method?"

"Assuredly," he replied.

"Ah Sir," I entreated, "teach this method to me, I beg of you."

"You will not find it out to-day, and it please you," said he smilingly, "I wish to avenge the People of the Elements for your having been so hard to undeceive regarding their supposed deviltry. I do not doubt that you are now recovered from your panic terrors. Therefore I leave you that you may have leisure to meditate and to deliberate in the presence of God as to which species of Elementary Beings will be most appropriate to His glory and to your own, as a participant in your immortality."

"Meanwhile I go to meditate in preparation for the discourse you have made me long to deliver to the Gnomes to-night."

"Are you intending to explain a chapter of Averroes to them?" said I.

"I believe that it might be well to introduce something of the sort," said the Comte, "for I intend to preach to them on the excellence of man, that I may influence them to seek his alliance. Like Aristotle, Averroes held two theories which it would be well for me to explain, one as to the nature of the understanding, and the other as to the Chief Good. He says that there is only one created understanding which is the image of the uncreated, and that this unique understanding suffices for all men; that requires explanation. And as for the Chief Good, Averroes says that it consists in the conversation of Angels, which is not Cabalistic enough. For man, even in this life can, and is created to, enjoy God, as you will one day understand and experience when you shall have reached the estate of the Sages."

Thus ends the Discourse of the Comte de Gabalis. He returned the next day and brought the speech that he had delivered to the Subterranean Peoples. It was marvellous! I would publish it with the series of Discourses which a certain Vicomtesse and I have had with this Illustrious Man, were I certain that all my readers would have the proper spirit, and not take it amiss that I amuse myself at the expense of fools. If I see that people are willing to let my book accomplish the good that it is capable of doing, and are not unjustly suspecting me of seeking to give credit to the Occult Sciences under pretence of ridiculing them, I shall continue to delight in Monsieur le Comte, and shall soon be able to publish another volume.

The Queen of the Hairy Flies is a nineteenth century magical text, known as a Cabala (indicating a magical secret, rather than Hebrew mysticism). Among other authors it was mentioned by Waite in his *Book of Black Magic* in common with *The Green Butterfly*, *The Black Pullet* and the *Black Screech Owl*.

For the first two of these see my *True Grimoire*; as regards the second, Waite mistook the grimoire of that name for the 'Cabale' that is the nearer relative. The latter of the three, a larger and handsomely illustrated text, is crying out for an edition at an affordable price. Then its relationship to the earlier Solomonic texts and the later French magical books can be assessed without forfeiting major limbs in the name of bibliophilia. More than one author has suggested a connection of all these texts with elemental spirits, which is not entirely misplaced. Nor are all of them utterly spurious or lacking in interest for serious occultists.

Needless to say this text has no connection with either Agrippa or Pietro de Abano. It is interesting nevertheless to see them named, as pseudonymous successors to the great Solomon in a more modern era. Despite this, and the comparative unseriousness of the text, it is a rarity which few students will have had the opportunity of examining. I am grateful to Dan Harms for providing a good scanned copy, and my friend Brendan Hughes for his work on the translation.

—*Jake Stratton-Kent*

THE MAGICAL SECRETS OF HENRY CORNELIUS AGRIPPA PUT INTO FRENCH BY PETER OF ABANO, TOGETHER WITH THE SECRETS OF THE OCCULT, INCLUDING THAT OF THE QUEEN OF THE HAIRY FLIES. APPROVED BY [THE DEMON] SARGATANAS. ROME. 1744.

The Great and True Natural Secret

of the

Queen of the Hairy Flies

WHO AIDS IN LOCATING PLACES
OF PRECIOUS OBJECTS

Translated by Brendan Hughes
Edited by Jake Stratton-Kent

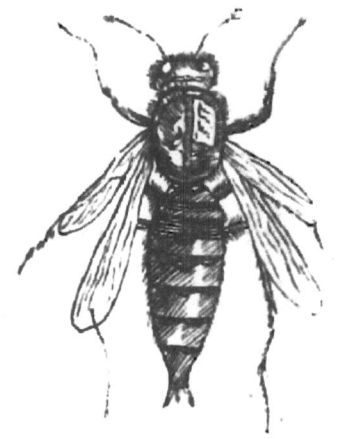

Amongst the numerous acrobatic winged insects, there is one most remarkable; the Queen of the Hairy Flies. This fly is in size and shape just as the one shown. You usually find it in summer on the flower of the common water-plantain which we have pictured, but smaller compared to this fly.

The common water-plantain which is also called mad-dog weed [Fr. crude flute] grows in ponds, lakes and upon river banks.

It is in these places that we urge our readers to look for the Queen of the Hairy Flies. To catch it alive, they are to chase it with a butterfly net.

When you have one of these flies in your possession, shut it in a transparent box like a glass sweet jar or a box made of window panes joined together with strips of paper stuck to the glass. Give it air twice daily and feed it with leaves from the plant on which it was at the start of the chase. This fly can live for about a month if carefully looked after.

To discover locations containing precious objects, possibly hidden at some depth, you need fine settled weather. Then, take the jar or box containing your fly in your hands, and off you go keeping your eyes on the jar, seeing every one of the fly's movements.

When you find yourself on land containing gold or silver, the fly will flap its wings, then, the more or less it flaps, the nearer or further you will be from where the gold or silver is buried. If the land contains precious stones, like emeralds, turquoises, topaz etc. the fly's trembling will be in its feet and the horns by its antennae. If on the other hand, there are only other common metals, be it copper, iron, lead or other minerals of lesser value, like coal, marble etc., the fly will walk without convulsion, always quicker or slower depending on the materials depth or distance.

It is with the same kind of fly that the Hindus search for the places which are most abundant in precious objects, the principal wealth of their country.

By the method we are revealing to you, you can at least avoid often futile and sorely expensive searches. With perseverance you can make your fortune a thousand times more quickly than those who rely on chance.

As you can see, there is nothing magic here, simply natural means, inexpensive and very readily employed.

BOTSINA DE-QARDINUTA
orignal painting by Johnny Jakobsson

The aureate elixir of Astaroth
original painting Johnny Jakobsson

The Language of the Birds

by Humberto Maggi

An example of Medieval Art, showing demons with mixed animal and human forms, and angels with animal heads, after the *Book of Ezequiel*. Source: *Commentarius in apocalypsin*, from Beatus de Liebana, XIII century, Spain.

> *The significant powers of the high-priesthood comes from the world of the spirits as gifts to those who have dedicated themselves to the spirits. These powers are instruments for the worker in service to the spirits so that the worker may participate entirely in the world of the spirits without any limit. One of the most significant of these powers is the esoteric vision, occult imagination, or inner sight, known as "la prise-de-yeaux".*
> Michael Bertiaux

I ONCE HAD AN INSIGHT ABOUT THE TRUE, RADICAL NATURE OF HERMES.
What is the base of communication, of every kind? It can be summarised as matter or energy being received, by a patient able to transform the experience into knowledge.

Of course, you can narrow the definition by including an agent that will send the matter or the energy to the patient. That adds purpose to the phenomenon. Every perception that hits the patient brings knowledge, but not necessarily every perception carries intent or will from an agent.

Hermes, seen in this archetypical form, can be defined as being manifest in the Universe at a certain stage of life evolution, when a patient arose being capable, not just to react to the environment, but also to learn from the reaction. There are, however, more primordial deities at work in the history of life: *Ares* and *Eros*.

Yes, and the truth, that I will abstain from qualifying, is that in the origins of life Ares came first.

Remember how life started: the first individual cells, and the act of feeding. To wrap and digest a particle of nutrients, that was the first manifestation of Ares. The second happened with the first cell that discovered that to wrap and digest *another cell* could be a much more efficient way of feeding.

The primordial birth of Cain…

And then, Ares gave birth to Eros. The very act of wrapping and digesting another cell became the blueprint of sexual reproduction, with the cells mixing their DNA to divide in changed forms. This blueprint repeats itself every time a spermatozoon gets inside an ovule. We have to revere much the wisdom of Heraclitus then, the enigmatic philosopher who recognized strife and conflict as the origins of everything:

> *War is the father of all and king of all, and some he shows as gods, other as humans; some he makes slaves, others free.*

And then comes forth Hermes. In the precise moment when two cells, instead of competing for food or eating one another, started to act together for mutual benefits. Cells had to find a way to communicate and share, the most basic kind of communication that exists, and in which rests the functioning of every superior form of life we know.

There are very mysterious steps in the process of life evolution. We tend to concentrate our ideas of evolution on the development of man and on the development of specific traits in the known species, but there are question marks in the initial steps of life awaiting answers:

How did the first cells to form a proto-organism decide on the differentiation of functions?

How did these cells manage to specialize themselves to fill the different functions?

And, the question mark of all question marks:

How did the cells develop the means to communicate all the different functions of all the different cells to one single cell, becoming able to reproduce?

Because, when we have the first multicellular organism, we have cells that just move the body, cells that just digest the food, cells that just perceive the environment, and, of course, cells that just deal with excretion. How did that happen?

First, we must suspect the use of the verb "to decide" used above. Can isolated cells *decide* anything? Is there intelligence in isolated cells to coordinate the process of specialization by themselves? To communicate the results to the cell in charge of the reproduction process?

Of course, this is the point where almost everyone on this planet will jump to the conclusion that *life has guides*. To be able to influence the pattern of life, the guides must be – of necessity – intelligences arisen *before* the first cells appeared on the surface of Earth.

It was the trend in the beginnings of the science of anthropology in the XIX century to analyze the development of Magic in the misunderstandings of perception and thinking of primitive peoples. Primitive people were supposed to believe in spirits after dreaming with dead relatives. They made wrong assumptions regarding cause and effect, so believed in sympathetic links, and that similarities could be exploited. They were just poor dumb asses. Or not?

It is ironic that actual propositions from Science seem to vindicate what was supposed by the first anthropologists to be the most erroneous suppositions from our ancestors. See, for instance, the theories about the phenomenon known as *"quantum entanglement"*. They say that it is really possible to affect at a distance a part taken from the whole. And the research into telepathy raise the question about how efficient symbols and similes are in helping and guiding telepathic efforts.

It is not that I am denying that to dream with the dead did not lead in many cases to a belief in the survival of the soul, neither do I disagree that primitive people erred in many assumptions regarding the cause and effect of many phenomena. But, the fathers of Anthropology left outside the equation the experience of contacting the spirits through ecstasy and concentration – they viewed all such happenings merely as symptoms of mental diseases, when in fact they can be experienced by people considered sane by any known psychiatric standards. A more updated anthropological approach to the "magical consciousness" issue can be seen in the works of Susan Greenwood, as for instance in her *The Nature of Magic – An Anthropology of Consciousness*:

> *"Magical consciousness, as an aspect of human cognition, may be equated with what Lévy-Bruhl has termed 'the law of participation'. Lévy-Bruhl*

> *saw participation as a psychic unity, a fundamental state of mind, that included individuals, society, and the living as well as the dead; he described it as a type of thinking that created relationships between things through unseen forces and influences. Magical consciousness is based on analogical rather than logical thought, and involves the association of ideas, symbols, and meaningful coincidences. Described variously as 'altered states of consciousness', shamanic states of consciousness, or non-ordinary reality, magical consciousness is usually brought about through the application of one or more techniques, such as dancing or drumming (or a combination of these); it may occur in or out of a ritual setting. Primarily concerning a shift in consciousness to an expanded awareness, it may involve the invocation of spirit beings."*

Hermes became the patron of Magic in recognition, I believe, of the fact that most of the time Magic deals with communication: the communication of intent from the magician to the world, and the communication of the magician with spirit beings. Outside these scopes we find just the cases in which the magician sends energy towards a subject, aiming not to communicate but to effectively affect someone. If the sending of the energy to cure, to harm or arouse is void of information, in the same way when we inject a medicine, shoot someone or put drops of a stimulant in a drink, we have stepped outside the communication side of Magic. In any other circumstance, however, *communication is the key*.

Take for instance the alterations of reality a magician looks for when doing practical magic. Unless we are talking about something like weather magic, I believe any other set of circumstances involves someone doing something that helps the result to manifest. This is telepathy, the communication of an intent directly by the magician or through the help of the spirits.

As I indicated in my previous text *The Tree of the Grimoires*, the contact with spiritual entities became one of the major features of Western Magic. Many historical reasons contributed to that, but what I need to emphasize here is the fact that the phenomenon of spiritual communication is too recurrent to be avoided or completely suppressed. If the enemies of Magic succeeded in killing all the mages and burning all the books of their age, just one generation ahead people would start to talk again with the spirits, new grimoires would be written and the very old and always new Path of Magic would be open once more.

The base of any communication rests on the *content* of the message. This is where the whole tradition of Magic comes to a halt, because from the Stone Age cave to the modern paranormal laboratory, no one ever produced a communication of which the content could prove the objectivity of the spirits. On the other hand, dozens of times it was justly the content of the so called spirit communications that enabled skeptics and researchers to prove the error or the intentional fraud of the mediums.

In 2008 I came upon the *Grimoire Shamanism* article written by Aaron Leitch. It was important for me just for the fact that he effectively addressed something I had intuited before: that every single technique or experience in Western Magic has its blueprint in the magic of primitive peoples. Aaron's paper was also very important at the time for the mention he made of the work done by Kathleen McDonald with the *Ars Paulina* grimoire.

The *Ars Paulina* is the third book in the collection of grimoires known as *Lemegeton* or *Lesser Key of Solomon*. Divided in two parts, it deals with the Angels of the Hours and the

Angels of the 365 degrees of the Zodiac. The legend surrounding the book says it was the fruit of the revelations the apostle Paul received during his ascension to the Third Heaven. The sigils of the astrological signs are borrowed from Paracelsus *Second Treatise of Celestial Medicines*.

Kathleen McDonald researched extensively on the craft necessary for the ritual, and what appealed strongly to me was the prospect of establishing a permanent link with a spiritual being, which by then I saw in an even more shamanic style. Of course, I lacked the proper conditions to follow as closely as possible the instructions in the grimoire, as she did. Instead, I opted for very simple methods, relying mostly on the concentrated reading of the invocations. I calculated the Angel of the Ascendant as Ajiel, and had one of my strongest magical experiences up to then.

The Invocation of Ajiel impressed me, for the level of the energy I felt and the alteration of consciousness it brought, and also for the amount of time I remained affected by it. After that, I decided to invoke *all* Zodiacal Angels from the book, a task which I did not finish, but in which I endured for some months.

In *The Tree of the Grimoires* paper I mentioned the neurological description given by Van James in his paper *Spirit and Art: and the Puzzles of Paradox*. This description should not be seen as unique, and it did not fit the pattern of the experiences I had, that I describe as follows:

- *The creation of a sacred ambience,* which means an alteration in the way the place is perceived, through vesting the robe, lightning candles and incense, performing preliminary rituals.
- *Concentration on the invocation,* stopping the mind and focusing on the effects of the reading.
- *Perception of the presence,* felt as a specific field of energy whose strength grew with time.
- *Establishment of communication,* feeling the energy being concentrated in my mind and body, actuating over it, and causing images and ideas to form.

The series of invocations with the Angels of the *Ars Paulina*, being so impressive for me, are the reason I started looking for one possible explanation for the objective existence of the spirits. I faced the content of communication problem described above, and came up with the idea that the spirits, being non-organic beings, organize intelligence and memory in a different way than we are used to. *That* would explain away the lack of specific content in the communications, and allow the objectivity of the result of my practice to remain an open question.

The objectivity of the spirits being proven or not, is not essential to successful practice. One of the most important facts for me is the high level of ecstasy I felt during the ceremonies. The invocations of the Angels of the *Ars Paulina* and the series of rituals I made with HRV are the most important events in my life up to now. The memory of them, which I feel not just in my mind but also in my body, is with me all the time and everyday I live in the expectation of acquiring such experiences on even higher levels.

I see the content of the invocations I will transcribe as strongly shamanic. As it can be seen, most of the time the Angels were curing me or teaching me how to work with energy. To learn *how to communicate* with them was also a prominent feature of the process.

The communication with the spirits was always a prized gift, and humans have been creating myths about this since we wandered the plains and took shelter in the caves. Much before the Jewish compilation of foreign myths in the Bible, and in other cultures far away in America and Oceania, the legends about the time when people could communicate with the angels and the animals speak of the vision of man as a complete and superior being, with superior communication abilities.

The loss of this ability is also prominent in the legends of many people. The pride of the First Shaman, mentioned by Eliade, and the sin of Adam are testimonies to the loss. Shamans, mystics, magicians and alchemists have all quested after the language, which had been called by different but associated names; this remained the golden grail of the Western Traditions. They called it the *Divine*, *Green*, *Adamic*, *Enochian*, or *Angelic* language.

The language of the birds.

The language of the birds was thought by the Greeks to be learned or received by magical means. That sits well with my vision of the magical development in two steps: acquiring the conversation and knowledge of spiritual beings, and then learning from them. Tiresias, the Greek prophet consulted even after his death, was said to have received the language from the goddess Athena. Other known initiates into the language of the birds were Democritus, Anaximander, Apollonius of Tyana, Melampus and Aesopus.

When we use the expression "conversation and knowledge" most of the magicians nowadays go straight to the Abramelin book and Aleister Crowley. In fact, deriving it from the grimoire, Crowley made the concept one of the cornerstones of his evolutive Magic. It was what he called the next step in human evolution, and in later works he mentions it as the acquisition of an ability not limited to one single guardian angel, but to any kind of spiritual beings.

The discovery of the lost language was associated in the minds of the Renaissance magi with the hopes of the New Age, and it figures prominently in the works of John Dee. Ironic, if the possibility of spiritual communications is as I hypothesize, to acquire the language of the angels as their knowledge and conversation is not a matter of learning a new vocabulary or rediscovering an ancient alphabet, such as Dee sought. It is a matter of learning to listen to this special kind of communication, as Dee expected his seers to do. Doing this, he missed the best part of Magic, for this reason I believe Crowley preferred to see Edward Kelley, Dee's seer, as his past incarnation, no matter the other resemblances we might see between the two mages.

The Angels of the Ars Paulina

What follows now is the description of the invocations I made in the period between July and October in the year 2008. The descriptions are in italic and, when due, are followed by some remarks. Some entries about other magical operations made during the time that I think are relevant are included. I used to calculate beforehand the time in which the Sun would be in the Angel's degree, and did the invocation during this period.

The ceremonial preparation usually included doing the Star Ruby, *the* Star Sapphire *and the* Liber Samekh *rituals.*

I used the Lemegeton *version edited by Mitch Henson.*

The Angels of the Sign of Leo

Mechiel
23/07/08
Between 06:30 and 7:30

A bit difficult, but towards the end some of the presence with a lesser degree of that magical joy I experienced with Ajiel a few weeks ago, which was one of the best experiences in my life, better than anything earthly. Mechiel showed me he is the Angel that opens the Water/Night of Cancer, to the Dawn of Leo. The Signs have a cycle like the day, getting stronger until the middle, and then decreasing. I tried to use the black mirror; the vibration of the stone seems to intensify etheric perceptions, but I could do nothing with the reflex.

Satiel
24/07/08
Between 06:30 and 07:00

The First Manifestation of Magnificence. I did not perform the Star Ruby and the Star Sapphire, only the prayer for the Ten Archangels. Felt an intrusion of a dark energy, as if trying to profit from my openness to the contact. First Section of Liber Samekh. The idea of not giving due importance to the invocations came to me (inspired by the Angel?). In fact, I was supposed to rise early to do the practice. A loud argument outside my room involved two men, the senior telling the subordinate he should be "humble" (see the text of the invocation). I gave the Angel license to depart, but felt the Angel wanted to stay longer, but my Holy Guardian Angel did not, because it was time for me to leave for work. Energy good, but not as strong as the last time.

The text of the invocation I used to call the Angels, from the Second Book of the *Ars Paulina*:

The Conjuration of the Holy Guardian Angel

O thou great and blessed *N.* my Guardian Angel, vouchsafe to descend from thy holy mansion which is Celestial, with thy holy Influence and presence, into this crystal stone, that I may behold thy glory; and enjoy thy society, aide and assistance, both now and for ever hereafter. O thou who art higher than the fourth heaven, and knoweth the secrets of *Elanel*. Thou that rideth upon the wings of your winds and art mighty and potent in thy Celestial and superlunary motion, do thou descend and be present I pray thee; and I humbly desire and entreat thee. That if ever I have merited Thy society or if any of my actions and Intentions be real and pure & sanctified before thee bring thy external presence hither, and converse with me one of thy submissive pupils, by and in the name of the great god *Jehovah*, whereunto the whole choir of heaven singeth continually: *O Mappa la man Hallelujah*. Amen.

Ajel
25/07/08
Between 06:15 and 07:00

Completely different from the first time. I felt a refreshing energy slowly getting over me, as if coming from the sides, and making slow/strong pressure to enter me. I still feel its effects, and it helps to dispel the fatigue. It seems also to carry some sort of communication. I remember it started with a sensation of rain. I learned before with my Holy Guardian Angel that the Angels do not allow me to get addicted to their energies and to be permanently changed by their energies/ presences. They withdraw so I can be myself, and learn to walk independently.

Mechiel
26/07/08
Between 15:30 and 16:30

Star Ruby and Star Sapphire ritually made. Robe, candles, incense. Difficult, with some dark energy again interfering. My energy also was not good. I kept banishing with the aid & help of my Angel with success, after some time. Some shamanic insights and perceptions – magical energies sometimes are much more near and material than I think. In the end, I called Mechiel again, saying Do What Thou Wilt. I had a flash vision, combining elements of the Ace of Spades and the Queen of Wands. I felt a good energy.

The perception of the magical energies being "much more near and material" than I thought became the starting point of my spirit hypothesis.

Sahel
27/07/08
Between 14:40 and 15:40

The Angel manifested with the energy/image of the Queen of Air. The presence was subtle. I see I was used to the strong presence and effects of my first and impressive invocation of Ajiel, I must see some manifestations as more subtle. The presence helped me to perceive and free myself of some unhealthy energies in the left side of my abdomen. The same interference occurred again, sprayed water with salt and submitted and banished with Liber Samekh Section E.

Aniel
28/07/08
Between 06:00 and 07:00

Subtle presence, the clear blue nature of some Air cards. It worked on my left side, with good results.

Masiel
28/07/08
Finished at midnight.

First, a mild manifestation of the clear blue energy, and some green like the Ace of Disks. I perceived again that these Angels give value to patience and endeavor. I have to accept what they want to offer, when they want to offer it. When I was going to read the Invocation to give the License to Depart, I in fact remade it, and the Angel manifested more strongly, and helped me in the Spiritual Combat, fighting the black energy that is opposing me like Michael with the Dragon. I had signs about that in the Mount Saint Michel. A stronger Conversation with the Angel followed, and he helped me with the internal Spiritual Combat, and helped me to establish a stronger ability of Conversation.

Between the first invocation with the *Ars Paulina* and the beginning of this series of invocations, I travelled with a friend to the Mount Michel in France. Up to this point, we can see the Angels helping me with works typical of shamanism:

- Effecting health enhancing practices.
- Helping against bad magical presences.
- Improving my abilities of magical communication.

Segael
30/07/08
Starting at midnight.

The presence strong and subtle at the same time. Inspiration more than conversation. I learned to not give the License to Depart, but to stay in touch during the duration of the Sun in the degree, receiving the energy of the Angel. First Angel with a clearly Leonine manifestation, although still a trace of Air. Strong & subtle. The Angels want to know me, and they see through my body, emotions, energies and thoughts. They help to cure.

I can't explain the prominence of the Air in the previous invocations. That should be a reminder that the magical universe does not feel obliged to conform to our established criteria. This is the difference between elaborating a system after symbol play and effectively researching the reality.

Aphiel
30/07/08
Between 23:00 and 00:00

Images of the Fool appeared a couple of times. This Angel was the most light-minded and pleasant up to now. Great variety of colors.

Metziel
01/08/08
Started at 21:00

The Angel showed a strong interest in some problems I have. I used the crystal falcon head over the black mirror, surrounded by the golden serpent bracelet. The stones had a strong effect on my Ajna, and I had a glimpse of a very beautiful vision of the Angel.

Sekiel
02/08/08
Between 19:50 and 20:30

Strong manifestation. The Angel spotted a dark love spell in my lower back, and helped to dissolve it. A beautiful but not very precise vision of the Angel as a Man in Warrior attire, red cape, standing erect upon the back of a Lion.

This is a good example of how the images of spirits in the books of Magic are created.

Ariel
03/08/08
Between 18:00 and 18:30

A vision on high, but somehow blocked by an iron/earth image of one Angel below. The Angel taught me to close my magical field to get rid of the black substance on my upper left side. He said I have been tested (I had a demonic presence during the night).

Gnethiel

I slept and lost the opportunity.

Sagiel
06/08/08
Between 00:00 and 00:40

Very strong but subtle. Helped against bad energies (parasites?) in the left abdomen (mainly stomach). Sometimes a burst of his energies opened more my perception for one moment. Advised me to buy one book about John Dee I saw in London.

I saw two books in the Atlantis bookstore which could match the vision; one was the Deborah Harkness's *John Dee's Conversations with Angels: Cabala, Alchemy, and the End of Nature*, the other Milo DuQuette's *Enochian Vision Magick*. I bought and read both, just to be on the safe side, and both were useful.

Abiel
07/08/08
Started 01:15

I made the preliminaries in Lotus, very tired. The Angel manifested with a fresh presence, bidding me to write.

Magiel
07/08/08
Between 22:00 and 23:00

First a beautiful image of the Angel. In profile, facing to the right. All details of the image had meaning, but I am not able to decode. The Angel instructed me about how to follow the Way of God, which includes the health of body and energies. The Angels like my fancies, when I forget what I am doing and I am taken by thoughts and images, because they see them and learn about me. The Angel helped to clean myself, like the Angels before him.

Gadiel
09/08/08
Between 03:00 and 04:00

The Angel showed me another aspect of a magical dilemma. He helped with cleaning my energies (I've being annoyed by opposing energies/spirits). I felt his influence more on the Etheric than in my mind.

Athiel

I slept.

Muviel
10/08/08
Between 08:45 and 10:10

The Angel helped me to expand my aura, and with the process of purification.

Saviel
11/08/08
Between 22:00 and 22:40

The Angel directed his presence to the crystal in the Altar. I stayed on my feet facing the Altar, instead of sitting in Lotus in the South. The energies of the Angel had Earth and Air qualities. There was some small disturbance, but I am considering making a trap and having this lesser spirit as a familiar. The Angel helped with the process of purification and expansion of my aura. I had a brief contact with the Soul of the Earth.

Achiel
Starting at midnight of 12/08/08
Finished at 01:00 of 13/08/08

I was oriented to invoke again on the Stone over the Altar. The oppositions are more distant and my energies are better. Sex magic energies of the Angel being Earth and Air, more Earth. Clear mind effects. Also a Leonine manifestation. Ideas and visualization for a ritual with the Scarlet Woman.

Metiel
13/08/08
Between 21:40 and 22:35

The Angel cleaned and closed the energy of my back. I think there were still demonic remains there. He helped me to expand my aura, and taught me about the inevitability of Magical War and the need for being prepared for it, due to the existence of many dark entities. He showed my problem is due to an opening in my aura (upper/left), and taught me to close it, at the same time "to bite" with my aura the intruding energies. The Angel was Fiery & Leonine. Before that, I had a new kind of manifestation of HRV as my Angel, receiving me now that I am forty years old. I was moved to offer the Ring to him, and then left it for a time charging over the crystal (one of the Angels before that had alerted me that the Ring needed to be recharged).

It is an Enochian Ring of Aemeth.

Siel

Slept.

On the 17th of October during a practice with *Liber Samekh* I had a strong contact with the Sigil of Babalon. The next day I received a message from a friend telling me about the launching of the *Red Goddess* by Scarlet Imprint. The experience with the sigil allowed me to buy one of the 49 edition copies of the book, and this contact led later to writing a contribution for *Diabolical*, which in turn led to this contribution in the *Conjure Codex*.

Aviel
18/08/08
Between 21:40 and 22:30

The Angel helped me with the Purification process, also working in the energy of the Temple. Talked with me about my daughter, and showed how to use the Candles to clean and burn undesirable energies.

Savael
20/08/08
Between 22:40 and 23:20

The Angel already manifests the energies of Virgo. It seems that the energies of Virgo begin to manifest in the end of Leo in a very subtle way. I was bathed in the refreshing energy, and the Angel learned, seeing my thoughts, about daily human concerns. Before, during Liber Samekh Section A, the Angel helped me to see and be free of some fears and concerns.

The Angels of the Sign of Virgo

Celiel
22/08/08
Between 22:30 and 23:10

First a beautiful Vision of an Angel with white Butterfly Wings on a Tree. I learned how to keep my Head in the proper position to receive the Images from the Angels (the Angel of Leo also taught me that). The Angel told me I was going to learn a different kind of Magick, meaning the Magick of Virgo is different from the Magick of Leo. The Angel told me that the Virgin is a State of Being. The Angel also showed me that the Roars of Leo make the communication more difficult in the beginning of the Sign of Virgo. It was a very short Conversation.

Senael
24/08/08
Between 19:00 and 19:40

The Angel showed me a Vision of the Gate of Baphometh. His presence was very subtle. He taught me Caffeine is not harmonic with Virgo energies, it is better avoided during these practices. Another good example of grimoire in the making.

Nasael
25/08/08
Between 21:40 and 22:40

Contact with HRV★RA★HA during Liber Samekh Section A. To cut all links to the past and start the A∴A∴ anew. The Angel showed interest in my books, identified and helped me to remove something that was sapping my energies to Work. I thanked all the Angels of the Ars Paulina for helping me, and manifested my Will to become more able to Converse with then.

Sangiel
26/08/08
Between 21:00 and 21:40

The Angel was difficult to contact, seemed a bit impatient and not willing to talk about himself. He asked to see one sexual fancy in my imagination. Before, some hints about manifesting myself and the magical practices of Atu XX.

Gnaphiel
27/08/08
Between 22:50 and 23:40

The Angel was very subtle. I made a good meditation, with dream-state.

Gnasiel
02/09/08
Between 22:20 and 23:20

I am getting more used to the patterns of the Angels of the Ars Paulina, and allow my mind to wander so they can indulge themselves looking at my thoughts and learning from them. They seem to be interested in human matters. The Angels are kind. It seems that my energy is all right, there was no cleaning. I meditated, it is good to meditate in their presence.

Zachiel
08/09/08
Between 22:30 and 23:35

The Angel was present since the beginning of the Prayer; I felt that carrying on reading when he was already present was not good. The Angel showed interest in my thoughts, he does not know much about humans, like the others. The Knowledge & Conversation is developing more to some kind of ecstatic experience. Before, I had a greater contact and assumed the god form of RHK. Yesterday I worked again with the fasting and the Great Invocation.

Vaziel
17/09/08
Between 21:30 and 22:30

A little interference of the usual black/green energy; but it was less inimical, more spiritualized. I invited the Angel; the Conversation was subtle, not very strong. I think they are teaching me to perceive more, which would not happen if they manifested with more force. He showed the usual interest in my thoughts & facts of my life. He showed to me why it is difficult for Angels to move or inspire people who are too closed, and then Demons should be used to move them, and how this must be approved by the Angels.

Zachiel
18/09/08
Between 22:50 and 23:50

The incense of erva-cidreira was much more in harmony with this Angel of Virgo. His presence was all around, but less Conversation than Presence. The meditation lasted longer; I think a Door is being opened in my Mind, which will allow me in time to have a different kind of contact with the Angels. More instructions about the Demons; I had the idea that each Angel has one Demon under his service.

Tajael
21/09/08
Between 09:50 and 10:44

Good presence of the Angel, but contact mainly through the energy. Gave me a suggestion about my daughter. The dark energy, exiled to the entrance of the room, was more agitated, so I lighted one Ananda incense there, and sprayed with water and salt. The first Action of the Angel was to bless the water and salt.

Jachiel
21/09/08
Between 18:00 and 18:47

The Angel attended my request, and took unhealthy energies from me (left arm and stomach). I saw the correct position of the two Lion Guardians of the Temple of HRV.

The Angels of the Sign of Libra

Ibajah
22/09/08
Between 21:00 and 22:00

Before, a very Strong & Beautiful rapture with RHK during Liber Samekh Section A. The Angel manifested very powerfully, opening my aura with the contemplation of Love Symbols. The Angel was very Venusian. He opened myself to the Universal Love, and opened and fought very hard against all the shells in my back. I helped invoking the Archangel Gabriel and EL, at the request of the Angel. It was the most powerful purification made by the Angels up to now.

I discovered that the Universal Love is something totally different to what we imagine. It is a shame I can't recollect the experience, but I remember it as being one of the more important in the sequence of results.

Chaiel
24/09/08
Between 01:00 and 02:00

The Angel showed me how some spirits try to diminish the effects of an Invocation creating interruptions, worry and fears. The Angel taught me to not create a self-image after the external images, but to accept and manifest my own image. Also how Angels can protect from accidents. The Conversation & Presence were more mental and subtle than yesterday. After that, I made the meditation and Invocation of Babalon.

A short time after that I escaped a car accident very similar to the one I saw in the vision.

Sahael
24/09/08
Between 22:40 and 23:30

There was a Conversation, but I went off a couple of times and don't remember. I went off also during the Meditation of Babalon.

Gnamiel
03/10/08
Between 22:20 and 23:20

The Angel liked the incense of Cassis and Green Apple. Very Venusian in nature. The Angel cleaned my diaphragm area. His presence was strong, he read my mind for a good time, and attending my request helped me to improve my ability to listen to them, and gave me a brief but beautiful Vision, but with no specific images. I remembered the Meditation of Babalon, and went to do it. I was briefly instructed about the Wonderful Visions that can allure in the Abyss.

INFERNAL CONJURE CRAFT

" *...the approach offered here is indeed biased towards a hoodoo practice style and setting along with its magical outlook and assumptions.*

Chad Barber

Introduction

It is my intention with this article to offer a small set of tools and ideas that might introduce hoodooists and other interested magical practitioners to working with the *Grimorium Verum* in a hoodoo-based style. This is to say, artfully including goetic magic and spirits in hoodoo spell craft – not only from a practical perspective but perhaps also a mythic one. The important distinction between the way of working described herein and the ceremonial form that goetic magic normally takes is that the emphasis of this style of work is patterned around the magical system found in traditional African American conjure and lore. That patterning is infused with goetic spirit work as described by the *Grimorium Verum* – with the magical symbolism and technology of both systems dovetailed to create an integrated approach that includes both magical modalities in a new synthesis, but maintaining a distinct emphasis on practical spell craft. And from this perspective, the approach offered here is indeed biased towards a hoodoo practice style and setting along with its magical outlook and assumptions. Practically speaking, this might include candle work, doll-baby work, use of condition oils and powders, creating mojo bags and bottle spells, construction of magic lamps and the array of potent and practical magical techniques and tricks held within rootwork tradition. These spell systems then are adapted to "operate by means of the spirits" of *The True Grimoire*, using an approach which is gleaned from the grimoire itself. Whilst it would be impossible to give the reader a grounding in all these hoodoo techniques within the scope of this single article, it is possible to offer an outlook that can be applied to future research and workings.

When considering the practical implications of a goetically infused hoodoo style such as the one proposed here, a little adjustment to our conception of what might constitute practical goetic magic in this particular context seems natural. Firstly, as a form of folk magic – like so many other folk magical forms – hoodoo leans toward accessibility with less emphasis on elaborate ritual tools or complex ceremonies; instead it has a much greater emphasis on the use of roots, herbs and curios (both zoological and mineral), as well as magical geography. This goes hand in hand with a preoccupation with hands-on spell craft and the nuanced magically sympathetic gestures and components that constitute this sort of craft. And it really is a craft in the true sense of the word – as subtle and sophisticated as any form of ritual magic could be. It follows that working with the grimoire and its spirits in this way, one would adapt spirit work to follow a similar pattern – opting for a more nuanced understanding of the evocation system, which has spell craft as its primary focus.

Fortunately, the *Natural and Supernatural Secrets* in the grimoire clearly demonstrates that just such a practical form of goetic spell work had apparently been intended to function alongside the more complex ceremonial system of the grimoire all along: a system very similar to hoodoo and one that operates by means of the legion of the *Grimorium Verum*. Additionally, *Secrets* offers some very clear formulas which give us an insight into the very practical nature of its underlying principles. By coming to that with a working knowledge of the hoodoo repertoire we are able to flesh it out and develop it even further. Consequently, this goetic style of hoodoo is a *new* development and although its roots are as ancient as magic itself, we need to be respectful and differentiate it from African American hoodoo. This isn't traditional hoodoo, it is something else. I like to think of it as *infernal conjure*. This approach has some things in common with the magic of Brazilian *Quimbanda, Magia Negra, Brujeria*, certain streams of Haitian magic as well as historical witchcraft in its various forms all the way back to the dawn of the pre-Christian goetia. You could say that it taps the current of a form of chthonic witchcraft and sorcery traceable throughout history – sorcery which has at its core spirit-based spell craft.

Hoodoo, God, and the Devil at the crossroads

So you might ask, how can one work in this way employing a black grimoire as notorious as the *Grimorium Verum* and its seemingly diabolical 'pact-making' system when hoodoo is so firmly grounded in folk-Christianity? A good question, and to answer it we must direct our attention briefly to one of the most interesting, and possibly mysterious, elements of the conjure mythos, the rite of making a pact with the Dark Man at the crossroads – also known as the Devil.

It has been argued that this figure is a syncretism between the crossroads intermediary spirit that populates New World traditions and the slave master's Christian Devil, most likely the result of the demonisation of African ancestral spirits – much like the spirits of the *Grimorium Verum* which are often demonised forms of older pre-Christian spirits. Yet, despite his devilish character, this figure continues to occupy an important if deeply mysterious role in rootwork tradition. Certainly it is hard to refute that there is a current of diabolism running through traditional Christian hoodoo. Despite hoodoo's folk-Christian framework the crossroads rite persists as an enduring and important source of mythic wisdom and magical power. By its inclusion it can be argued that infernal symbols and the language of the 'diabolical' are legitimate sources of knowledge and magical power within the overall conception of the tradition. Further we find several traditional infernal and demonic substances, materials and formulas contained within the corpus of traditional hoodoo lore, substances with hellish associations such as sulphur (fire and brimstone), black dog hair (the devil is thought to have a black dog), mullein (used in hoodoo to conjure and control demons) and formulas such as Dark Arts oil, incense and powder – all geared toward conjuring infernal spirits and for use in black magic. Similarly, figural candles of devils, skulls, Baphomet and other chthonic forms have become commonplace in many conjure shops.

Considering all this we can see that a nuanced and multivalent New World conception of the 'Devil' makes him a very interesting figure in hoodoo, and in fact one of three key sources of a conjurer's spiritual contact and power – traditionally speaking: God, the Dead and the Devil. And while it cannot be said that this element is truly 'Satanic' in the modern sense of the word, there still remains a certain Luciferian quality to the proposition of meeting the Dark Man at the crossroads. Numerous accounts recorded by Harry Middleton Hyatt describe root-doctors entering pacts with the crossroads Devil to gain the ability to work magic – as did the famous figure Zora Neale Hurston by her own admission. Jeffrey E. Anderson draws a parallel to West African tradition (which along with Kongo influences had a major role in the formation of hoodoo) in which sorcerers would approach 'evil' spirits in order to gain power – remarking that African Americans followed a similar path entering similar pacts with the Dark Man in order to gain the ability to conjure.

Looked at from this wider mythic perspective one might say that a folkloric form of goetic magic, in some sense, has been part of hoodoo for some time already. This offers adventurous practitioners the opportunity for plausible inclusion of further goetic spirit work by following a similar magical trajectory. Admittedly, the rite of meeting the Devil has been met with a great variance of responses in contemporary and historical conjure, ranging from outright rejection as satanic to the full embrace of it as an essential aspect of the tradition, and on to the more recent fashion of collapsing the Devil, symbolically, as a syncretism of the ubiquitous African crossroads intermediary. However, there is no getting around the fact that in later hoodoo, which is mainly Protestant, the Dark Man was understood to be the Devil in an unmistakable, if nuanced, sense. In this regard then, hoodoo tradition might offer an illuminating and practicable approach for working with the infernal realm, one in which that which is commonly perceived of as 'evil' or 'demonic' instead becomes a valid source of skill, knowledge and power, while at the same time foregoing any of the outright dualism seen in mainstream Christian doctrine, and indeed western occultism. From the pragmatic perspective of folk magic, God, the Dead and the Devil are all legitimate sources of empowerment. Of course, my conflation of the folkloric concept of the Devil in relationship to goetic magic is meant to have him stand as a kind of mythological signifier for the entirety of the chthonic forces of the goetia, rather than the spiritual bogeyman that figures in mainstream imagination. Similarly, I do not propose that he might be any particular figure within the grimoire's hierarchy as such, but rather a mythic doorway through which a goetically inclined hoodooist might step into the chthonic dimension described by the grimoire.

What is of particular interest to the work discussed here is that, quite remarkably, while the system of the *Grimorium Verum* is framed in a pious Christian theology and retains those religious trappings in its ritual system, it simultaneously embraces 'diabolical' devices such as sacrifices and blood pacts, seemingly without any apparent conflict or dissonance. Additionally, there is no method of coercion or torture of spirits but rather they are befriended. These two points alone are profoundly illuminating and one could speculate that this is why the grimoire was so readily absorbed in many New World traditions where sacrifice and contracts with spirits are commonplace. More importantly, the way that the *Grimorium Verum* frames its theology offers hoodooists a useful formula and framework for incorporating goetic work into conjure craft without getting into an adversarial theology themselves – or any need to abandon the Christian symbolism and underpinnings of traditional hoodoo either for that matter. At the heart of this perspective lies the insight that the infernal, or chthonic realm, is not at odds with the Divine but *part* of it.

Further, we might observe how the pact with an enigmatic Devil at the crossroads rhymes with the pact of the *Grimorium Verum* both in terms of its mythic narrative and its magical ramifications. In turn, the *Grimorium Verum* brings a workable, non-adversarial philosophy to dealing with infernal spirits that is deeply resonant with hoodoo's own traditional methodologies for petitioning the aid of spiritual entities – whether these be the dead, saints or the Dark Man at the crossroads himself. Spirits are petitioned and bargained with and rarely if ever are they bullied or coerced. They are usually paid in exchange for their services, often deals are made, and as we can see in the famed crossroads ritual the Dark Man, or Devil, is approached respectfully and seen as an initiator. These attitudes are entirely sympathetic to the overall conception of the *Grimorium Verum* which similarly places a great emphasis on pleasing the spirits and paying them for any magical favours.

Finally, and very importantly, there is the matter of the key role of Scirlin, the system's own intermediary spirit, who puts one in touch with all the spirits and grants the operator a form of non-coercive control over them. The intermediary function of this goetic entity is a rather unique feature of the *Grimorium Verum* when compared to the rest of grimoire tradition, but what makes this facet of the system most remarkable and useful for the work described here is that it is yet another characteristic that this fascinating grimoire shares with both New World and African spiritist systems. As such, an intermediary spirit constitutes a core mechanism in many of these spiritist traditions. Interestingly, often enough the intermediary spirit is syncretized with the Devil when he reaches the New World, as seen with hoodoo's Dark Man at the crossroads. As is evident, these kinds of symmetries open up a host of fertile magical and mythological avenues for creative synthesis and spell work, whilst still offering the possibility of remaining true to the spirit of both systems.

Natural and Supernatural Secrets

As mentioned, the grimoire's *Natural and Supernatural Secrets* offers a clear glimpse into the kind of goetic spell work that had been intended to function alongside the greater conjuration system of the grimoire. It also offers several insightful formulas which can be unpacked to reveal the core principles of what might constitute a functional 'goetic' hoodoo. This is especially so if one approaches *Natural and Supernatural Secrets* with a working knowledge of the hoodoo and folk magic repertoire. Upon closer inspection, much of what seems like straight-up malefica, which is to say capricious spells that hurt or kill, are revealed to be clever conjure systems that can be used in variety of ways to help or harm, especially as one begins to examine the versatility of the underlying principles of these spells. It then becomes as straightforward as changing spirit names, sigils and orations in alignment with the new intentions to have entirely different effects. Needless to say these spells use the grimoire's spirits to expedite their effect, providing what experience has proven to be the most efficacious means to practical magic: spirit-driven spell work.

PACTS: IMPLICIT AND EXPLICIT

> *"There are two kinds of pact, the tacit and the apparent, otherwise said the implicit and explicit. You will know the one from the other, if you read this little book. Know, however, that there are many kinds of spirits, some attractive and others not attractive. It is when you make a pact with a spirit, and have to give the spirit something that belongs to you, that you have to be on your guard."*
> — The True Grimoire, page 59

Before we get into some examples of spell adaptations drawn from the principles underlying *Secrets,* we may need to discuss some of the basic assumptions we can make about how to approach a 'goetic' hoodoo. To do that we need to look at a few practical approaches that might be taken with regard to goetic spell craft and its relationship to the full conjuration system of the grimoire.

One approach would be to become an operator of the full ceremonial system outlined in *The True Grimoire* by constructing the tools and going through the formal conjuration and pact procedure and then on to working goetic hoodoo spells of the sort described here alongside, or in conjunction with, the full ritual system. Certainly this would give one a firm footing with the spirits as well as the magical current of grimoire. In this way long-term pacts with various spirits appropriate to the conjurer's areas of interest would be cultivated

There is another strategy suggested implicitly by the *Secrets*, however, whereby one engages the spirits in magical work on a spell-by-spell basis – as appears to be the case in the *Secrets* operations. From this perspective each spell could be viewed as a short term implicit 'pact', where terms are negotiated for each spell. This approach is much closer to traditional hoodoo methods which place less emphasis on elaborate ritual and more situational spell craft. Further, spirits are not understood to be conjured to 'full appearance' in these sorts of spells, but rather their power and influence is petitioned and woven into the constitution and construction of each spell itself, which is a subtle but very important distinction. This is done by various means, such as including spirit seals and orations in the spells along with verbal or written petitions as well as other symbolic gestures during the manipulation of materia magica, which we shall get into a bit later.

The former requires the construction of the tools and a ritual circle, and the latter can be done at the kitchen table, graveyard or crossroads for that matter, using basic spell ingredients and a little cunning. Similarly, the former approach is more structured with all the benefits that this brings whilst the latter can be more freeform, with a little more risk. Additionally, working with short-term implicit pacts in these sorts of spells, the practitioner can get to know the various spirits a little better and well-informed decisions can be made with regard to longer term pacts based on these sorts of working relationships. The latter strategy is also quite evident in the way material from the *Grimorium Verum* was introduced to magical approaches of the New World, where it has been creatively adapted to plug into indigenous folk magic and religion – usually to hair-raising effect. As the principles underlying the *Secrets* reveal, this sort of adaptation is done easily enough and quite naturally if the system is applied artfully. Nonetheless, we should also be aware that the spirits might be a little more unpredictable if they are not bound by the full pact form of the main system, but rather the short-term implicit 'pact' of a spell. Special care needs to be taken that the terms of these short-term pacts are met, and the spirits are paid their dues.

In either case, from a practical perspective it is vital that a good working relationship with the intermediary spirit Scirlin be cultivated, and especially so in the looser framework of the second approach, because it is Scirlin who maintains control of the spirits, constrains them to come and intercedes on behalf of the petitioner. In a very real sense Scirlin is the lynchpin of the entire system. To this end a special altar space for Scirlin might be constructed and furnished with items dedicated to the work: devices such as a spirit pot, dedicated divining tools, votive candles and offerings could all be included in cultivating this sort of connection. This then would be an appropriate place to perform infernal conjure-craft, following the New World practice of setting up dedicated altar spaces for spirit work.

Goetic Seals and Petition Papers

In its simplest and most historically resonant form, the inclusion of goetic sigils or seals in hoodoo spell-work should be our first port of call. Solomonic seals have been included in various forms in hoodoo since the introduction of grimoires to the tradition by the mail order suppliers in the early twentieth century, although there appears to be a few references to Solomonic material earlier than this in the Hyatt material. Interestingly, we find inclusion of spirit seals from the *Grimorium Verum* in Robert Pelton's *Complete Book of Voodoo* and while this particular text is not the most reliable source, it does seem to have drawn on actual accounts of conjure work circa 1960. We also find the use of seals from the *Black Pullet* employed frequently in conjure-making for yet another serendipitous connection – especially considering that this interesting little grimoire is structurally and historically related to the *Grimorium Verum*. Such seals are generally dressed with condition oils and then used as petition papers, placed under candles, or placed inside mojo bags and in other container spells, or along with any other conjure work in which petition papers might usually be included.

Similarly, in the *Natural and Supernatural Secrets* almost all of the spell craft, and especially sympathetic magical procedures such as the manipulation of wax dolls, driving nails into footprints and so forth, we find that these workings are empowered by the inclusion of spirit seals in the material construction of each spell, either on parchment or drawn on the ground or some other material.

This then in its barest form is the core 'system' we can most expediently adapt for 'goetic' hoodoo, and as such we can make the very useful assumption that the seals have the power to implicitly evoke the influence of a spirit into a working. It is then up to the conjurer to divine which spirit would be most appropriate to the work at hand, petition the spirit with the help of Scirlin and perform the spell under its aegis. The complexity need not necessarily even be that great as we can deduce from the spells in the *Secrets,* and most importantly this is the key feature in both hoodoo tradition and the grimoire that perfectly overlap, creating our first vital link.

Working in this way then, one might select an appropriate spirit from the hierarchy using preferred divinatory tools. The spirit seal would then be drawn on blessed parchment, Scirlin petitioned in order to make contact with the spirit successfully, and using further divination arrange the terms of the spell with the spirit. These might include the desired effect of the working and the payment offered to the spirit upon completion of the work – and following common hoodoo protocol, the petition might be written out in full on the back of the seal, including the terms of agreement, which then could be dressed with appropriate condition oils such as, say, Dark Arts oil. Finally, the seal is included in the construction of a spell – whether this be a simple candle spell, mojo hand or a more elaborate working such as a magic lamp – giving the intrepid goetic hoodooist a familiar and very accessible approach to working with goetic spirits. This approach becomes in essence an implicit spell-based pact, and can be elaborated on with more ritual complexity according to taste and ability.

Further techniques employing Spirit Sigils

Considering the important role that the inclusion of spirit sigils takes in the material construction of a spell it is worth noting that there are numerous practical ways in which these can be introduced into a working to empower spell-work other than being inscribed on parchment.

Taking chalk and drawing a sigil on the ground or work table, for instance, to set the stage for magical work is a potent and effective way of incorporating these spirit-figures. Chalk holds a special place in New World ritual symbolism, often associated with bones and therefore the underworld and the dead. A chalk sigil can then be 'activated' by blowing cigar smoke onto it – keeping in mind that tobacco smoke is an important tool in many New World magical systems – viewed as a means of contact and offering but also 'heating' or 'stimulating' spiritual entities. In hoodoo mojo bags are sometimes fed tobacco smoke for this reason. Similarly, a swig of whisky or rum might be mouth-sprayed across a chalk sigil, with sharp and powerful blast to ensure that it forms a fine mist like spray rather than a messy squirt!

The mouth-spray technique, too, is found in numerous of these systems as a means of activating spirit markings, or pots and so forth, and acts as part offering, part spiritual stimulant. In conjure, whiskey is sometimes mouth-sprayed onto mojo bags to 'feed' a mojo, for instance. In either the case of blown tobacco smoke or mouth-sprayed alcohol, expelled breath figures as a vital component in the technique, infusing the object or sigil with the operator's own life-stuff and is therefore closely equitable to blood in both the organic and magical sense. Once a sigil is potentised, spell craft can be performed atop such an area – a magic lamp for instance might be created and left to burn there, or a mojo bag tied, herbs chopped or ground.

Such sigils could of course be drawn in the dirt using a stick or wand whilst working at the crossroads or elsewhere outside. By the same token, magical powders – which are commonplace in conjure (containing powdered herbs, roots, oils and talcum) – with some practice could be used to 'draw' a spirit sigil on a work surface. Such powder-sigils might become 'activated' by puffing smoke on them, or burning candles down over them accompanied by the petitions, and thereafter might be gathered up once again, empowered by the process, and deployed elsewhere to expedite their magical aims near the target of the work (place of business; path of an enemy or lover, etc.).

Goetic Doll-babies

Highly adaptable and amenable to further goetic spell-work are the wax doll spells found in the *Secrets*, used to torment or destroy an enemy. Using 'dollies' in a similar manner is a staple of many traditions of folk-magic: European, New World as well as African, and is certainly a widespread practice in hoodoo. This kind of work is done to harm often enough, yes, but also to influence, dominate, confuse, bind or imprison, send away, seduce or heal. Interestingly, doll-babies are not traceable as having entered hoodoo tradition through the Kongo roots of hoodoo. Instead, doll-babies most likely were brought to rootwork from European witchcraft. In *The True Grimoire* wax dolls are manipulated using spirit sigils along with some interesting gestures and spoken formulas which when unpacked further are revealed to be highly versatile methods with a host of useful applications in various contexts. Considering the wide range of uses to which doll-baby work can be put, this single *Secrets* adaptation could be used for nearly any conceivable condition from love or healing work to hotfooting and enemy work.

Of course the use of wax images suggests that *all* other cognate forms of image-based sympathetic magic might be employed in a similar way, whether this be the use of cloth or vegetable poppets, photographs, name papers or any of the symbolic representations of a target found in hoodoo. Additionally, the use of wax itself suggests another highly appropriate hoodoo-centric material for this adaptation, namely figural candles. These have been popular in conjure tradition ever since their introduction by spiritual retailers. Figural candles take a variety of forms: male and female figures, genitalia, skulls, devils, cats, bride and groom and many other useful surrogate shapes. These candles are used in moving-candle spells, dressed with hoodoo condition oils along with herbs and petition papers and are manipulated in a variety of potent ways to affect a target – all of which could be enhanced and adapted by using the *Secrets* principles. Further these can double as an offering of flame for the spirits. This naturally results in goetic candle work!

Let us examine the original wax doll spells in order learn more about their underlying magical principles:

Death Spell by Magic Image, p95, The True Grimoire

Make a wax doll representing the person you wish to destroy, slit the head, chest and stomach and insert the sigils of Frimost, Guland and Surgat.

Impale the image head to foot and turn over the brazier saying:

It is not my hand that scorches thee, it is the hand of Frimost which scorches thee. It is not wax which I scorch it is the head, heart and spleen of N… that I scorch.

The Principles:

From this remarkably compact yet clever spell we can draw a few very useful underlying principles at work in the *Secrets*:

Principle #1:
An image affixed with appropriate spirit seals can affect specific areas of the body and their associated symbolic values in a target.

Principle #2:
The representation can be manipulated in some fashion (here scorched) to direct the spirits influence to effect a symbolically related outcome.

Principle #3:
Verbal formulae can be employed to empower magical gestures performed by the conjurer so that these are effectively carried out 'as-if' the spirits perform them – hereby producing a magical outcome directly related to the gesture in question.

SEDUCTION DOLL-BABY: EXAMPLE

Now let us take these principles and adapt them to a goetically powered doll-baby spell for seduction:

Firstly with some divination and common sense we should select two spirits appropriate to the work at hand: Frimost, and Huictigaras – noting that Frimost excites passions in men and women and Huictigaras can cause insomnia or sleep and by association all forms of sleep related effects.

One should wait 'till late at night and the target is most likely asleep – midnight being a potent magical hour in hoodoo. The operator might open the spell work very simply with purifying and protection prayers followed by an invocation to Scirlin along with an offering of mace on coals in his name and honour. After the invocation the conjurer would request that Scirlin bring the attention of Frimost and Huictigaras to this working. This could then be followed by an offering of frankincense in the name and honour of these two spirits.

The written petition of intent for the working along with the appropriate seals as well as the 'terms' – which should include the payment that the spirits can expect upon completion of the work and other details – could be placed under a red vigil light decorated with the Scirlin seal. The candle then would be dressed with appropriate condition oil, fixed and given as an offering of flame to the spirits. We are now ready to begin spell-work.

Looking to conjure tradition for the herbal symbolism and other details to flesh out this working, we might create a wax image and within the wax include personal concerns such as hair or nail clippings from our target. Additionally, we might include herbs and roots appropriate to our amorous aims such as tonka bean, damiana and lovage root, and knead these into the wax as the figure is sculpted, calling our petition and the influence of the spirits into the work. A tiny pinch of red-pepper or ginger can be moulded into the doll's genitalia to 'heat' and arouse the target sexually. Taking principle number 1 into account we select appropriate areas to (gently) insert spirit sigils drawn on parchment into the wax dolly. In this case, the genitals, heart and head. The doll should be then be 'baptised' and named after the target.

This could quite simply involve the operator making the sign of the cross over the image, saying:

In the Name of the Father, the Son and the Holy Spirit I baptise thee N...

The operator can then take the dolly and begin 'working' it, by manipulating it in variety of ways – the options really are infinite. In this example the operator could take attraction condition oils and proceed to sensually smearing oil over the doll's genitals, saying:

It is not my hand that caresses thee, it is the hand of Frimost that caresses thee. It is not wax I caress it is the genitals of N... that I caress.

In this way we bring both Principle No. 2 and No. 3 into the working. The operator might go further and take the dolly up close to his mouth and gently blow into its neck and ear, kiss it and whisper saucily:

It is not my lips that kiss thee and stir thee from thy sleep, it is the lips of Huictigaras. It is not wax that I kiss it is the soft flesh, neck and ears of N... that I kiss.

It soon becomes clear that the possibilities this way of working presents are manifold – in this case exciting passions and sleeplessness in the target, creating an erotic night-time obsession and lustful longing. This might be continued for a set period (days or weeks) for extreme results.

When the operator concludes the spell-session he could take his own used and assumedly musky underwear and wrap this around the dolly saying:

It is not my hand that envelops thee in desirous scent, but the hand of Frimost. It is not wax I envelop but all thy body and senses.

The dolly then would be stored somewhere safe. The conjurer would conclude and give the spirits an offering of incense and thereafter giving them leave that their attention might be dismissed, followed by thanks and an offering to Scirlin, closing the rite appropriately. A cleansing rite of some sort might be in order thereafter – a hyssop bath, for instance – as is the custom in hoodoo following any working of black magic.

Using a photograph or name paper: A Green Devil 'pay-me' spell

Extending this idea we can develop it once more in a simplified but analogous way by using a photograph of the person along with a figural candle. Let us adapt a classic 'pay-me' compelling spell. For this all the worker would need is a green devil figural candle (or in a pinch, a plain green candle), commanding and compelling, or 'pay-me' condition oil and a photograph of the target. The spell's aim is to compel the target to pay a monetary debt owed to the operator. Taking the photograph the operator in this case would draw the spirit sigil upon the forehead in order to influence that area and its associated symbolic value – in this case the target's mind. An additional petition and spirit seal along with the Scirlin seal would in this case then be placed beneath the Green Devil candle. The candle is dressed with compelling oils and inscribed with the appropriate spirit seal in some way.

The rite is opened as before (prayers, invocation, offerings and so forth), and the candle is lit as an offering to the spirit chosen for this work; Claunech seems a suitable candidate. The operator takes up the photograph and lightly singes a corner of the picture, saying:

It is not my hand that scorches thee it is the hand of Claunech. It is not paper I burn but your thoughts that burn with fear and anxiety until you repay your debt to me!

The photo is placed beneath the candle which is left to burn for a while, then pinched out. The candle is relit at the same time the next day and the spell is continued daily like this, gradually burning up the photograph until the money owed is paid to the querent. Naturally, this spell could be adapted to compel the target to do nearly anything, and a figural candle might not be essential, but I do find the dovetailing of Devil symbolism here pleasing and appropriate. Similarly, if no photograph can be found, a name paper with the name repeated (in tiny letters, to make the target small and vulnerable) all across the paper. The name-paper then is inscribed with the sigil and manipulated in the same way.

Not my hand but the hand of Frimost: further tricks using Principle No. 3

Verbal formulae can be employed to empower magical gestures performed by the conjurer so that these are effectively carried out as if the spirits perform them – hereby producing a magical outcome directly related to the gesture in question.

The seemingly simple oration contained in the previous *Secrets* spell is revealed to be incredibly powerful and versatile after some practical work with it. With some creativity it can be adapted to a host of workings and contexts ranging from spell work to oil and powder creation to simply laying down tricks or otherwise deploying it in spell work.

One might blend a condition oil or powder under the aegis of an appropriate spirit from the hierarchy; perhaps the spirit's sigil is inscribed in chalk on the work table and as one blends, grinds and works in other ways manipulating materials and herbal ingredients one can empower these processes with the spoken formula, adapting it to the spirit whose aid is solicited.

Here are a few examples:

It is not my hand that grinds this money powder but the hand of Claunech.
It is not my hand that blends this healing oil but the hand of Heramael.
It is not my hand that dresses this candle for destruction of N... but the hand of Surgat.
It is not my hand that ties this mojo but the hand of Sustugriel.

Similarly when deploying spell work, or laying down tricks near the target of the spell, the oration becomes a potent activator:

It is not my hand that casts these powders of confusion but the hand of Sergulath.
It is not my hand that buries this bottle but the hand of Musisin.
It is not my hand that dresses this envelope to attract N... but the hand of Hicpacth

Any kind of magically significant gesture could be imbued with force in this way, working in accordance with power of the spirit whose influence is being woven into the work.

Goetic Candle-work

Looked at in a certain way a candle can be understood to be a kind of wax figure, with the area near the wick being the head, the middle the body and the base of the candle the feet. There is an image-based approach to candle work, for instance, where a mouth or eyes are carved into the area taken as the 'head' of the candle. The mouth then might be loaded with 'shut-up' type herbs to stop gossip, or conversely 'loose tongue' type herbs to get someone to talk, or the eyes bound to blind the target. Similarly, the 'foot' of the candle may be loaded with red pepper and similar material seen in hotfoot class of spells to set the target running. Naturally, therefore the use of the candle in its simplest form can be adapted to the aforementioned *Secrets* principles by carving, or inserting spirit sigils in the appropriate area of the candle, baptising the candle, fixing it and lighting it to expedite the spell. Thus combining the wax image spell, fire offering and candle spell into a single form! When the approach is applied to a figural candle the options become quite numerous and creative.

Interestingly, the *Natural and Supernatural Secrets* already seems to contain a form of candle work in the spell *To Make a Girl Come to You, however Modest She May Be.*

Goetic Container Spells

The container spell in its various forms such as the bottle spell or mojo bag is understood to be the result of one of the more influential aspects of Kongo magic in conjure. The concept of the *minkisi*, or indwelling spirits of magical charms, was carried over into hoodoo in the form of these magical packets and bags which are understood to be inhabited and 'fed' in order to be kept alive and working. These pouches function as a magical charm but in another very real sense as spiritual locus for a kind of familiar spirit given to a task ascribed to it by the conjurer. Further, in Kongo belief gnarled roots were believed to house the first and most powerful *inkisi* (singular) called Funza, and we thus find a great emphasis placed on roots within conjure tradition – the American derivative of the African concept. This is especially emphasised in mojo bags which quite often will contain a large root (such as the famous High John the Conquer root). Here then we find fertile ground for dovetailing the technologies of the grimoire and hoodoo.

To do this we need to consider the spirit Sustugriel, as he not only promises to be a very powerful ally in the art of magic but specifically in the endeavour of creating mojo bags and other container spells. He is described as "imparting familiars for all purposes" which in his domain is connected to the mandrake root. I won't detain the reader by discussing the complex role of mandrake in European occultism, but I would like to point out the meaningful resonance here between the grimoire and hoodoo tradition, which interestingly also sees the inclusion of mandrake root in its corpus of herbal lore. More importantly, it is the mandrake root's connection to familiar spirits in the grimoire (and historically) that is of most interest in the construction of goetic mojo bags. One could argue that this is an analogous concept to the Kongo concept of the *minkisi* spirits associated with gnarled African roots and therefore the spirits of mojo bags.

The Devil's Mojo Hand

A carefully selected piece of mandrake root will become the centrepiece of this goetic 'hand' – our 'midnight' equivalent of the ubiquitous High John root and thus the locus of the familiar. Base ingredients for the mojo could include:

Crossroads dirt
Mandrake root
Black dog hair (the devil is thought to have a black dog)

Further herbal, mineral and zoological ingredients specific to the aim of the charm should be included: lodestone to attract, pyrite for money work, tonka beans for love, sulphur for protection, etc. Some care needs to be taken with the crossroads dirt that it's collected from a crossroads that is suited to the work – most importantly, dirt should not be taken from a 'troubled' crossroads or it will bring a similar effect into the work. Sites to avoid are places where many accidents occur or that suffer some from geographic affliction – be it historical or social. An offering needs to be left for the spirits of the crossroads to pay for the dirt; one Hyatt informant recommended whisky and salt as payment to the crossroads spirits, but small change, cigars and various forms of strong alcohol all seem to be acceptable.

Once the material basis of the bag has been selected, the spirit sigils and petition need to be formulated. For this task we should look to the spirit Sustugriel with the aim of procuring a familiar spirit to inhabit the mojo hand and work for the operator. To do so the function of the familiar could be sigilised using traditional methods such as Agrippa or Spare's monogram method. Alternatively Sustugriel could be contacted via Scirlin and the sigil for a familiar appropriate to the bag might be procured by means of scrying. In these matters it might be prudent to consult Scirlin directly. The main point here being that the sigil for the familiar that is to inhabit this infernal mojo hand needs to be procured or created by suitable means. Once this is done the petition paper may be drawn on parchment in an appropriate way along with the Scirlin sigil, the sigil of Sustugriel and the newly procured sigil of the familiar. An appropriate offering to Sustugriel should be arranged; similarly the needs of the familiar need to established, as it will need to be fed. This could include traditional methods such as feeding the mojo whiskey weekly, or a grimoire based approach in which the mojo could be fed blood at certain intervals.

To execute this working Scirlin would be conjured following working methods outlined in the grimoire or those the operator has arranged with the spirits, then asked to bring in Sustugriel who then would grant the familiar. The mojo would then be constructed during the 'charge' to the Sustugriel, resulting in the potentised and living charm bag.

A Goetic Money Mojo: Example

An example might give the reader an opportunity to see what such a bag might look like in practice – once again combining hoodoo herbal symbolism and methodology with concepts from the grimoire.

INGREDIENTS:
Mandrake root
Lodestone
Pyrite
A bank note: (a potent form of which would be a lost note found by chance i.e. 'lucky money', alternatively a perfectly crisp, new note from the bank)
Magnetic sand
Cinnamon
Sassafras root
Crossroads dirt collected from an intersection with a bank at it
Personal concerns
Green thread
Three vigil lights
Money-drawing condition oils
Florida water or other strong spirits
A red flannel bag

The money-bringing familiar's name and sigil will have been procured by suitable means beforehand. The three vigil lights are arranged in a triangular configuration on the work surface – these affixed with the sigils of Scirlin, Sustugriel and the familiar-to-be-granted. The candles are dressed and fixed appropriately with condition oils. The sigil of Sustugriel additionally might be drawn on the work surface in chalk and 'activated' in the centre of these.

The rite is opened appropriately (prayers, invocation, offerings and so forth). The three vigil lights are lit in the name and honour of each spirit inscribed upon them after Scirlin is 'invoked' and Sustugriel's attention is 'brought in' by Scirlin.

The bank note might then be taken and the petition along with the 'terms' may be written carefully on one side of the bank note. The other side of the note then is inscribed with the Scirlin seal (the small one is more practical here), the seal of Sustugriel along with sigils of the mojo bag's money familiar. The note is dressed with condition oils. The mandrake is 'fed' condition oil, smoke and whiskey. Along with a nice pinch of bank dirt the root may be placed on the note and tied into a packet with green thread, folding and tying *toward* the operator, to bring the influence toward the one. This might be accompanied by extemporised petition calling Sustugriel to pass the familiar and his power into the work. The packet tied like this is placed inside the bag along with the herbs and some personal concerns of the client. Next the lodestone may be fed some magnetic sand oil and along with the pyrite put into the flannel bag.

A small splash of Florida water or other strong spirits such as rum then might be poured in a saucer. One may then take a match and give the formal 'charge' to Sustugriel to grant the familiar and so doing light the Florida water, letting an offering of blue flame flare up. As it does one symbolically 'scoops' three handfuls of flame into the bag, after the third scoop very quickly closing and 'capturing' some fire and then firmly tying the mojo with three knots, saying:

It is not my hand that ties this mojo bag but the hand of Sustugriel. It is not a mojo I tie but the familiar spirit N… that I bond to this money work.

The mojo then may be passed through the offering of incense smoke to Sustugriel. This should immediately be followed by the full offering to Sustugriel in return for granting the familiar (as would have been arranged through divination before-hand). The rite can then be concluded, and then appropriately closed. The bag is left between the candles 'till these have finished burning down over the next few days – 'working' the mojo daily as it does. This can be done by feeding it smoke daily, or whiskey along with prayer. The bag should then be 'fed' whisky or whatever else has been arranged for the familiar's nourishment weekly or at agreed intervals and worn on the operator's person, ensuring no one ever touches it.

Magical geography: the crossroads

An important feature in hoodoo's 'magical geography', the crossroads offer us numerous useful possibilities for working with the spirits and potentising spell ingredients. Additionally, this site's important position in both New World and European mythic thinking makes it a potent nexus for further mingling of the grimoire current with that of hoodoo. Performing spells at the crossroads would become the most obvious opportunity for this kind of work – especially when taking into account the symbolism and magical properties of the site itself. In hoodoo the crossroads are deeply intertwined with its conceptions of magic, both as spiritual locus of the crossroads Devil but also more broadly as a site of spiritual ingress with the otherworld – the place where the numinous and ordinary intersect. The concept was carried over into the tradition from Kongo and West African beliefs which revered the crossroads as important sites and symbols for the these same reasons. Crossroads dirt then becomes a potent ingredient connecting to us to this numinous intersection, and therefore a substance that offers spiritual forces a point of egress to move through from the other side into the work the practitioner.

Along with the use of dirt in spell work, further techniques that suggest themselves are the burying of spell ingredients – roots, charms, curios and coins – at the crossroad to empower. This could be done by inscribing the appropriate spirit sigil over the material's burial site in the dirt along with a petition and an offering of some sort to the spirit in question, and then leaving the materials for a numerologically significant number of days, perhaps taking into account the phase of the moon or other astrological factors and then later exhuming the fully potentised materials to use in spell craft (mojo bags, lamps, bottle spells, etc). Similarly, disposal of spell remains as a form of deployment at the crossroads is another traditional and appropriate way of working – taking the remains of goetic candle-work for instance and leaving it at the crossroads with a petition that the spirits involved 'take' the work and finish it. Parallels to this approach can be found in Brazilian quimbanda, Haitian Vodou as well as hoodoo.

Conclusion:

I have tried to illustrate a few approaches that require a minimum of ingredients and ritual elaboration – in an effort to remain succinct and true to the spirit of conjure craft – which above all things favours accessibility and directness. Nothing should get in the way of doing your work, as one of my teachers likes to say. Naturally this approach can be elaborated on – increasing in complexity, incorporating the orations, tools, magical timing and other specifics from the *Grimorium Verum* and hoodoo tradition – according to the practitioner's taste and inclination. But I am of the opinion that the formulae in *Natural and Supernatural Secrets* ratify a straightforward approach – low in ritual complexity whilst dense in material and gestural symbolism. It's an approach that fits well within the hoodoo oeuvre, too.

In this light it worth noting that whilst conjure does retain a corpus of lore, dealing largely with the use of botanical ingredients and typical sympathetic processes and gestures that a rootworker might employ, what truly distinguishes it as a magical craft is the specialised improvisational approach that flows from that lore. It could be compared to jazz which has improvisational musical elements, but these are always performed in a highly developed and skilfully executed expression of the jazz form. And this is where spectators get confused – it is assumed that because hoodoo has an improvisational form it means an eclectic range of disparate elements that appeal to the magician can be thrown together to create a working. This would be like mixing polka, folk and Latin elements into a jazz session – at best odd, at worst noise! A skilled jazz musician *could* however introduce some Latin flavour to a session artfully if he is versed well enough in the form that it becomes a valid artistic expression. It becomes a personal flourish or a style.

Similarly, when approaching the notion of 'goetic' hoodoo we need to cultivate a mindset that is familiar with the basic form so that our goetic inclusion is a useful expression and not a half-baked, hodgepodge affair. At its heart pure conjure work is a certain way of thinking about magic, spell ingredients and the world itself, and whilst it is not within the scope of this article to elaborate too much on all of that, it would be helpful to familiarise oneself with that perspective as much as possible. A clearer picture can be gained by studying reliable historical sources such as the Hyatt material, or going further by learning from experienced rootworkers first hand, examining spell examples and perhaps more broadly investigating European and New World folk magic as a genre. By looking at these kinds of examples, a clear insight can be gained into this particular way of working which then becomes fertile ground for actual practice.

LESSONS FROM

A personal perspective on Haitian Vodou and its influence on my practices as a pagan and occultist.

Introduction

"A small building trembles with the sound of African drum rhythms somewhere on the small Caribbean nation of Haiti. White clad initiates sway to the drum beat and sing songs to the spirits. Suddenly one of them starts to stagger and spin violently, till they are steadied by those around them. They no longer bear their normal expression as they are being 'ridden'[1] *by spirits. The initiates quickly bring the spirit its favourite clothes, foods and drink. After feeding the spirit proceeds to give advice to those present before departing with the promise it will return soon. This is what is at the very heart of Vodou."*

The preceding paragraph I originally wrote for an article on Haitian Vodou back in 2002 and I still feel it conveys the essence and beauty of Vodou. The article came about after a trip to Haiti the previous summer. I had travelled there to undergo Kanzo, a two week series of initiation ceremonies, with the Roots Without End Society.

Despite being a witch (of a primarily pagan variety), I had been working with the lwa (Vodou spirits) for a few years. During a certain piece of work I had asked the lwa involved what they wanted in return for their aid, as is quite normal in Vodou and other similar traditions. The answer came back that I should Kanzo. I had been in contact via email with Mambo Racine (an American woman

GINEN

by Drac Uber (Bon Houngan Lamp DeNwite D'Ginen)

who had been Asogwe, the highest rank in Vodou, for many years and had settled in Haiti's cultural capitol, Jacmel) for some time. So having discussed it with her, six months later I followed the spirits and found myself sitting in her peristyle (temple) with various other prospective initiates (mostly from Haiti and the US). It was an amazing experience and I learnt a lot (both about spirits, magick and my relationship to both).

I wrote my article back in 2002 for a popular pagan magazine, as I felt there was a lot modern neo-paganism could learn from Vodou. Back then spirits (and other otherworldly entities) were far too often talked at rather than to, or worse seen as purely aspects of self. As for working with the ancestors, that was far too much like necromancy (and what's wrong with that I hear you cry) for most pagans' liking. And occultist of the time weren't much better. The only ones who seemed genuinely interested in spirit work at that time were chaos magickians.

Thankfully things have come a long way since then (this present volume should be proof enough of this). In this current essay I will explore the theology and techniques of Haitian Vodou, and try and give you a personal account of how these have influenced and enhanced my practice and understanding as a pagan and occultist. To save confusion (I hope) the term *spirit* will be used to denote any spiritual entity (including gods, lwa, demons, elemental, angles, fairies, etc).

SECTION A
(FROM ALBION TO EDEN)

THEOLOGY OF HAITIAN VODOU AND RITUAL IN THEORY AND PRACTICE

Vodousants (followers of Vodou) believe in an ultimate source of the divine, who is the Creator of everything. This being is called *Gran Met* (Great Master) or *Bondye* (Good God) and is identified with the Christian God. As *Gran Met* has to run the universe s/he is far to busy to get involved with the affairs of mankind, so s/he has lesser aspects of him/herself, called lwa, who rule over various areas of human life. Each of the lwa have their own characteristic behaviours, colours, items, images[2], favourite foods and drinks. The lwa are divided into three main families (or nations), Rada, Petro and Guede. These then have various sub-families, such as Nago (who are practically a family on their own) Ibo or Kongo. Vodousants also work with among others *djabs*[3] (devils), *les morts* (the dead), the spirit of all the people associated (during their life) with a particular place and assorted ancestral spirits.

One theory I have heard from some Houngans and Mambos, is that the lwa represent different spiritual vibrations (if God is the entire spectrum, then each lwa is a single frequency) and that by using the songs, images, offers and sacred items associated with a particular lwa you can tune into it.

So where do the lwa live? For the most part the answer is Ginen. Ginen is a sort of idealised 'ancestral' Africa. Alternatively, after death the souls of the dead are said to descend into the abysmal waters, but can later be reclaimed by their living family or by Baron and become Guede. However there are also places within our world where the spirits reside. For the most part these are sacred rocks, trees, waterfalls, springs and other natural features. Some of these places are places of pilgrimage (such as the waterfall at Saut d'Eau and Ogou's mud bath in Plaine Du Nord) at certain times of year.

Most Vodou ritual follows the same structure, the only difference being how elaborate it is. The best way to demonstrate this is to describe how a full-scale 'dance' is performed. I will then talk about the underlying structure and how this is scaled down for use in a personal ritual.

The ceremonies usually start in the morning with the sacrifice of animals, so that there is plenty of time to prepare and cook them in time for the main service in the evening. During this ceremony the animals are washed with water scented with perfume and fresh, crushed basil leaves. The lwa are invoked to bless the sacrifice and may even possess a Vodousant to take part in the sacrifice. When the animals are killed their blood is collected. The blood is then given to the lwa along with a portion of the cooked animal[4] and other food offerings during the main ceremony during the evening.

The evening service is started with the initiates renewing the sacred space of the Peristyle, by saluting the four directions and other sacred areas within it. This is followed by various prayers. These start with those prayers addressed to God, such as the Lord's Prayer, the Hail Mary and the Apostle's Creed. Next is the Priye Ginen (Prayer of Africa), which is a long prayer that starts with an entirely Catholic content and gets progressively more 'African' as it goes on. After this Legba[5] is called on to open the gates to Ginen. The rest of the service consists of songs and drumming for various lwa. Normally three songs are sung for each lwa included. The first group of lwa to be sung for are the Rada Lwa, followed by the Guede Lwa and finally the Petro Lwa. When the last song for the last lwa is sung the service is over.

The basic structure here is fairly straightforward. First everything needed is gathered together and properly prepared (this includes setting up the altar/s). Sacred space is marked out and defined, and spiritual focal points within it are honoured. Prayers are said to the ultimate source of all spirit, thus raising ourselves up from everyday life. Honour is given to the roots (racine) of the tradition and the spirits that represent it. The gate keeper between the material world and the spiritual world is honoured and asked to 'open the ways'. The spirits are called on and given honour (at this point offerings are made and any 'work' is done). Finally the ritual is closed.

So how does this ritual structure apply to a small personal service? Let's say you wanted to create a charm with LaSirene's[6] aid. You would gather together everything you need for the ritual. This may include a white or blue altar cloth, a large white candle, a selection of white and or blue candles (tea lights will do), a small quantity of rum, a set of blue or white clothing, sea shells, an image of Stella Maris, a mirror, suitable offering for LaSirene (melon, anisette[7], sweet cakes with blue or white icing, champagne, corn meal porridge with molasses, etc.) and all the materials for making your charm (selected through divination or directly prescribed by one of the lwa). Having showered or bathed first, you'd dress in the clothes you'd prepared. Spread the altar cloth on a suitable surface and arrange all the other items on it (except the rum and assorted candles, which should be put to one side). Salute[8] the four directions (east, west, north and finally south) and then the altar. Light the large white candle, cross yourself and perform a simplified '*action de grace*'. Traditionally this consists of three repetitions each of the Lord's Prayer, Hail May and Apostle's Creed. However, while I use the first two I don't use the Apostle's Creed, as it is very Catholic. I know one Vodousant, and member of the O.T.O., that uses Crowley's Gnostic Creed instead. Myself I favour Jack Parson's Gnostic Creed[9] or William Gray's reworking of Psalm 23[10]. But you could simply replace all three with the Invocation of the Bornless One. Then you'd pour out the rum, as an offering to Legba, and ask him to 'open the gates'. Light a blue candle and call on LaSirene and present to her the offerings (with each offering, light another candle and place it with it). Next you'd construct the charm and leave it and the offerings on the altar. After a while you'd close the ritual by thanking the spirits and snuffing out (don't blow them out) the first candle you lit for LaSirene and the large white candle. All the candles with the offerings should ideally be allowed to burn out. After the ritual, offerings should ideally left somewhere appropriate to the lwa they are for (crossroad for Legba, the sea for LaSirene or Agwe, etc.) or, if this is not possible, in the bushes somewhere.

The above should give you a rough idea of how Vodou ritual works. I'm sure most of you will be able to see how these principles could be applied to 'pagan' spirits or deities, but I will return to this later.

Haitian views on the structure of the human soul and its implication in necromantic work

Unlike in the modern western view of the soul, which is seen as singular, in Haitian Vodou the human soul is believed to be made up of five main parts and influenced by other spirits that accompany us through life. What happens to each part on death is different and so is approached differently.

The first part is the *gran bon ang* (big good angel). This is identical in each individual and could be viewed as a personal manifestation of the universal soul. This returns to 'the source' upon death.

Next is the *ti bon ang* (little good angel). This part of the soul is closely linked to the individual's intellect and personality. This part can be seen as the individual soul. After death this part descends into the abysmal waters. After a year certain rites can be performed that call the spirit back to their family (biological or spiritual). The spirit is then housed in a terracotta vessel and served with other ancestral spirits. A number of things can happen to those spirits which are not claimed by their family. They can be claimed by the Baron and become Guede, they can choose to be reincarnated or they can become absorbed into the general 'ancestral current'.

Then there is the *nanm*. This is your spiritual life force. This is similar to the Yogic prana or Taoist chi, but is 'imprinted' with the individual's personality. This part of the soul is retained in your physical remains (especially the skull) after death. Any magic using human bones is calling upon this part of the soul.

This brings us to the *zetwal* (the star). While this is part of your soul, it is not housed in your body. This part of your soul is guardian to the collective spiritual experience of your lifetime. Personally I believe that the *zetwal* is the Vodou equivalent of the Holy Guardian Angel of modern ceremonial magick.

Finally is the *met tet* (master of the head). While in neo-paganism most people choose their patron deity, in Vodou you are believed to be born with a ruling lwa. While this spirit is separate from yourself, part of its essence is believed to reside within you and to strongly influence your personality.

As well as the various parts of the soul, in Vodou it is believed that you also have a 'spiritual court' that is said to 'walk within'. This is made up of lwa that are strongly associated with you, *lwa racine* (root spirits) those spirits that your ancestors served (and you have inherited) and general ancestral spirits. While these do not assert as strong a pull as the *met tet*, they still are believed to influence an individual's personality.

GUEDE, THE ANCESTORS AND LE MORT

As you have probably gathered from the preceding sections (especially the last one) in Haitian Vodou there are various types of spirits that were once living people. The three main groups are the Guede Lwa (the unclaimed dead the Baron has raised up), the Ancestors (those dead that have been reclaimed by their 'family' and the more general ancestral current), and *les morts* (literally the dead, what we would probably call ghosts).

The Guede Lwa are one of the three families (or Nations) of the lwa. They are headed by Baron and Madame Brigett. In fact there are many Barons; the main three are Baron LaCroix (the cross), Baron Samedi (Saturday) and Baron Cimitiere (cemetery). Strictly every graveyard (and cemetery) has its own Baron and Brigett[11]. The Guede are ironically the most 'alive' of all the lwa. Being dead and therefore not bound by the consequences of their actions, they do not have to conform to social norms. They laugh at and expose our pettiness and moral conceits. They will often do this with humour and they love a dirty joke. They also enjoy drinking, smoking and generally partying. They are known for their down-to-earth advice and matter of fact approach.

Les morts are most often associated with the spirits called forth from skulls. Whereas the Guede are as likely to be called for advice as for aid in magic, the use of *morts* is almost exclusively magical.

Finally we come to the Ancestors. It is believed that by maintaining good relations with the Ancestors, they will draw good fortune and repel bad fortune. Unlike the Guede and Les Mort, their power and wisdom is normally of a more general nature[12]. In Haiti ancestral rites are closely linked to and very similar in form to those of the Guede. This is because like the Guede they have been 'under the water', but have been re-claimed by their family (rather then by Baron). This process of re-claiming the dead starts shortly after death. Certain funerary rites are performed for the deceased family member. Then a year later a big 'dance' is held for them and rituals are performed to call them back from 'under the water'. Their spirit is then housed in a specially prepared clay pot wrapped in white cloth.

SECTION B (THE JOURNEY BACK HOME)

Applying Vodou ritual technology to neo-paganism and western occultism

I think the main lesson to be learnt from Vodou is to really 'live with' the spirits. All too often with the highly intellectualised, and often psychoanalytical, approach of the modern western mind the entities we work with can become far too distant. The main two ways to close this gap are by talking with them (through divination) and feeding them (through offering).

So let's start with divination. There are numerous ways to speak to the spirits. I will not go into them in depth, as there simply isn't room and other writers have already covered them far better than I ever could. However, I would suggest you have a few methods under your belt, as different situations and spirits suit different divination systems. Personally I use tarot cards[13], dice, bibliomancy[14], dream interpretation[15] and a system using four flat stones with a black spot on one side, based on the *Ifa obi* oracle. Divination should also not be reserved purely for gaining advice from the spirits. Divination should be used to consult the spirits whenever you are considering performing any sort of 'working'. They will be able to advise you as to whether it is worth doing anything, what type of working you should do, what materials and ingredients you should use, which spirit you should be working with and what offerings you should give them.

This nicely brings us to the subject of offerings. Don't worry, I'm not suggesting that you go out and sacrifice a fatted cow. While I have no problem with animal sacrifice in the right setting and done the right way[16], killing some poor animal just because you want to be hardcore and then just chucking its body in the bin is just plain disrespectful. Most spirits are very happy with much simpler fare.

In Vodou it's easy to know what to offer, as each spirit's likes and dislikes are well known. With pagan gods and the spirits of the western occult tradition, it is a lot more difficult. Most of this information has been lost in the sands of time. Some clues can be found in archaeological and historical evidence. However, for the most part you'll have to go on gut instinct and by asking the spirit itself. Generally, appropriately coloured candles and incense are a good starting place. I tend to find that most spirits like alcohol (although fairies prefer milk), but of what kind varies from spirit to spirit. However, through regular consultation your spirits should be able to tell you what food, drinks and other items they would like.

Finally, it is always good to have a good relationship with a spirit of the gates – those that stand in the doorway between the material and the spiritual world. In Vodou he is Papa Legba, for the Greeks and Romans it was Hermes or Mercury and in Hinduism Ganesh fulfils this role. This seems to be a very widespread concept in most polythemic traditions, but has somehow been lost in most neo-paganism.

ANCESTRAL REVERENCE AND NECROMANCY (THE WHITE TABLE AND THE DIRTY WORK IN THE GRAVEYARD)

In Haiti the Ancestors would normally be honoured together with and in the same manner as the Guede. However, personally I honour them separately and this is not uncommon among international Vodousants. Although ancestral shrines vary from practitioner to practitioner and tradition to tradition, there are some items that will be found on any ancestral altar in Afro-Caribbean religion. These are a white altar cloth, a glass of clean water[17] (usually scented with a few drops of perfume or cologne[18]) and a white candle. My ancestral shrine is very simple and contains the above three items, my grandfather's bible (which I use for bibliomancy) and an ancestral *pwen*[19]. Other items that are common are photos and pictures of ancestors, further glasses of water (some traditions use seven or nine in total), items that belonged to deceased family members, flowers (ideally white), dolls or statues (to house the spirit of specific ancestral spirits).

Over the years I have developed my own method of serving the ancestors and I will attempt to give you an overview here[20]. After having set up an ancestral shrine[21] (in the same manner as setting up a Lwa altar, described earlier) I put three splashes of Florida Water into the glass on the shrine. I then dip two fingers into it and sprinkle some to each of the four directions and make the sign of the cross on myself (this could easily be substituted for the quabalistic cross). I then light the candle and begin with the Lord's Prayer (although I am not Christian the majority of my ancestors were). I then recite the following prayer:[22] "I pay homage to the ancestors in the east, I pay homage in the west, I pay homage to the ancestors in the north, I pay homage to the ancestors in south, I pay homage to all the ancestors in the realm of the ancestors. I pay homage to my blood ancestors[23], I pay homage to my clan ancestors[24], I pay homage to all the ancestors." I would then ask the ancestors to guide, strengthen and empower me. After this I'd give any ancestral offerings[26] I had and finally spend at least five or ten minutes meditating (and possibly performing divination) before the shrine. I would then close the session by saying "I give thanks to the ancestors, I give thanks to the ancestors, I give thanks to the ancestors" before kissing the front of the shrine three times and snuffing the candle out.

The other place to work with the dead is in a cemetery or graveyard. Obviously such work is often of a more necromantic nature[26]. The most important thing to remember when working in a cemetery (or any of the 'kingdoms', as they are called in Brazil) is to pay respect to the spirit that rules it. In Haitian Vodou this is Baron Cimitiere and an offering should be made to him at the largest cross in the cemetery[27]. There are two main ways that you can proceed with this sort of work. You could work with the spirit from a particular grave[29] and this would be working with *Les Mort* or you could work with the general spirits of the graveyard (along the lines of the Guede or Ancestors). You can either work with graveyard spirits directly in the cemetery or bring 'something of the graveyard' home and do it there (however, you will still need to leave the offerings in the cemetery afterwards).

Each of these spirits will be different, so it's hard to give a description of how to work with them. However, if you use the general ancestral rite described above as a starting point, the spirit you are working with should be able to tell you how it would like to be served and what offerings it would like.

Pan-cultural spiritism and conclusions

I hope this essay has given you some insights into Haitian Vodou and some inspiration to aid you in developing your spirit further. We live in very exciting times to be occultists, pagans and spiritual questors. The information age has opened up avenues of wisdom previously available only to the few. Translations of ancient texts are now more widely available than ever before. The internet has allowed us to easily speak to people all over the world, including people that practice spiritual traditions that in the past have been open to very few born outside them. This in turn has led to an explosion in published material (of mixed quality) exploring them. We all now have an opportunity to expand our horizons and deepen our understanding of our own practices and spirituality. To quote Aiwass in Ch1, Ver37 of *The Book of the Law,* "Also the mantras and spells; the obeah and the wanga; the work of the wand and the work of the sword; these he shall learn and teach."

Notes:

(1) In Vodou when someone is possessed, they are said to be ridden as the relationship between the person and the spirit is similar to that of a horse and its rider.

(2) Most usually an image of a Catholic saint that features an item linked to the Lwa.

(3) While the term *djab* is usually to describe an aggressive spirit lower than a lwa (similar to *djinn* of Arabic legend), it can be used to describe any spirit (including a lwa) that is considered hard working.

(4) The majority of the cooked sacrifice is eaten by those present at the evening service.

(5) Lwa of gateways. Who is honoured before any other lwa, as he holds the keys to Ginen.

(6) Literally 'the mermaid'. She is the queen of the ocean and mother of the fishes.

(7) A white liquor flavoured with anise, similar to ouzo or sambuca.

(8) There is a traditional way of doing this, but a simple nod will do.

(9) *Freedom is a Two-edged Sword* (New Falcon, 1989)

(10) *Magical Ritual Methods* (Helios 1969)

(11) The first male buried becomes the Baron and the first female becomes the Brigett.

(12) This is based purely on my own experience of the Ancestors.

(13) I actually have different packs for different types of spirits.

(14) Divination through opening a book (traditionally the Bible) at a random page and sticking a pin (or your finger) in on a random paragraph.

(15) Strictly it's not me that uses this, but my wife. She regularly speaks with her lwa in her dreams. They give her advice and have even taught her how to make *wangas* (charms) to help with certain problems.

(16) As per the above section describing a full-scale Vodou 'dance'.

(17) Tap water is fine for this and what I normally use, but spring water (traditionally associated with the underworld) or holy water would also be good.

(18) Most often Florida Water is used, but otherwise I would recommend your favourite perfume or cologne.

(19) Like many terms in Vodou *pwen* has a general and specific meaning. Generally it denotes an item used to draw and focus spiritual power, but specifically it refers to a packet constructed to house the energy a particular spirit.

(20) Alternatively *Awo: Ifa and the theology of Orisha divination* by Awo Fa'Lokun contain excellent instruction on performing ancestral services.

(21) In fact I keep a shrine permanently set up on a book shelf in my living room.

(22) I wrote this prayer, inspired by one in *Awo: Ifa and the theology of Orisha divination*.

(23) Those ancestors that I am related to by blood.

(24) Those ancestors that I am related to by marriage or adoption and the ancestors of my extended family (including my spiritual family).

(25) Traditional offerings include sweet black coffee and bread. However it is also good to give them food and drink they enjoyed in life or that they have asked for.

(26) Although the Guede are often served there and their offerings should ideally be left there.

(27) Of course different traditions will honour different spirits. In Kimbanda (an Afro-Brazilian with heavy Congo influences) it is Exu Caveira (Exu Skull) and he is honoured by lighting a black candle on the third grave on the left as you enter the cemetery. Also Hades, Kali or any similar deity could be honoured instead.

Further Reading:

- *Haitian Vodou: Spirit, Myth & Reality*, edited by Patrick Bellegarde-Smith & Claudine Michel (Indiana University Press 2006).
- *Kiumbanda: A Complete Grammar of the Art of Exu*, Nicholaj de Mattos Frisvold.
- *Goetic Divination*, Jake Stratton-Kent (Hadean Press, 2009).
- *Awo: Ifa and the theology of Orisha divination*, Awo Fa'Lokun Fatunmbi (Original Publication 1992).

DRAC UBER is a servant of the Old Gods and a child of the Lady of the Stars and Sea. He has been studying various spiritual paths for over 15 years, including Witchcraft and Haitian Vodou for well over 10 years. In 2001 he was Kanzoed (initiated) as a Houngan Sur Pwen (junior priest) of Haitian Vodou by the Roots Without End society in Jacmel, Southern Haiti, but has since been adopted into La Sosyete Fos Fe Yo We (based in Chicago, USA). He is also initiated in Witchcraft by the Hearth of Brighid (of the Clan Coranieid) and now runs a hive of this coven, the Hearth of the Sangreal (of the Clan Coranieid).

He lives in a seaside town in Southern England with his wife Ivy and provides various spiritual services through his website: www.dracuber.co.uk

An Interview with England's Most Notorious Necromancer

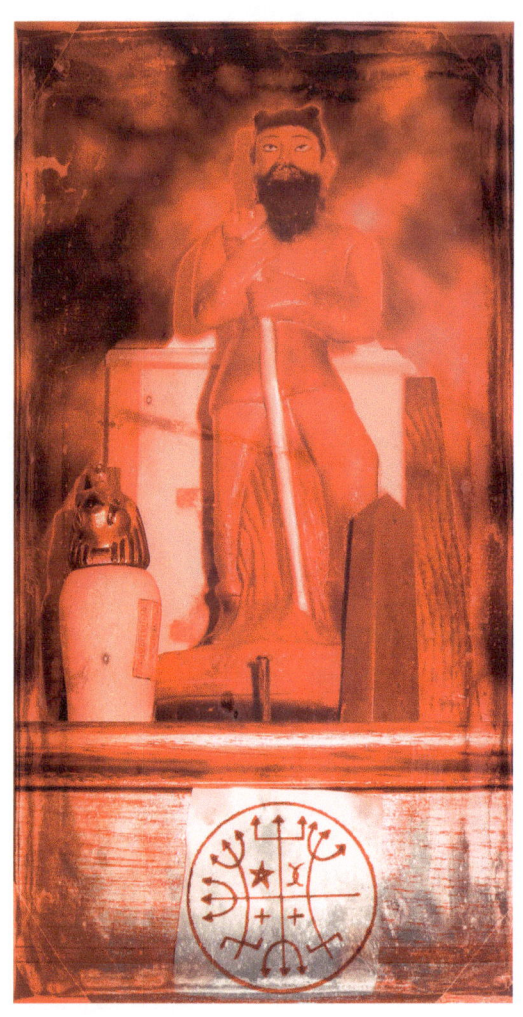

Co-editor Erzebet talks with
Jake Stratton-Kent
about his practices and his beliefs

First of all let's get this pesky word 'necromancer' out of the way. You know how people are, they'll think you're out there shagging the dead or some other such rubbish. Classically, the term *necromancer* means the consultation of the dead for purposes of divination. This practice was quite the rage in antiquity, with perhaps the Graeco-Roman style being most well-known. Poor Tiresias! He never got any rest. It was our friends Scarlet Imprint, publishers of some notorious texts themselves, who first branded you with the title 'England's most notorious necromancer'. It is a fitting nomen for you, but tell me, how much necromancing in the traditional sense of the word is going on these days? (We aren't interested in people who are actually out there shagging the dead. That's not magic, it's gross.)

For sure, lets not confuse necromancy with necrophilia.

Divination by the dead is certainly the main meaning, though the dividing line between divination and magic has often been rather thin. Sorcery, for example, is derived from a word meaning "divination by casting lots" (sortes). So magic involving the dead naturally follows from the divinatory connections.

In terms of iconography of course, magic has its fair share of skulls, grim reapers, etc., and the once central role of necromancy has a lot to do with that. I say "once central", because despite the fact that the dead, particularly ancestors, are pivotal to most magical and religious systems around the world, they have taken rather a back seat in Western magic for some considerable time. Especially, oddly enough, in the very areas where their presence was once strongest. The grimoires derive directly from the Greek traditions you mention, where necromancy was central to procedure and outlook. So too our other Greek inheritances, Hermeticism and Neoplatonism, in the more 'popular' forms known today, retain little connection with the dead.

Now, when we put aside the gruesome images of necromancy as demonised in the past, there are some very serious issues here. If we examine Christianity for example, we find that eschatology is pivotal to its entire message. The Resurrection, redemption, heaven and hell, penalties for and forgiveness of sin, all concern the Afterlife. The crisis facing the established churches is precisely due to the loss of meaning or interest in these ideas. This is **exactly** analogous to the situation facing Western magic. For whatever reason – and there are straightforward historical explanations, medieval and more recent – magic lost sight of the role of the dead in its origins, theory and practice, and as a result a lot of meaning has been lost.

So for example, there is no sensible explanation of why spirits would take any notice of magicians in the first place, without the conceptual background which magical eschatology once supplied. What are spirits? What is the spirit realm? What is in it for them when it comes to communicating with humans? All these questions – or rather their answers – once revolved around the matter of Death and the Afterlife.

In short, it doesn't take too much to be England's most notorious practitioner of necromancy, as many magicians have forgotten that is what they are meant to be doing!

It doesn't help that the human dead have been stripped of all credibility, does it. The great Victorian-era scam involving table-rapping left its mark on the Western psyche, and anything involving ghosts has been relegated to the much besmirched 'paranormal'. I'm not entirely convinced that ancestor veneration is a dead art in the West – think of all those stately homes and castles full of paintings of the owner's family line, sometimes spanning back for centuries. This kind of thing happened on a lesser scale in the immigrant households of the American east coast, and I do include those who made their way over in the 1600s from Britain in that word 'immigrants'. I personally own an entire large trunk full of old photographs, some of them from the early days of photography, and I know I'm not alone. So why is it, do you think, that we've lost some of the art of working with the dead, particularly our own ancestors? How did we lose that connection?

Not all C19th Spiritualism was as phony as it is often depicted, though certainly the more interesting aspects were outside the English Speaking world. You make a valid point about the instinct for ancestor veneration; a lot of that interest is nowadays directed into *where do you come from?*, but the empathy certainly remains. Historically there are two main reasons the occult lost its connection with the dead. One was the antipathy of the Church; which while accommodating to many aspects of popular belief, made a major exception of funerary practices, which were completely taken under its wing.

The other was, indeed, connected to Spiritualism. There was a great magical revival in the C19th. This had Oriental and Occidental modes: Theosophy in the first case, and movements like the Golden Dawn and OTO in the second. Both modes were careful to distinguish themselves from contemporary Spiritualism, with the result that when Spiritualism faded out, the occult field deriving from these movements had little capacity to reclaim its old connections with what we might call 'the Higher Necromancy'. Not that it was un-involved with working with spirits, but these were generally angels, demons and elementals. It is worth noting – incidentally – that distinctions between these were a lot looser in earlier periods.

We've spoken mostly of the human dead so far, but spirits encompass a whole range of entities. We should probably make it clear right now that we, the editors of Conjure Codex, believe these spirits exist as separate entities, rather than being some manifestation of our inner psyches (though they can be that as well). You mention the distinction between types of spirits: historically, if there was a division, it was more one of celestial spirits and

chthonic spirits, rather than holy angels and infernal, evil demons. We'll talk about that shift in perception in a moment, but first, in your own experience, when it comes to these inhuman entities, is it really so cut and dried as 'good guys vs bad guys'?

It is not cut and dried at all. For one thing, on a historical level perceptions of specific entities have shifted endlessly. Sometimes this could be seen as evolution (either of the entity or some aspect of the culture concerned). In practice, which is more to the point, the nature of the entity, in planetary or elemental terms, is more important than any arbitrary Manichean division into good and evil.

Take the 'angel' Cassiel for example – he's an angel, right? Should be one of the good guys then, by the imposed dualism hypothesis. That isn't how it works though; he is an angel of Saturn, and the nature of Saturn includes malefic or unpleasant aspects. Cassiel has shown himself to be very able in that respect, angel or no angel.

Then there are supposed demons whose nature or role determines their performance the same way. Frimost, for example, is very helpful to men in matters of love. This can manifest in quite exploitative ways, even vengeful. That isn't anything to do with his demonic categorisation, but his role. Equally, a man in emotional pain can ask Frimost to relieve it, with no malicious intent, and get over a sour relationship, which most of us would conclude was a good thing. This isn't any kind of contradiction. In fact it is simply the kind of thing his skills or natural abilities cover, for good or ill on a subjective level as seen by the recipient. So really what determines what a spirit does isn't their place in some cosmic war of good versus evil. Rather it consists of what their particular individual nature enables them to do. After all, we are not discussing Star Wars or comic books, but the practical aspects of sophisticated ancient philosophies and shamanic religions.

Let's briefly talk about that shift in perception then, especially as it does (or doesn't) appear in the grimoires. Solomon is possibly one of the best-known names when it comes to the grimoiric tradition, and as with most of the ancient magicians, the myths and legends about him are far more entertaining than the actual fact. Especially considering that historians and archaeologists have yet to definitively prove the man even existed. But Aramaic incantation bowls do exist, and they form a sort of corpus of early Jewish magic, where angels are conjured, or called upon, to help with everything from childbirth to protecting one's household against other angels. By the time the written grimoires came along, angels had been planted firmly on the side of good by the Church, with demons and other 'base' spirits on the side of evil, which in practice only served to exoticise them. Do the grimoires themselves reflect this false good vs evil dichotomy? In your grimoire of choice, how are the spirits represented?

It is fairly common, though not invariable, for supposed demons to be conjured by the authority (and with the protection) of angelic forces. My favourite grimoire, as is tolerably well known, is the *Grimoireum Verum* (GV) or *True Grimoire*. There the spirits are dealt with rather differently. One seeks to make oneself one of the 'intimate friends and confidants' of the superiors, through a pact. From there one proceeds to conjuring by the authority not of angels but of the chiefs. A similar process, with some extra drama, is present in the *Grand Grimoire*. I see this as analogous to the Greek papyri where spirits are conjured by authority of rulers of the underworld, rather than the angelic process we are accustomed to taking for granted.

The spirits of the GV are certainly not fluffy bunnies, but this process is as traditional in its way as the other more familiar one. It also makes a deal more sense than adopting a spirit negative paradigm of an isolated point in the past. For example in a folklore textbook I was reading recently it remarked that many Elizabethans saw *all* fairy folk as demonic. Two things stood out, one this was not all Elizabethans (nor all occult authors, Agrippa for instance would have disagreed). Two was, this paradigm was of one point in time, other attitudes existed before, as well as contemporaneously and subsequently. It is considerations such as these that lead me to prefer the *True Grimoire*, where at least you can deal with the spirits from within their own 'family', rather than impose ideas of fear, domination and dualistic conflict on the process before you even start.

This is not to say there are no conditions where those attitudes are appropriate. Nevertheless, the idea of spirit allies is at least as important, and there is no good reason for restricting this to angels from a monotheistic religion you scarcely believe in.

I'm glad you mentioned the pact. In popular culture this is often referred to as a bargain of sorts (I'm thinking Robert Johnson meeting the devil at the crossroads, etc.), wherein one gambles with the spirits – or even the devil himself – and may the best person win. It doesn't quite work like that, does it?

The pact is often represented as a late development of 'sensationalised' grimoires, drawing on Christian misrepresentations. Certainly it can be found in accounts of the Sabbat and so forth before its **return** in the *Bibliotheque bleue* grimoires. In fact however that notion of its origin is erroneous and superficial.

The early Church Fathers represent the process as part of pagan religion, and archaeology fully supports that. The gods received written petitions (offering, for example, temple service in return for recovery from illness). Later on there are resemblances – close to the point of identity – between the 'Book of Spirits' and the Pact. Once one removes or diminishes the idea that all spirits are devils (including the gods of the pagans, where the notion of bargaining started), it becomes more a matter of forming a relationship with spirits. There are mutual aspects to this, and it is by no means a contest for the soul of the foolhardy or desperate sorcerer. That idea is a polemical invention; the pact itself is a venerable concept, fully deserving of restoring in modern practice.

Quite simply a pact is a mutual agreement, and a similar idea is implicit in the word 'conjure' which literally means 'swear together'.

I'd add, if I may, that in many respects the *Bibliotheque bleue* grimoires deserve a major reappraisal. In my opinion they represent a **revival of goetia** in its own right. The fact that they differ from the 'aristocratic angel magic' of the earlier Solomonic manuscripts is no reason to dismiss them. There is a more solid fusion with folk magic, as well as a return to some classical ideas. Certainly this lurks behind some antinomian imagery, but it is none the worse for that.

For readers who may be unfamiliar with this genre, *Bibliothèque bleue* refers to the collection of pamphlets that appeared in France during the late 17th/early 18th centuries. These inexpensive texts made available to the general public knowledge that had previously only appeared in the 'gentlemen's' grimoires, thereby expanding the use of magic exponentially among the masses. I'm very interested in this fusion with folk magic that you've mentioned. Can you tell us more about that particular trend in spirit work?

Certainly, it's important to recognise that the connections of grimoire magic with folk magic, rather than being a recent development, were simply increased and renewed by the *Bibliotheque bleue* genre. So too there was a new influx of classical themes, which however had been there from the beginning. Richard Kieckhefer (*Forbidden Rites*) underlines a point I consider evident, that Iamblichus was the major influence on spirit hierarchies throughout the grimoire genre.

The folk magic links straddle ancient, medieval and early modern phases. The anonymous additions to Scot's *Discoverie of Witchcraft* emphasise the links between grimoire spirits and numerous lesser figures of ancient mythology that also persisted in folk magic. These range from household spirits, the *lares familiaris* of Rome being essentially identical with British brownies and Scandinavian and German equivalents. These same links are present in the *Three Books of Agrippa*, as well as the *Fourth Book*, whoever we might believe wrote that. So too in the grimoires themselves the presence of elemental spirits is a long-standing theme. This again we must realise was renewed rather than initiated by Paracelsian influence, being present in such influential early texts as the *Sworn Book*. These are of course identical with nature spirits of antiquity as well as figures from fairy lore and folk belief.

> Let's get to the good stuff. You've been a practicing magician for quite a number of years. What first attracted you to spirit work? Has working with the spirits in this manner changed your life? Why is this type of work important to you?

You're right, this is the real nitty gritty. My magical career has developed from good instincts about retaining traditional ideas and procedures, to an informed appreciation of those same elements. Most of my instincts were borne out by research and experience and have become all but axiomatic. Spirit work was certainly one of my earliest interests and pursuits, and the *True Grimoire* was always my favoured text within that genre. Somehow I also grasped fairly early on that Voodoo was a living tradition and thus a superior resource than revivalist ideas from the C19th. The intimacy of spirit/practitioner relations in that tradition made a strong impression and influenced my earliest approaches to spirits in a Western context. I also made use of handmade statuettes of gods and spirits I wished to communicate with, as well as performing grimoire style evocations.

Later on I departed a little from this direction in pursuit of Thelemic magic, working the A∴A∴ curriculum etc. While fruitful and not a subject of regret, there was nonetheless a very notable contrast when I eventually reverted back to the grimoires and my interest in African Traditional Religions (as an influence on my goetic work rather than an alternative to it). My later involvement with Thelema was centred on the highly valuable current of astrological magic associated with English Qaballa. This work was completely transformed and its effects maximised beyond belief by integrating my work with *True Grimoire* spirits into the established praxis. The central rite of the EQ tradition (at least for myself and my co-workers at the time) involved an ecstatic invocation of astrological forces to possess a priestess of Nuit. Identifying these same forces with a spirit or spirits of the grimoire that might be expected to attend the rite was a revelation.

The roots of this transformation are fairly simply explained; we'd previously defined EQ praxis as 'Astrologically Timed Magic in English', with magic semi-defined as tantric worship, which in turn empowered magical intentions. We were ahead of our time as regards astrological magic; some of the advances made await appreciation by modern occultism when they are done revising Renaissance astrological magic. So too our Qaballa represented a decided advance, no longer hinging upon the generic 'Hebrew' system (again a product of Renaissance occultism, filtered through Mathers and Crowley). However, the invocation of prevailing astrological forces was essentially flying blind: the priestess would personify a nameless aspect of the goddess matching the chart, on which we had few handles other than experience. In other words, we had the astrology and the Qaballa down like nobody else at the time. However, like the rest of modern occultism we had wrongly assumed we knew what 'magic' was. We imagined that these advances in astrology and Qaballa were all that was necessary to overcome historical losses in Western magic.

Reverting to the traditional definition of magic as centred on traffic with spirits produced very striking results. This enabled the priest and assistant magicians in these rites to ascertain who was responding, what they liked and disliked and how to handle problems arising in the ritual. This simply by knowing which spirit or spirits might at least be expected to attend a given astrological invocation of this type, and acting accordingly. The results of ditching vague ideas about astrological archetypes in favour of a meaningful dialogue with a known spirit hierarchy supplied many deficiencies in what was otherwise a very advanced system. This made a very powerful impression upon me, and has informed my practice with both traditional and modern approaches ever since.

What tools do you use in your personal practice? I assume your grimoire informs your choice of materials, but do you also incorporate items and rites from other sources?

Well yes, naturally my primary tool kit relies very much on the *True Grimoire*. This incidentally is one area among many in which this grimoire scores, and gives the lie to those who consider it 'spurious' compared to Solomonic manuscript tradition. Every tool in the *True Grimoire* has a defined or ascertainable purpose, none are superfluous or undefined, as they are for instance in several manuscript Keys and their published counterparts. Both wands are defined, in that their use in the opening stages of the rite are given, and that one is obviously the wand of evocation while the other is readily identified as more 'receptive', concerned with divination and so on.

This said my 'liturgical transplant' reforms the *Verum* rite on the skeleton of Crowley's *Pyramidos*. Consequently some ritual equipment from that has entered my toolkit – just as 'instruments' associated with Catholicism might be implicit in the performance of many grimoire rituals or their preparation. More importantly however I have certainly followed up some implicit connections between the grimoire and other praxis. The presence of graveyard dirt (the only grimoire known to mention it) and lodestone in *Verum* practice has led me to extend further into 'hoodoo' style practice with herbs, oils and so on. This has not been merely eclectic, as said before my practice is informed by other traditions but remains goetic in root and branch. So the use of these oils and other materials is informed by the concept of Sympathia; this is present in the work of Empedocles and other *goes* upon which my tradition was developed prior to its temporary decline. The correspondences involved in my use of hoodoo 'power oil' for example are at least as Western as they are African. The incenses I compose for individual spirits are inspired by correspondences to various Fixed Stars associated with those spirits. Rather than simply imitate Palo Mayombe I make use of trees and plants from traditional Western magic; elder and hazel and other trees, mugwort, hellebore along with the three purifying herbs from the grimoire, and so on. On the other hand magicians living in America, Australia or elsewhere should follow the lead of the African Diaspora in identifying suitable plants, trees and so on in the environment into which their tradition has been transplanted.

The commonalities between African traditions in the New World and magic of the Western Tradition are manifold. Most striking and well known is the performance of magical rituals at the Crossroads. Obviously this involves the Classical past of Western magic, rather than originating in the Judaeo-Christian milieu. So too this older stratum of Western magic is the best vantage point from which to compare traditions and appreciate their commonalities. This vantage point is necessary in order to revitalise Western magic by reconnecting with its roots. Not to produce a static re-enactment of the past but to move confidently into the future in whatever environment we may find ourselves.

There seems to be some argument as to how spirits, in particular 'demonic' spirits, should be handled. What this argument boils down to, as far as I can tell, is a concern about the magician's relationship with the spirits he or she is conjuring. What kind of relationship do you have with the Verum spirits, and are your relationships with spirits limited to those of the Verum?

Yes, I work primarily with spirits from the *True Grimoire*, and have a pact with the majority of them. They are not the only spirits with which I work, however; indeed some of them assist me to work with the spirit world in general. They do constitute essentially a mini-pantheon of sorts, and higher gods are implied; without necessarily involving any division on dualistic lines.

This approach is informed by the papyri, African Traditional Religions and the grimoires, as well as European folklore. It is a response to those influences and to experience in equal parts. The spirits I work with are analogous in some respects to familiar spirits and some encountered in New World cults who are welcome participants in rites. While I generally avoid the coercive element I don't wholly 'blame it on the Christians'. On the contrary I see where, when and why it may be necessary, and where it is simply misapplied. On the other hand I do see goetic magic as involving religious modes as well as practical magical work. Rituals of purification, even penitence, are as Classical as they are Christian, and have a major role in my preparations and in the more formal rituals.

Western demonology has two main strands, the others dovetail more or less happily. Straight Christian demonology has little role in the grimoires aside from colouring the spirits. It is the Classical schema that defines the hierarchies and many characteristics of the spirits. Within those parameters spirits as such (distinct from say angels or gods) can be divided into three main categories, all of whom might be termed demons in this or that source. These are elementals, the dead and 'evil spirits'. The first two can overlap with the second, but essentially it means evil spirits. All are fairly broad terms, and might be subdivided endlessly, but they'll do in the context of the question.

I don't accept the 'Crown of Creation' doctrine that is held to give humans automatic dominion over nature and by extension spirits. I do however subscribe quite strongly to the concept of the pact – an agreement between magician and spirit. Not of course involving surrendering the soul to hell or any of that nonsense. This implies a relationship, and for my purposes excludes 'evil spirits' as such. This leaves the dead and elementals; beings of fairly benign nature, at least as regards yours truly. Relations with these involves offerings where appropriate, or regular work and payment where they are not.

Evil spirits are more of a special case, the genuine ones that is, not those who are merely the victims of theological confusion. Generally they'll be encountered in exorcism rather than conjured as such. They might be enlisted temporarily on occasion, usually through another spirit.

My attitude to most spirits is respectful, rather than domineering, and this involves some departures from the old grimoire model. In some cases coercion is appropriate, but this usually implies dealing with the more unpleasant types, where a pact is not involved.

While I have enormous respect for the African Traditional Religions my tradition is goetia. As a continual current this precedes both the Orphic books and the papyri. It then continues on through the grimoires to the present day. Goetia need not be limited to a particular phase of religion influential upon it in one particular period. So it is to the goetic tradition as a whole that these ideas belong, and within which I operate.

You mention spirits of the dead – as I said earlier, this area of spirit work seems to me to be one of the most overlooked in the entire Western ceremonial tradition of magic. I'm curious as to how often you find it necessary to work with such spirits, or how much they play a part in your general practices.

The role of the dead is absolutely the single most neglected aspect of Western magic. This was not always the case. Briefly, although the early Church was fairly accommodating to some local customs and survivals of pagan lore, this specifically excluded the dead and all concerning them. Burial rites were taken firmly under the authority of the Church, and all old customs concerning them were largely eradicated as a matter of priority. This naturally included Ancestor cults and so forth. A consequence of this for magic was that less benign spirits of the dead were replaced by 'fallen angels' and other more 'orthodox' agents. The transition from understanding 'Spirits of the Air' as dead to such demons is readily traced in the literary tradition. Tellingly dealing with these was often still referred to as 'necromancy'; frequently altered to 'nigromancy' as the original context all but disappeared.

In this process Western magic, insofar as it tried to adapt to the new environment, lost something vitally significant. There is probably no other magical tradition in the entire world where the dead are so absent. Indeed generally the dead are close to the core of the tradition in question. Magic could even be defined as 'practical eschatology'. It is dealing with the dead, whether in assisting them, protecting from them or employing them for knowledge or other purposes, that lays at the core of magic. This includes the much misunderstood tradition of Goetia, which is the most ancient core of much Western practice.

Incidentally, the loss of this feature renders much of magic virtually nonsensical, except in very stereotyped terms. What have spirits to gain from working with magicians? The dead have very clear reasons, say being laid to rest or assisted to move on in return for cooperation. Even – more critically to a coherent philosophical basis for magic in general – working with initiated magicians assists spirits to evolve. An eschatological context is very important to understanding the relationship between the living and the dead, and magicians and spirits are no exception, indeed their relationship is the most illustrative and central to such a paradigm.

I'm curious as to how often you find it necessary to work with such spirits, or how much they play a part in your general practices.

The simple answer is very often indeed.

There are various levels of dead spirit, with radically distinct roles in magic:

Firstly, hostile or unpleasant spirits of the dead, generally of a low level of evolution or having degenerated to a minimal level of intelligence and volition.

These are employed in aggressive magic, which can include 'love magic' where compulsion is employed. As I see things magic is largely amoral; magicians however are as likely as anyone else to subscribe to a moral philosophy, religious code or personal set of ideals. So as I don't find this particular application morally acceptable it forms no part of my repertoire. Other purposes, such as confusing, impeding or destroying enemies, are equally traditional and to me – given appropriate motives – are perfectly acceptable morally. After all, with the possible exception of the last of these we'd have no objection to employing 'conventional' means. Destruction of enemies generally requires some kind of sanction when conventional means are involved, and are then accepted as moral by some portion of a given community. Just the same, in many contexts, and dependent on the system of morality doing the judging, these purposes might be considered 'black magic'.

Anyhow, back to the question. When we consider magical roles for more evolved spirits of the dead, divination is high on the list. A variety of methods varying from mediumship to 'throwing the bones' are easily identified, and most of the methods underlying modern skrying also belong in this category. My own work reflects this historical background very strongly.

Bear in mind also that the dead have been supplanted – or disguised – in late Western magic. Instead various kinds of spirit, often so called 'demons', serve a large variety of purposes. Much of this is readily transferred back where it belongs.

An important issue concerning these so-called 'Fallen Angels' is less readily avoided where the dead are concerned. This is the question of 'Restitution', where spirits anticipate an end to their torment or wandering, through evolution to a higher level (or mercy at the Last Judgement in stricter Christian terms).

The Christian equivalents to this idea arise in passing even in such late texts as the *Goetia of Solomon*. In a context involving the dead these elements become more important, to the extent where specialised workings become necessary. Incidentally this seems to apply in some respects also in Martinism, though in relation to more familiar conceptions of spirits in magic.

To give an example, say a benign spirit of the dead works on your behalf. This might well involve release from some lower condition, and 'works of elevation' then become part of the remit of the magician. This evolutionary context obviously embraces the living as well as the dead. A necromantic or eschatological context has obvious relevance to the benefits understood as bestowed by initiation, to spiritual development in occult work, in particular to expectations in the afterlife.

For you, is spirit work a practice or a lifestyle? How deeply embedded into one's personal life can spirit work – or the spirits in general – become?

Magic in my eyes is a vocation, a grimoire forms a preliminary training and introduction from which you proceed. A pact with a spirit, let alone a few dozen spirits, implies a continuous relationship. Some of these spirits will be daily contacts, others not quite so frequent but fairly regular, while others will 'be on call' without the same degree of intimacy.

The term 'familiar spirits' is readily understood from this perspective. In essence several of these spirits are akin to work colleagues, or even friends of a sort.

Do you have any advice or recommendations for people who would like to begin some type of spirit work? Are any sort of lengthy preparations required before one makes contact? In other words, what should beginners know before they set forth into this realm of work?

It's not fashionable to say so, but really the Western Tradition of Magic is still in a process of revival, so that the gap between beginners and experts may not always be very wide. The plainest and most useful advice is to find a 'toolkit', for example a workable grimoire process, and stick with it. Of these the best in very many respects is the *True Grimoire*, this has the advantages of simplicity and completeness, as well as having no overt antagonism to the spirits in its worldview, something many others do. The preparations specified by the grimoire in terms of tools, familiarisation with the process and the initial stages of forming a pact are useful and not overly onerous.

The advantages of having a 'toolkit' are manifold, not least engaging with the spirits through a traditional process that they recognise, and adding structure to your individual efforts.

Bear in mind though that every grimoire is essentially a means of getting started, providing an 'introduction' to spirit work. Once engaged with the spirits directly they and the experiences involved will provide other means and insights. This stage largely surpasses the text, so that trying to progress by reading between the lines over and over misses the point. Naturally there are pointers in the better grimoires for dealing with the later stages of one's 'vocation'. Nevertheless the relationship with the spirits should take first place, so that agreements made with spirits in the pact-making process must be rigorously fulfilled.

Do you have any closing comments for our readers?

While adhering as closely as possible to a grimoire is useful training, this is not about performance by rote after the point indicated above. Far from it, techniques and attitudes will inevitably progress.

In looking deeper into the nature of such work it is also useful to compare Goetic practice with traditions from the New World. Also to be aware of the precursors of the grimoires in the Greek magical papyri and Chaldean starlore. There are many advantages to this extra-curricular study, as among other things these traditions have a broader and less negative view of spirits, including the dead and elemental daimones.

NEFARIOUS OCCULT DEALINGS

necromancy, ghosts and spirit expeditions
in the
GRAECO-ROMAN, HOODOO
and
VODOU
magical traditions

by KIM HUGGENS

A MAN, CLOTHED IN NIGHT, looks both ways before entering the cemetery grounds. He makes an offering at the biggest and most important-looking grave, before pouring libations to the spirits of the dead that surround him – the untimely dead, those dead before marriage, those dead by violence. Then he begins his invocations and chants, binding the spirits of the dead, by now swarming around him, to his will, sending them out into the world to do his bidding. Through the streets he sends them, searching, through houses and locked doors and barred windows they peer, looking for the target. The man has given them a way of recognizing the target already – a piece of clothing from her hem, a lock of her hair, a rag soaked in her blood – and so, like sniffer dogs, they eventually track her down.

Back to the sorcerer they drag her, by the hair, by the guts, by the liver, by the heart, by the soul, and she is powerless to resist lest she be driven insane. When the spirits of the dead have done the deed, the sorcerer allows them to depart, releases them from their bondage, and they return to wandering cold and bereft amidst the graves.

This image, as much a feature of Hammer horror classics as of modern occult conjure practices, is an evocative one. Yet to apply it to a single tradition of magic would be incorrect – firstly, the necromantic rite above is found in a fully formed version, attested to frequently in the contemporary literature, in the Late Antique Graeco-Roman and Romano-Egyptian practices; lastly it is also practised, but seldom written about, in the hoodoo and Vodou traditions of the African Diaspora. Where the former provides us with a vast body of literature to explain the various techniques and features contained within the magic, the latter remains relatively silent on the subject. This would seem in direct opposition to the fact that the Graeco-Roman magic of the Late Antique period is, by nature, now rarely practised and if it is, it is a recreation or attempted reconstruction out of its original context, whereas the hoodoo/Vodou traditions maintain an unbroken practice.

This leaves modern practitioners of hoodoo and Vodou, especially those picking up the tradition outside of Haiti, the Dominican Republic, Brazil and America, in the dark about practices that are both a part of the tradition's wealth of history and a deeply entrenched technique of magic. This paper seeks to illuminate the shadowy practice of necromancy – in particular of "Spirit Expeditions" – from the hoodoo/Vodou traditions, along with associated necromantic methods, using the literature surrounding the Graeco-Roman practices.

It is, however, important to note that I do not seek here to prove an influential link between the Graeco-Roman practices and those of the African Diaspora religions. Whilst there is some evidence that may go towards such a conclusion (via the medieval Grimoire tradition) I seek rather to use the Graeco-Roman writings to elaborate upon the inner workings of the hoodoo/Vodou techniques so that those practising the latter are better equipped to understand it.

Necromancy 101: Some Basics

In both traditions there appears to be a set of almost uniformly practised traditions that form a foundation for necromantic practice and hexing (also called "fixing", particularly in the New Orleans hoodoo tradition.) Due to the nature of hoodoo and Vodou it is wrong to say that these practices are found across the board, but certainly they appear almost all the time even if their manifestation is slightly tweaked by the practitioner. For many people approaching these traditions from outside their context, these practises can seem strange, and since they are never usually explained, nor their inner workings revealed, we find ourselves left in the dark and this can lead to performing the magic as though it were a prescription, rather than an heartfelt and energetic act. So, why the black hens, black roosters? Why graveyard dirt? Why leave payment at a grave?

Black as Night

Many hexes in the hoodoo tradition use black exclusively – black candles are burned, for instance. Black cat hair, black dog hair, and a black hen's egg are all said to cause break-ups of a happy relationship, bring trouble to somebody, move somebody away, "goofer" an enemy, and more.[1] It is such a prevalent practise that it is even referred to in the old blues songs:

"My baby, she got a mojo, tryin' to keep it hid
Papa Weaver got somethin' to find that doggone mojo with

My Mama, she told me,
I's a boy playin' mumble-peg
'Don't drink no black cow's milk,
don't eat no black hen's egg.'" [2]

In the song, the singer's girlfriend is trying to hide a mojo that he knows she has put on him, and "Papa Weaver" may be a *bokor* (magician/sorcerer) or Houngan (Vodou priest) who can do magic to locate such an item and thereby destroy it and the magic. The second verse continues, and indicates that the singer is distrustful of his girlfriend, and thinks she is trying to hex him through underhanded means with this mojo, and therefore recalls the advice his mother gave him when he was very small and playing a childrens' game: don't eat certain black foods. Magical survival advice hidden in mother's playground wisdom.

In the Vodou tradition the colour black is traditionally associated with the spirits of the dead and with the lwa that are in charge of them – the Ghede lwa and the Banda nation of spirits. The family of Ghede include such well-known spirits as Baron Samedi, Bawon La Croix, Manman Brigitte, Brav Ghede and Ghede Nibo. Bawon La Croix, Baron Samedi, and Manman Brigitte are all well-known for liking black roosters and black hens respectively as their offerings. This is in contrast to the "cool" and "light" spirits in the Rada rite, who – if they do accept animal sacrifice at all – take white birds, and the group of warrior spirits in the Ogou family who prefer red roosters.

Since the Ghede lwa are all associated with death (or are, themselves, resident in cemeteries), it should come as no surprise to find that in the Graeco-Roman tradition black animals are given as offerings to the Chthonic Gods and Goddesses. In the first century CE, Ovid writes of a rite to Hekate that sees Medea making an offering of a black sheep:

"...then two turf altars [she] built,
The right to Hecate, the left to Youth,
Wreathed with the forest's mystic foliage,
And dug two trenches in the ground beside

And then performed her rites. Plunging a knife Into a black sheep's throat she drenched the wide Ditches with blood..." [3]

In particular Hekate is associated with black bitches, and her sacrifices usually consisted of a black bitch or puppy offered at the crossroads.[4] Similarly, sacrifices to Seth-Typhon (a prominent deity called upon for curses, particularly erotic-separation spells, in the Romano-Egyptian handbooks of the Greek Magical Papyri) are of the body parts/fluids of a black donkey, and Seth-Typhon is imagined and depicted as the animal. Thus, in one spell under the auspices of Seth-Typhon, the magician calls upon the God to separate a loving couple by causing them to hate each other:

"Another...of a black donkey, and you put a ... which is..., and you leave [it] in it for three days... it. You should cook it for one night..., and you should bring a / strip of..., and you should write... the names on it with donkey blood, and you should gather outside... saying, "Separate NN, born of NN, from NN, born of NN!" And you should... and you should... the urine..." [5]

Although the spell is fragmented, it is clear that the magician is using the blood and urine (if not more) of a black donkey in this rite.

It seems that in the Graeco-Roman magical tradition black animal sacrifices were not only offered to the Chthonic deities, but also to the denizens of the Chthonic realms: the spirits of the dead. In Homer's *Odyssey* Odysseus promises to sacrifice an all-black sheep to the ghost of Tiresias in exchange for the dead seer's wisdom,[6] and in Horace's *Satires* a group of witches (and devotees of Hekate), dig pits and pour the blood of a black lamb into the pits as offerings to the dead so that they might consult them.[7]

From this there arises a number of references in the magical texts to black animals as sacrifice, thought it may not be explicitly stated in all cases that the rites are necromantic – although they are all to be considered curses. One erotic-attraction spell, for instance, prescribes:

"You should bring a shaving from the head of a man who was murdered together with seven grains of barley buried in the grave of a dead man; you should grind them with ten oipe of apple seeds; you should add <u>blood of a tick of a black dog</u> to them together with a little blood of your second finger and the little finger of your left hand and your semen..." [8]

Another spell, "Love spell of attraction performed with the help of heroes or gladiators or those who have died a violent death", tells the sorcerer to offer up dung from a black cow along with ashes of flax and seven pieces of bread from which he has eaten in order to draw the dead spirits to his will.[9]

It is also a feature of necromantic rites to be performed at night and/or in complete darkness. Firstly, in today's society this may be simply practical – we don't want to be interrupted in our Chthonic acts by a little old lady walking her Yorkshire Terrier in the cemetery on a nice Spring afternoon, nor be discovered trying to conjure up the spirit of a dead man who just so happens to have a weekly visit from his granddaughter due. However, it also seems that nighttime is preferable not just for practical reasons but also because the spirits of the dead are more comfortable coming out in the dark (which we all knew from horror movies anyway!). When the Greek witch Erictho raises a dead spirit out of Hades to consult him, she draws night around her like a cloak, choosing as the site of the proceedings a particularly dark and dank cave:

"There the ground fell steeply down, almost to the sightless caverns of Dis. It was pressed close by a colorless wood, its foliage drooping down. Yews, never raising their tops to the sky, impenetrable to the Sun, cut off its light. Within the cave is a morose darkness and gray mould, the product of protracted night. No light is shed except that which is manufactured with a spell. The air in the jaws of Tainaron is not as stifling as here. It is the dismal boundary between the hidden world and our own. It is such that the kings of Tartarus do not fear to let the dead pass to it. For, although the Thessalian prophetess does violence to the fates, it remains uncertain whether she is able to look upon the Stygian shades by virtue of drawing them up or by virtue of going down herself to them." [10]

Here it is clear that the witch has created a point in the world where the dead do not fear to come to the realm of the living, because it resembles the darkness of their native Underworld. It may also be that darkness is preferred for these rites because the Gods who rule over the dead are destroyed by daylight, as Erictho threatens to expose Hades himself to daylight should he fail to co-operate:

"Upon you, Hades, worst of the world's rulers, I shall send Titan, the Sun, bursting your caverns open, and you will be blasted by the instantaneous light of day. Do you obey?" [11]

The timing of a magical operation in hoodoo also has great significance. If you are performing a spell to increase something e.g. passion or prosperity, the time of the rising sun is best; if your aim is to cause the depletion of something, e.g. remove sickness, you may perform the rite at sundown; but to do something truly nefarious – such as a curse to cause death, madness, or sickness, the time when the sun is at its lowest and when light is dimmest is best.

PAYING THE FERRYMAN

It seems, then, that the reason for giving offerings or sacrifices of black animals, foods, and items in necromantic and malefic magic is because that is what the spirits of the dead, and those that take care of them, accept. However, another practice regarding offerings is worth commenting on here: the custom of leaving an offering by the graveside or at the cemetery gates before or after your working.

In the hoodoo tradition it is customary to leave an offering at the cemetery gates as you enter, as payment to the spirit that guards the gateway – in many traditions this is Bawon Cemitye, but can also be Bawon La Croix or Baron Samedi. Often this offering takes the form of money – particularly shiny pennies. Since these spirits guard not only the cemetery grounds but also the realm of the dead, it is they who stand at the liminal point and who can control whether the dead spirits you wish to work with will respond to your request or not. This practice is not mentioned in the Graeco-Roman sources, however a similar concept arises in the magical texts where the dead are believed to be placed under the special patronage of the Chthonic deities – particularly Hekate, Hades and Persephone. It is these deities, but especially Hekate, who are petitioned first, before the dead, and who are asked to send the dead spirits up from their abode in the underworld to aid the magician, or to send them back down again.[12]

*"O primal Chaos, Erebos, and you
O awful water of the Styx, O streams
O Lethe, Hades' Acherousian pool,
O Hekate and Pluto and Kore,
And chthonic Hermes, Moirai, Punishments,
Of the eternal bars, now open quickly,
O thou key-holder, guardian, Anubis.
Send up to me the phantoms of the dead
Forthwith for service in this very hour."* [13]

In some cases the text reports the magician having problems getting the Chthonic deities to send spirits up from the underworld, and the magician then resorts to threats to induce their co-operation:

"Tisiphone and Megaera, you who scorn my calling, do you not drive this hapless soul through the emptiness of Erebus with your cruel whips? Any moment now I shall call you up by your true names and make you stand as Stygian hounds in the light of the upper world. I shall pursue you through tombs, through burials, ever hanging on your heels, I shall drive you from barrows and keep you from all urns. You, Hecate, decaying and colorless in appearance as you are, are in the habit of showing yourself to the gods above only after first making up your face. I will show you to them and forbid you to alter your hell-face. I shall blurt out, Persephone of Henna, the meal that traps you beneath the vast weight of the earth, the agreement by which you love the somber king of the night and the corruption you experienced that induced your mother to refuse to call you back. Upon you, Hades, worst of the world's rulers, I shall send Titan, the Sun, bursting your caverns open, and you will be blasted by the instantaneous light of day. Do you obey?" [14]

This indicates that the spirits and deities associated with these liminal points between the world of the living and the world of death are – in both the Graeco-Roman tradition and the hoodoo/Vodou tradition – less friendly than might be assumed by modern Pagan practice, that they require payment for their services, that they may even react with hostility towards the magician. After all, what the magician is trying to do in these practises is unnatural, against nature, against the laws of death – those in charge aren't going to let just anybody dredge up the dead and bind them to their will!

Once the spirits and deities that watch over the dead have been propitiated and their co-operation in the rite secured, it is also common practice for the magician to make offerings to the spirits they are going to be working with – usually left at the graveside. This often takes the form of a food or drink offering, flowers, or money. To many modern practitioners this can be viewed as "paying" the spirit for their services, of giving as well as taking, and indeed this can be part of it. However, the Graeco-Roman tradition usually prescribes that the magician make offerings of wine, milk, seasonal flowers and barley. As Ogden observes, these offerings were also traditional graveside offerings from mourners at a loved one's funeral, and that in such cases they are less payment and more soothing and honorary towards the dead spirit.[15] It should come as no surprise when we read in the Greek Magical Papyri:

"You place it [the figurine of your victim], as the sun is setting, beside the grave of one who has died untimely or violently, placing beside it also the seasonal flowers." [16]

This also reflects the practice of Hercules in the *Odyssey*, when attempting to call up the shade of Tiresias from the underworld:

"Draw near to this spot, hero, and, as I bid you, dig a pit a cubit wide this way and that. Around it pour a full libation to the dead, first with honey-milk, then with sweet wine, and third with water. Sprinkle white barley on top." [17]

Why the need to propitiate the spirits of the dead with such offerings and soothings? Modern pagan practice might have us believe that Gods and spirits are just sitting around waiting for us to call upon them for their aid, eager to help us with any task we might place upon them. Whilst this may be true of some of the more approachable and accommodating deities and spirits, it doesn't appear to be true at all of the Chthonic deities, spirits of the dead, or those who watch over them. Particularly in the Graeco-Roman tradition these deities are there for a specific purpose: take care of the spirits of the dead, guard them, and in most cases keep them imprisoned in the Underworld. They are not there for our purposes, as evidenced by the above quoted threat of a magician who is finding the Chthonic deities uncooperative.

The nature of ghosts in both the Graeco-Roman and hoodoo/Vodou traditions is one of simple indifference, keen malevolence, or desperation and mourning resulting in accidental harm of the living.

On the coast of South Carolina, the Gullah people still practice the rootwork traditions that survived when their ancestors were brought to the New World as slaves from West Africa, and still carry with them remnants of the old African beliefs of their forefathers regarding the soul, afterlife, ghosts, and burial practices. Pinckney writes:

"This familiarity [with ghosts] has its origins in Africa, where many tribes practiced the ritual of the second burial. Because a corpse decomposes quickly in the tropical heat, the initial burial took place within a day or two of death. The time was too short for a gathering of the dead person's relatives, or for adequate rituals. A year or two later, the relatives were summoned for a great feast, the bones were exhumed, carefully wrapped in leaves or cloth, prayerfully and lovingly put in their final resting place. No property could be transferred until the second burial and until this time the spirit could not rest easy. But once in America, plantation masters did not give their slaves the luxury of two funerals – burials took place quickly, often at night by torchlight, so as not to take valuable time away from fieldwork. And the exhuming of a body was one African ritual Christian elders would not tolerate.

And so spirits were condemned to suffer an eternity of unrest, becoming in the Gullah lexicon 'trabblin' spirits'. And the living would bear the consequences." [18]

In the above case, the second – "proper" – burial of a body resulted in a ghost being laid to rest. If a body was not given the appropriate burial rites, the resulting ghost became angry, hostile, or simply restless. This concept is found throughout the Graeco-Roman tradition as well, in which there was a specific class of ghosts called *Ataphoi* – those denied proper burial. These ghosts were usually restless, sometimes malevolent, and tended to either cause harm to the living should they accidentally wander into the spot where the ghost's body had been discarded (often a battlefield or site of a murder). They also appeared to the living as hauntings – usually in an attempt to inform the hauntee of the location of their body, so as to incite a proper burial.

Virgil gives us a vision of the souls who stand on the banks of the river Styx, trapped and unable to progress fully into the their final rest, due to being denied burial:

"All the crowd you see here is destitute and unburied. This is Charon, the ferryman. These, whom he transports over the wave, are the buried. He may not carry the souls across the awful banks and the rumbling waters before their bones have found peace in a resting place. They wander over and flit about these shores for a hundred years. Only then are they admitted to the pools they have longed for and can revisit them." [19]

Pausanius writes of a particular battlefield that saw awful bloodshed, where the ghosts of those whose bodies still lie there, now decayed and buried in shallow graves without proper rites, torment any who pass by:

"All night long there one can hear the sound of horses neighing and men at war. It has never been good for anyone to go there in the deliberate attempt to get a clear look, but the anger of the demons is not directed against those who find themselves there accidentally and for some other reason." [20]

Of particular interest are the related ghost-laying practices, nearly all of which prescribe a second burial – like that of the West African practices – or even the symbolic funeral rites given to figurines made to represent the restless spirits in cases where the body is unavailable.[21]

For the Gullah people, most ghosts (or "hants" – hauntings) would never directly harm a person, but they might scare somebody to death with their presence, cause somebody to harm themselves, or accidentally bring about harm – such as disease – to any loved ones they visit. In this tradition spirits can be placated and made calmer by placing decorations on the grave of the deceased – sometimes these decorations take the form of the last objects the deceased used (this practice still continues today and the addition of modern technology to grave decorations is common e.g. phones and television sets.)[22] It is also known to the Gullah people that certain kinds of spirits – called plateyes (ghosts that guard items or treasure) – can be placated with offerings of whiskey (or at least slowed down in their pursuit of a thief of the guarded objects.)[23]

So it seems that when offerings are made to the spirits of the dead in hoodoo and Vodou, it may be a combination of funerary offerings to mimic a second burial, thus placating the spirit, and diversions to keep the ghost well-fed on food and drink instead of being tempted – either through hunger or boredom or malevolence – to attack the magician.

GRAVEYARD DIRT

In hoodoo you can traditionally use dirt from an array of places, such as from outside a courthouse, jail, or bank if you want justice, incarceration, or business/money luck respectively. However, graveyard dirt is a vast and complex subject, since it is usually mentioned only in a glancing manner, the mechanics behind it not discussed or explained.

The Greek and Roman sorcerers tended to use certain kinds of spirits for their aggressive magic, four in particular: *Aoroi* ("those dead before their time"), *Bi(ai)othanatoi* ("those dead by violence"), *Agamoi* ("those dead before marriage") and *Ataphoi* ("those denied burial"). In their own ways, each of these kinds of spirits had been deprived of the full extent of life, either because their time had been cut short, or because they had not had the chance to fulfil what was viewed as the reason for their being (particularly in the case of women dead before marriage or childbirth.) There is also mention of benevolent ghosts in the Graeco-Roman tradition, usually those of family members who died content and at a reasonable age, that could be brought in to protect the family. There is some discussion regarding the Lares, deities that protected the home and the family and whose blessing was required at all important family events – Taylor suggests they are spirits of the departed, identifying the typically chthonic nature of their rites at Compitalia and Larentalia.[24] The second century CE author Festus suggests directly that they are gods of the underworld, and the first century BCE author Flaccus stated that the Lar (singular form of Lares) and the Genius (here understood to be an ancestral Genius) were one and the same.[25] Interestingly Lucius Apuleius, writing in the second century CE, made a distinction between the Lares as benevolent ancestral spirits and the vagrant, malevolent ghosts he called Lemures. To Apuleius the Lares belong both to the Chthonic realms of the underworld but also to the surface world of human affairs – they are willing to aid the living. Since they are benevolent, and have physical domains that they rule over, they are set apart from the Lemures that have no domain and no control, who are unwilling to help the living. [26] Not only the Graeco-Roman sorcerors, but also their non-magical counterparts, were using the aid of dead spirits in their everyday life, and they were keenly aware of the difference between the benevolent spirit of an ancestor and the malevolent, vagrant spirit of the untimely dead, unburied, dead by violence or dead before marriage.

Similarly, in hoodoo it is traditional to obtain the help of certain kinds of dead spirits for certain kinds of magic, and this seems to be done through the obtaining of graveyard dirt from the graves of suitable spirits. You may take the dirt from the grave of a loved one or family member and use it for protective magic towards yourself. But you may also take the dirt from the grave of a thief, murderer or rapist to hex somebody; you may take the dirt from a young woman's grave to attract a man to you or the dirt from a young man's grave to attract a woman. It can be suggested that the gravedirt simply carries with it the symbolic essence of what its dead owner represents, and is therefore used in contagious or sympathetic magic – "Just as this dirt is from the grave of a thief who knows all the secrets of hidden, stolen items, so I use it to get NN to return the items they have stolen from me." However, this kind of prescription is rarely given and used with graveyard dirt practices in hoodoo. It seems, instead, that the dirt brings with it the co-operation of the dead spirit from whose grave it is taken. Portable magic at its best! Thus, you take with you to the comfort of your own home the protective spirit that is your grandmother; you carry to the doorstep of your enemy the aggressive and destructive spirit of a murderer; you send after your desired partner the young, sexual spirit of a woman dead before marriage.

"The dirt should be gathered at midnight from the spot on the grave just above the corpse's heart. The gatherer should choose a person he or she knows – ideally one who has not been dead for more than three or four years. Like in dirt gathered for rootwork, the personality of the departed is important – a goodly man for good, a bad man for evil, a successful businessman for financial acumen, a gambler for luck with cards or dice. Money must be left at the graveside and prayers to the dead must be spoken, though in the case of a ritual at an evil person's grave, a good cursing will suffice, instead." [27]

Here we find the nature of the deceased from whose grave the dirt comes important, but also the location in the grave is mentioned: in this case, above the corpse's heart. The reason for this is not given, and no clues are found in the Graeco-Roman sources either. However, many cultures have viewed either the heart or the brain as the seat of the soul, knowing how vital the beating heart was for the continuation of physical life and – presumably, by extension – for the existence of the soul in its body. However, in some Vodou practices the head (in the form of the skull) is given this honour, with some communities keeping skulls from very famous and powerful Houngans or Mambos as advisors and valuable members of the community long after their death. Instead, it could be that the heart is viewed as the place where intentions lie – to have a good heart is to live well and treat others kindly and do good things. To have a bad heart is to think badly of others, to act out of anger, spite, vengeance and bitterness, and to do bad things. So, the dirt taken from above the corpse's heart might be seen as containing within it the essence of the deceased's "goodness" or "badness", enabling the dirt to effect such qualities in the magical working.

One spell from the Greek Magical Papyri, "Love spell of attraction performed with the help of heroes or gladiators or those who have died a violent death" makes use of the dirt from the place where such people were slain:

"And go to where heroes and gladiators and those who have died a violent death were slain. / Say the spell to the pieces of bread and throw them. And pick up some polluted dirt from the place where you perform the ritual and throw it inside the house of the woman whom you desire, go home and go to sleep." [28]

This is interesting because the dirt is specifically called "polluted" in the text – probably because the violent deaths upon that place have stained the earth with negative energy, all the blood seeped into the ground has made it unclean. So, in this case, not only the ghosts being called upon are aggressive and polluted, but the very dirt itself is also. Further, it is then deposited in the home of the victim of the spell, who is tormented by the ghosts of the untimely dead until she relents to the magician.

In the above we also find offerings are to be made to the deceased, and prayers spoken at the graveside – in much the same way as they might be spoken at a funeral. These prayers in the hoodoo tradition would likely take the form of Biblical passages and Psalms, particularly Psalm 23, a popular verse for funerals and comforting the bereaved:

*"The LORD is my shepherd; I shall not want.
He maketh me to lie down in green pastures: he leadeth me beside the still waters.
He restoreth my soul: he leadeth me in the paths of righteousness for his name's sake.*
*Yea, though I walk through the valley of the shadow of death, I will fear no evil: for thou art with me; thy rod and thy staff they comfort me.
Thou preparest a table before me in the presence of mine enemies: thou anointest my head with oil; my cup runneth over.
Surely goodness and mercy shall follow me all the days of my life: and I will dwell in the house of the LORD for ever."* [29]

The Graceo-Roman sources are quiet on any appropriate prayers or hymns to be given to the deceased, but the placing of grave offerings and seasonal flowers remains the same and are suggestive of funerary rites.

An interesting note in the quote above is that the grave from whence the graveyard dirt is taken should be no older than three or four years. This is presumably because the spirit is still "fresh" and still retains more of a semblance of its old self. In the Graeco-Roman practices the magical operator frequently calls upon those "untimely dead" – those who have died before their allotted time had run out, as it is believed that these types of spirits loiter around their own graves or are stuck closer to the earth:

"One must imagine this corporeal element to be burdensome, heavy, earthy, and visible. The sort of soul that has it is weighed down and drawn back to the realm of the visible, in fear of the unseen [aïdous] and of Hades [Haïdou], as it is said, and rolls [kulindoumenê] around gravestones and tombs, around which in fact some shadowy manifestations of souls are seen, such as are the ghosts that souls of this kind produce, souls that have not been purely released, but still participate in the realm of the visible, and for that reason are seen." [30]

So a spirit who has been dead for decades or centuries may have moved on, or become completely disinterested in helping with any human affairs. In some ancient sources it was believed that those dead before their time wandered the earth until the time they would have originally died, so the sooner the magician works with them, the more likely they are to still be present at the gravesite.

However, this is in direct opposition to another account of the retrieval of graveyard dirt from Hurston, one of the foremost commentators on the Vodou religion. Hurston states that the link between the dirt and the power of ghosts to harm the living is mere superstition, and that the "magic" actually lies in the composition of the dirt itself. She quotes Dr. Domingo Foriero:

"If each corpse is the bearer of millions of organisms specific of ill, imagine what a cemetery must be in which new foci are forming around each body! More than twenty years after the death of a body, Shane found the germs of yellow fever, scarlatina, typhoid and other infectious diseases." [31]

Hurston suggests that the most effective gravedirt comes not from the recently dead, but rather from decades-old graves, getting the soil from corpses that *"...had sufficient time to thoroughly decay..."* [32]

For Hurston, the deadly composition of diseases in graveyard dirt is what caused the deadly results of most hoodoo hexes – hence "goofer" dust (which is made up of graveyard dirt) that can kill people if it is laid on their doorstep or sprayed into their eyes and mouth. However, the question surely arises from this assertion – isn't the procurer of the dirt the one most likely to be affected by the diseases contained within it, positioned, as they are, an arms-length into the grave to retrieve it? (It is important to note that whilst many practitioners might be tempted to simply grab some topsoil from a grave for their workings, the old prescription is to take it from deep within the grave...) Of course, in modern Western society it is rare to find a corpse that has died of any of the above diseases, given our regular use of vaccines and the fact that the above are all extinct in most developed countries.

For any modern necromancer or hoodoo practitioner, the belief in spirits may come as a given, whilst the random hit-and-miss chance of attempting to infect somebody with a deadly disease by sprinkling minute particles of it on their doorstep may be more unbelievable. It seems that the mechanics of the use of specific kinds of graveyard dirt bring the aid and intentions of a particular spirit with it – it is not just a sympathetic magic aid, as has been assumed by many researchers. The qualities of graveyard dirt – cold, associated with death, heavy – are only partly what creates the magic. However, it is conceivable that one could use graveyard dirt based only on these qualities, regardless of any attached spirits – the burying of a figurine of somebody in graveyard dirt has symbolically potent imagery for a curse, for instance. The practice of burying a figurine in a grave is certainly widespread in the ancient Graeco-Roman world and earlier cultures, such as:

"You [the witches] have picked me out for a dead body,
You have handed me over to a skull,
You have handed me over to a ghost of my kin,
You have handed me over to the ghost of a foreigner,
To a roving ghost for whom nobody cares [...]
You have given figurines of me to a dead man,
You have picked out my figurines for a dead man,
You have placed figurines of me with a dead man,
You have placed figurines of me in the lap of a dead man..." [33]

Plato also commented on this practice in *The Laws* 933a, where he casts scorn upon superstitious men who are made uncomfortable by the sight of "waxen images" upon parental graves or at three-way crossroads. This is particularly interesting, as Plato specifies the graves to be those linked to the magician by blood – could this be a tantalizing hint that some sorcerers used their ancestors to aid them in their necromantic rites, instead of conjuring up the shades of strangers? Alas, there is no other mention of such practices in the Graeco-Roman sources, excepting the traditions surrounding the Lares, but since such traditions were public and state-sanctioned rites (as opposed to secret and occult) it is unlikely that the Lares would have been used for nefarious necromantic deeds.

However, it seems more likely that the burial of the figurine (and this is true of all examples found in the Magical Papyri as well) in the grave, once again, has less to do with the symbolic qualities of the dirt in the grave than it has to do with the presence of the dead spirit near or within that grave. To give figurines of somebody to a grave is to give them over to the power of the dead spirit that resides there – hence the figurine in "Wondrous Spell for Binding a Lover" is placed by a graveside and the dead spirits are called up from there to go a fetch the victim for the magician.

In this vein, the "Mnesimachos doll" – so called for the name "Mnesimachos" that is written upon the right leg of the figurine – was discovered buried in a grave in the Athenian Ceramicus cemetery, entombed in its own miniature coffin crafted – rather ingeniously – from lead curse tablets. The curse tablet that formed the coffin lid bore an inscription of a legal curse for binding the tongues of witnesses in court. Its burial in a grave could have been intended to rouse the ghost of that grave (from which bits had been taken, indicating the ghost in question was also being compelled by the magician that held its *ousia* – discussed below) to stop the tongues of the witnesses.[34]

In the hoodoo tradition the sending of the spirits of the dead after your desired victim is called an Expedition – examined in the following section.

Expeditions and Envoi Mort: Sending out the Dead

There is a traditional curse used in Vodou and Hoodoo Conjure to kill somebody or make them very sick, done in the name of Bawon Lakwa (Baron the Cross). The magician will go to a cemetery and to a major cross there – this can be the oldest cross, or the biggest and most impressive, as this is most often where Bawon Lakwa will be served. The magician will then pour Florida Water (a citrus-smelling cologne that is used in many Petwo and Ghede rites, and is also highly flammable) all over that cross and light it on fire. They will then take a whip or something that can be used for flogging, and will whip the burning cross three times for each dead spirit they want to raise to send after somebody, while telling those dead spirits who they need to go to. For a Western practitioner this might be viewed as the "energy raising" portion of a magical rite, but it serves a far greater purpose than that (examined below.)

When the practitioner feels that they have raised all the dead spirits necessary for the work, they will then take a stone for each one of the dead (preferably a stone from that same cemetery), get an image of St. Expedite and turn it upside down. They will leave the stones in front of this image – probably overnight, placed in the cemetery by that big cross – then place these stones on the victim's property. If the practitioner does not know where the victim lives, they can place the stones at a crossroads.

Note that it is not necessarily the setting of the cross on fire that aggravates and raises up the spirits of the dead in this curse: setting a cross aflame is sometimes used in Vodou service for Ghede spirits. Instead, the act of whipping or flogging the cross seems to act as a charioteer's whip goading his horses into action. In this case, there does not seem to be any concern with respect towards the spirits of the dead. No prayers are spoken and no offerings are made – the idea is to make these spirits angry so that when they are sent after the magician's victim they will easily carry out the deed.

The name of such a curse is an "Expedition" – partly because the spirits of the dead are being sent out on an expedition of sorts, but also partly, perhaps, from the Saint that is used in the curse – St. Expedite.

A similar curse, called *envoi mort* (literally, "Sending out the Dead") takes the idea of raising the spirits of the dead and using them to cause sickness and death, but uses it in a more specific manner. In *envoi mort* the magician will call up a single spirit of one who died young or in a violent manner. Kenaz Filan writes:

"*The basic operation involves going to a cemetery, to the grave of a person who has died young or by violence. After petitioning the Bawon for his aid, the Vodouisant then 'sends' that dead person's spirit against the target. If this spell is successful, the cursed person will begin to manifest the symptoms of whatever killed the mort. If the mort died of AIDS or cancer, the target will begin losing weight despite the best efforts of doctors. If the mort was shot, the target will suffer from intense pains in the area of the wounds, and so on.*" [35]

This *envoi mort* does not send out any old spirit, but rather it focuses on the cause of death – much like the Graeco-Roman sorcerors who put such faith in the untimely dead and those dead by violence. Here, an Expedition raises the dead through heating them up and goading them, making them angry, and an *envoi mort* petitions Bawon to send out the spirit concerned. Whilst the latter seems less violent, the results are the same.

A few interesting features of these spells give us clues as to the mechanics at work in the magic. Firstly, the stones used in the Expedition; secondly the act of sending out the dead at all; finally the act of setting the cross on fire and whipping it.

Sending out the Dead

There are many accounts of the dead being sent out to harm the living in the Graeco-Roman sources, sometimes in packs and sometimes one specific ghost will be sent. A spell from the Greek Magical Papyri instructs the magician to write upon a papyrus the purpose and victim of the curse, and then to insert the rolled up papyrus into the corpse's mouth:

"*…arouse yourself for me, / daimon of the dead, and do not use force but fulfil what has been inscribed and inserted into your mouth, immediately, immediately, quickly, quickly.*" [36]

Apuleius gives us an account of a spurned woman who employs a witch to either achieve reconciliation between her and her [ex] husband, or to cause him violence and destroy him. The witch finds that the "powers" will not help her create a reunion between the man and woman, so instead she calls up the angry spirit of a woman and sends it to the man to murder him. Apuleius writes:

"*At around the middle of the day a woman suddenly appeared in the mill, disfigured by the sort of extreme misery affected by defendants in court. She was only semiclothed, by a pitiful piece of patchwork. Her feet were bare and uncovered. She was yellow like boxwood and foully emaciated. Her unkempt hair was partially grey and caked in the ashes* that had been scattered over it. It hung down and covered most of her face. In this state as she was, she reassuringly put her hand on the miller, as if she wished to share something with him in secret. She drew him aside to his room and, with the door put to, stayed there for an awfully long time. But when the workers had processed all the grain that they had to hand, and a further supply inevitably had to be sought, the boys came to the room and called on their master and asked for new supplies for their work. They shouted out repeatedly and frequently, but no master responded to them. They began to beat more vigorously on the door. It had been carefully bolted, and so they began to suspect that something rather serious and rather bad was afoot. With a stout shove they pushed out or broke the hinge and at last opened a way in for themselves. There was no sign of the woman, but their master was there to be seen hanging by a noose from a beam and already dead."* [37]

This ghost, frightfully described with corpse-like features and the traditional signs of mourning (unkempt hair and ash upon her head), does not seem to kill the miller herself, but rather causes him to commit suicide. Ogden suggests that this is because the touch, presence or directed malevolence of a ghost is enough to pass on the state of death to a living person, as happens on the aforementioned Marathon battlefield. This would be similar to the envoi mort, in which the cause of the ghost's death also kills the victim. Death begets death.

In some cases the Graeco-Roman magician is advised not to take any chances about his power over the dead spirit he chooses to send out, and instead to create a dead spirit himself for use in the rite. This is usually done by sacrificing an animal and using its dead spirit, such as the "Love Spell of Attraction Over a Dog",[38] and a love potion that sends the spirit of a sacrificed scarab beetle to torment the victim.[39] In a rather sensationalised description of this, Lucan describes a witch who regularly creates dead spirits for her magical work by killing humans before their time:

"Babies are dragged out from a slashed-open belly, not the way nature intended, to be laid upon hot altars. Whenever she needs cruel and brazen shades, she herself manufactures the ghosts. Every human death is of some use to her. She tears the blooming cheek from the body of a young man. She cuts the lock with her left hand from the dying adolescent. Often too, at the funeral of a relation the dreadful Thessalian presses herself upon his limbs, dear to her as they are, and, while fixing kisses upon them, hacks bits off his head. With her teeth she releases the mouth, frozen shut, and, biting the end of the tongue that sticks fast in the dry throat, pours mutterings between the chill lips and sends secret and criminal orders down to the Stygian ghosts." [40]

Although this account obviously is not a good indicator of actual events, it does tell us that the Greeks were aware of the possibility of the creation of ghosts for use by magicians through acts such as murder.

It may be wise to ask how the magician might go about identifying and calling up an already-dead and specific ghost for use in such a spell. The mechanics for this are slightly different to those of calling up a group of anonymous ghosts, but share some features in common. The ancient Graeco-Roman magical texts suggest that the magician takes a piece from the corpse of the ghost they wish to raise, and literally holds it hostage until the ghost completes the task they set for it. In "A Wondrous Spell for Binding a Lover" (*PGM* IV.296-466) the magician is instructed to take such a piece from the corpse, and speak an accompanying prayer to Helios:

"...go to the depths of the earth and search the regions of the dead, send this daimon, from whose body I hold this remnant in my hands, to her, NN, at midnight hours, to move by night to orders 'neath your force."

It is not clear why it is Helios being called upon for his aid in a necromantic rite, since Helios is also not a Chthonic deity; however the section of the Greek Magical Papyri that this text comes from seems to have been written or collected by a redactor (or sorcerer) for whom the Sun God in his many forms was a preoccupation (it is this book of the Papyri which also gives us the infamous "Mithras Liturgy", for instance.) In Graeco-Roman magic, as in modern Vodou practice, a God or spirit that you are particularly close to can be petitioned for aid in any matters or concerns – they have specialities, but can still help their devotees or servitors in any area of life. What is interesting though is that, once again, a God or higher spirit is being called upon to find or release the particular ghost that the magician wishes to work with – Helios in this case, but Hekate and Bawon La Kwa above.

The remnant that the magician takes from the corpse is called *ousia* in Greek – literally translated it means "stuff" – and *materia magica* in Latin ("magical material") and is usually used in the sympathetic magic of the time to establish a link between the ritual act and the target of the spell. So, in the case of "A Wondrous Spell for Binding a Lover" the *ousia* of the target is also used by attaching it to an effigy of her that is then stuck with thirteen copper needles. In ancient Mesopotamia witches were said to take hair clippings, bits of clothing and dust of footprints from the victim:

"[The witches] have placed dust of my feet in a grave, have taken my measurements, have collected dust on which my feet have stepped, have taken my spittle, have plucked out my hair, have cut off my hem."

"... and you take the combings of their heads. You clothe them in the combings.
You bind them [i.e. the statues] together in a skein. You put them in a half-sila container...
...you bury them in the ground." [42]

However, not only does this *ousia* establish a link between symbolic representation and victim, it also acts as a scent trail for the ghost(s) that is/are commanded to go to the victim and harm them or bring them to the magician (in the case of love spells.) So we have a lead tablet from the Late Antique Graeco-Roman period stating:

"Don't ignore [these] names, nekydaimon, but arouse yourself and go to every place where Matrona is, whom Tagene bore. You have her ousia. Go to her and seize her sleep, her drink, her food, and do not allow Matrona (whom Tagene bore, whose ousia you have) to have love or intercourse with any other man, except Theodorus, whom Techosis bore. Drag Matrona by her hair, by her guts, by her soul, by her heart until she comes to Theodorus and make her inseparable from me until death, night and day, for every hour of time. Immediately, immediately, quickly, quickly, now, now." [43]

The lead tablet upon which this was inscribed was found accompanying an earthenware bowl that had also been inscribed with a love charm. In a second bowl found with these items, a pair of waxen images embracing was wrapped in a love charm written on papyrus. (Note also that the term *"nekydaimon"* is Greek for "dead spirit".) Further, other magical texts from this period state that to "give" the *ousia* to a ghost one must bury it in the appropriate grave, as in PGM XV 1.21 in which the magician places *ousia* from the victim in the grave of one untimely dead, asking the daimon of that grave to bring Nilos to him.

Thus, the *ousia* of the victim, when "given"

to the ghosts turns the ghosts into otherworldly (or underworldly!) sniffer dogs, hunting down their prey. This act also establishes a significant link between the corpse and its ghost, a link that is further exploited by many ancient sorcerors in their rites. By affecting the corpse in such a way that you effectively mutilate it – taking a remnant of the corpse to control the ghost with – you not only hold the ghost hostage but also make it powerless to act against you or in any other way that you decree. The Graeco-Romans had a practice known as "armpitting", in which it was assumed that the state of the corpse affected the state and power of the ghost. If a ghost were feared to come back in hostility and anger and wreak havoc upon the living, its corpse would have its extremities or important bits removed and sometimes placed in the wrong place in the grave:

"Consider whether the dead man in the grave appears to receive these gifts propitiously from the woman who killed him, dishonored him, subjected him to armpitting like an enemy, and wiped off the bloodstains with his hair to clean her sword." [44]

A spell from the Greek Magical Papyri appeals to the God Helios to send to the magician the spirit of the dead man from whom he has *ousia*:

"I beg you, lord Helios, hear me NN and grant me power / over the spirit of this man who died a violent death, from whose tent I hold [this], so that I may keep him with me, [NN] as helper and avenger for whatever business I crave from him." [45]

It is worth noting that this spell specifically requires a spirit from a man who died a violent death, this spirit falling into one of the four preferred categories of ghosts that are useful to the unscrupulous magician, in this case the *Bi(ai)othanatoi*. Here, the spirit of the dead man is clearly being placed under the control and power of the magician, with the permission of Helios and the use of the dead man's *ousia* as "hostage". Thus, the aforementioned "Mnesimachos doll" found buried in the grave of a corpse from whom body parts had been taken was probably part of an elaborate curse to not only bind the tongue of the victim(s) but also to send out the spirit of the dead man of that grave to enact some form of torment or silencing upon the victims.

As has been discussed above, many of the dead spirits that are worked with in necromantic curses and hexes are hostile; however they can be made more hostile and furthermore they can be made hostile towards a specific person (the victim or target of the curse) with the correct application of force. This force can also be applied to goad the dead spirit into action, threatening it with further torment until it has completed the desired task for the magician. In the case of spirit expeditions in Hoodoo Conjure, the force used is that of whipping and engulfing the spirits in flame.

Burning the Cross

The use of flame bears a problem for our examination. In Graeco-Roman burial rites corpses could be either buried or cremated on an open pyre. Cremation became a common practice from the 12th century BCE, when it was probably imported from Asia Minor, and survived as a well-loved burial option until the advent of Christianity when inhumation was preferred. Even then, those that remained pagans opted to cremate their dead, though as inhumation became fashionable they sometimes followed suit regardless of religion. According to Cicero, inhumation was sometimes the only option available to the poorer citizens, whereas cremation was for the middle and upper classes. In some instances the burning of the body allowed the spirit freedom, and in the case of the Roman Emperors an eagle was released above the pyre as the body was burned, symbolizing his deification and ascension to the place of the Gods. This would certainly fit with the concept of "armpitting" – a body not available to have *ousia* stolen from it, or unable to be mutilated, makes the accompanying spirit free to act in its own way, or free from the control of others – such as the unscrupulous magicians we are currently discussing! However, the burning of something in a ritual or magical context held an entirely different symbolic mechanic – fire could be used to both infirm and inflame a victim, injure them or make them whole, purify them or pollute them.

In much of the ancient world ritual use of fire represented a destructive force – it was used in the Maqlu texts ("Maqlu" literally translates from the Assyrian as "Burning") to destroy evil magics, witches, sorcerors, enemies and ghosts, in which the target is "given to Girru", the fire god.[46] It was also used by the people of Sardis in 165 CE under instruction from an oracle of Clarion Apollo to destroy and ward off a plague that had been causing immense death in the city:

"Bring in her [Artemis'] image, shining with gold, from Ephesus, and set it up in a temple, with joy in your hearts. She will ward off your sufferings and dismiss the man-destroying spells/poisons of the plague, melting the wax-moulded dolls by night with the flames of her fire-bearing torches, the evil tokens of the mage's craft." [47]

Most interesting in the above quote, perhaps, is the denoting of the flames and fire-bearing torches as tokens of the mage's craft – tools the evil sorcerers who had caused the plague upon the city may have used in the first place to cast the spell.

However, one of the most important clues to the intended mechanic of flames in the spirit expeditions is found in the use of fire to incite erotic feelings and love madness in a desired lover. Although many of the ritual texts surviving from the Graeco-Roman period often use piercing (with needles, nails or pins) as a means of inspiring love, the later Greek and Latin dramatists portray a number of witches burning and melting images of their desired lovers. In the 3rd century BCE Theocritus' witch Simaetha melts a wax doll of Delphis to inspire love in him:

"As I melt this wax doll with the help of the goddess, so may Delphis of Myndos at once be melted by love."[48]

Simaetha also uses fire to cause damage or torment to Delphis, in the same way that the nails piercing an image were intended to cause love sickness and wakefulness until the victim relented:

"Delphis has caused me pain. I burn this bay leaf against Delphis. As this bay leaf is set alight, crackles loudly in the flames, and quickly blazes up, leaving no ash for us to see, so may Delphis too shrivel his flesh in the flames." [49]

It is clear that this was not a unified account of a magical rite, but instead a drawing together of a number of rituals that nevertheless had the inflaming of passion and love as their goal. Regardless of the fictional nature of Theocritus' account, it demonstrates a knowledge of a wide variety of these practices, and as Faraone has shown it is easy to see the factual sources behind the drama.[50]

Virgil's portrait for a witch in his *Eclogue* from the 1st century BCE bears remarkable similarity to Theocritus', most likely due to the fact that Virgil had read Theocritus' work and sought to employ the motifs in his own writing. Instead of just wax being burned, however, there is an addition into Amaryllis' (the witch) fire:

"As this clay grows hard and as this wax melts in one and the same fire, so may Daphnis melt in his love for me." [51]

Not only is the melting wax intended to sympathetically melt the heart of Daphnis (and we can safely assume that the wax and clay are made into images of Daphnis), but it seems that the hardening of the clay has a particularly erotic function intended to harden Daphnis' loins and arouse passion in him.

Only slightly after Virgil's account, we find Horace's *Satires* providing us with an entertaining portrait of two older witches. At first it is unclear that they are performing love magic, probably due to the dramatic and bloody description of the rites, but we then read that:

"There was a woollen doll, and another one made from wax. The woollen one was larger, so that it could restrain the smaller one with punishments. The wax doll held the pose of a suppliant, as if it were about to be executed in slave fashion." [52]

This bears a resemblance to the love spell of PGM IV. 296-466, in which the magician is told to make two dolls, in the same pose as these. However, instead of the slave doll being pierced, it appears she is thrown into the fire:

"...how the fire flared up higher because of the wax image..." [53]

It would seem then, that Canidia and Sagana in this account are performing love magic using melting and burning techniques.

The extent to which burning images causes torment, and is thus intended to torture the victim in the same way as piercing until they give themselves to the magician, is discussed by Faraone.[54] Given the classical and Hellenistic view of *eros* (passionate love) as a mental disease or fever, it is easy to see how burning an image of a victim could be seen as tormenting them with love sickness. The Greek Magical Papyri even contains a love spell that asks the magician to carve upon a magnetic stone an image of Psyche being held by the hair by Aphrodite, who sits astride her, and burned with a torch held by Eros – a literal representation of this fiery love sickness: PGM IV. 1716-1870. The image provided by this spell is highly evocative:

"Take a magnetic stone which is breathing and engrave Aphrodite sitting astride Psyche / and with her left hand holding on her hair bound in curls. And above her head: "ACHMAGE RARPEPSEI"; and below / Aphrodite and Psyche engrave Eros standing on the vault of heaven, holding a blazing torch and burning Psyche." [55]

It is not hard to imagine this image with the magician in the role of Aphrodite and Eros, and the spirits of the dead in the role of Psyche, bound and controlled by the magician, and burned with the fires that inflame, agitate and goad them into hostile action. This is a symbolic concept supported by the fact that in modern Vodou practice and Hoodoo Conjure, setting something on fire "heats it up". To pass a mojo bag or other spellwork object through the flames of a fire or candle helps make it work faster, activate it, or make it more potent; when the warrior lwa Ogou Feray comes in possession he sometimes complains that "gren mwe fret" ("my balls are cold!") and in response he will be given a fire made in an iron or other fire-proof receptacle made from a mixture of Florida water and (usually) rum over which he warms his feet – the same substance, we should note, is used to set the cross alight in the spirit expeditions. When Ogou's balls are cold, any course of action finds a far slower resolution if any at all, the servitor's life becomes blocked in many ways or filled with obstacles, and problems do not resolve easily. However, heating him up too much – just as heating any spirit up too much – can make him aggressive and hostile, more prone to heavy-handedness in resolving problems. Vodou maintains this concept of heat and fire as representing agitation, fast action, aggression, hostility and hot-headedness throughout its praxis and belief system: the Petwo rite and its associated lwa are perceived as hot, fiery spirits, and as such they are traditionally more aggressive, they can be hostile in their worst states, but very quick to act and magically potent and strong workers when served correctly. In the Petwo rite we find spirits such as Ezili Dantor, the strong, independent single mother and patroness of lesbians, women who suffer domestic abuse, and the oppressed; we find Marinette, the once-human priestess (Mambo) who started the violent Haitian slave revolution by sacrificing a black sow to Dantor at the Bwa Kayman ceremony; we find Ezili Ze Wouj, the sister of Dantor who is so angry at the injustices of the world that her eyes turn red, she cannot talk with anger, and she vomits blood.

The Petwo lwa are strong allies for any that walk with them and serve them, and many of them – particularly Ezili Dantor – are extremely popular lwa among practitioners. However, it is recognized that too much fiery Petwo influence in your life can make you too hot-headed – an undesirable trait in traditional Vodou, in which remaining cool-headed, calm, peaceful and centred is desirable. As such, when a person's lwa Met Tet (Master of the Head, their patron spirit) is divined during certain initiation ceremonies, a Rada (cool, watery spirit) is sometimes placed upon their head for the duration of the ceremony (this is done in some houses, not all.)

As we have seen above, one way to lay a restless ghost or bring it peace in the ancient world and in modern Hoodoo practice was to perform a symbolic funeral ceremony for it, or give it funerary offerings. It could be seen, therefore, that any person therefore burning a cross in a cemetery during a spirit expedition might be going some way to symbolically cremating the dead spirits, releasing them from their bonds and bringing them peace much as the Roman Emperors were upon their funeral pyres. However, this is where the modern concept that the intention behind the act is more important than the act itself finds full force – since the magician setting the cross aflame during a spirit expedition has the express intent not of performing a symbolic cremation (and thereby laying the ghosts of the departed to rest) but instead of agitating and goading the spirits into fiery, angry hostility, it is this purpose that the fires serve. As shown by the frequent use of fire to cause hostility, goad a spirit or victim into action, torment the victims of a love spell until they relent, and cause madness, and supported by the measures taken in Vodou to maintain cool-headedness instead of hot-headedness, it would seem that the flaming cross serves to agitate and make hostile the spirits of the dead. Indeed, one line from a malefic spell in the Greek Magical Papyri hints that this is the understanding that the act of burning holds:

"You too as well, Lady, who feed on filth SYNATRAKABI BAUBARABAS ENPHNOUN MORKA ERESCHIGAL NEBOUTOSOUALETH, and send the Erinys ORGOGORGONIOTRIAN, who rouses up with fire the souls of the dead, / unlucky heroes, luckless heroines..."[56]

Adding to this the image of physically injuring – through the act of whipping or flagellating – the cross and therefore the dead spirits, the magician is putting himself in the role of torturer or tormenter, purposefully aggravating these spirits and then pointing them in the direction of the victim. This is vividly demonstrated by the Graeco-Roman sorcerors who, as we have seen, controlled and bound the spirits of the dead to their will, mutilated their corpses and took pieces of them – their *ousia* – to use as a magical insurance policy, ensuring the spirits would do as they bade. A defixione (lead curse tablet) that accompanied the famous Louvre Doll from the 3rd century CE, an effigy of a woman, kneeling and bound hands and feet, with thirteen nails struck through it in all the important places, says,

"Do not permit her to eat, drink, hold out, go out, or find sleep apart from me, Sarapammon, to whom Area gave birth… Restrain her food, drink, until she comes to me, Sarapammon, to whom Area gave birth, and do not permit her to be penetrated by any man other than me alone, Sarapammon. Drag her by the hair, by the guts, until she no longer disdains me, Sarapammon, to whom Area gave birth, and until I have her, Ptolemais, to whom Aias gave birth, Ptolemais the daughter of Horigenes, subservient to me for the full extent of my life, loving me, lusting after me, telling me what she has on her mind. If you do this, I will give you release."[57]

The Louvre Doll itself was discovered by a grave, immediately indicating that the target audience of the above inscription are the spirits of the dead, being asked to fetch the desired lover to the magician. If the dead spirits did as they were asked, the magician would "give them release" – release from a prospective afterlife bound to a mutilated corpse, or bound to a magician, or tormented by the magician.

So, whipping the cross during a spirit expedition might be seen as not only aggravating the spirits into hostility and then aiming them at the victim, but also threatening them with torture and torment until they have achieved the goal for the magician.

Of course, this poses a very distinct danger to the magician. You rile up a bunch of hostile dead spirits, get them to perform outrageous acts of cruelty upon the living, torture them with fire and flagellation, and when you're done you expect them to simply return to their peaceful state and leave you alone… There is a real danger here that once done, the spirits may turn on the magician as well. This is why the magician has already – as in the practice of *envoi mort* – attained "permission" or blessing (in this case, protection!) from the lwa that rules over the dead, e.g. Bawon La Kwa, or the Chthonic Queen of the dead, e.g. Hekate. By using the sacred names and power of these bigger, greater spirits or deities, the magician is able to threaten the spirits of the dead, as is done throughout the Greek Magical Papyri with the repeated use of sacred names, barbarous names, and in some cases the magician identifying him/herself with the invoked deities. In many of the rituals from the Greek Magical Papyri the magician asserts his/her superiority and power over the lesser spirits s/he is commanding by demonstrating his/her superior knowledge of the divine and the secret intricacies of the sacred. In the "Binding Love Spell of Astrapsoukos" the magician tells the commanded spirits all the secret names of Hermes, all his foreign names, his birthplace and his true name:

"Your names in heaven: LAMPHTHEN OUOTHI OUASTHEN OUOTHI OAMENOTH ENTHOMOUCH. These are the [names] in the 4 quarters of heaven. I also know what your forms are: in the east you have the form / of an ibis, in the west you have the form of a dog-faced baboon, in the north you have the form of a serpent, and in the south you

have the form of a wolf. [...] Your true name has been inscribed on the sacred stele in the shrine of Hermopolis where your birth is. Your true name: OSEGARIACH NOMAPHI. This is your name with fifteen / letters, a number corresponding to the days of the rising moon; and the second name with the number 7, corresponding to those who rule the world, with the exact number 365, corresponding to the days of the year. Truly: ABRASAX."[58]

Further, the magician goes onto identify himself as Hermes/Abrasax:

"I know you, Hermes, and you know me. / I am you, and you are I."

This spell also puts Hermes in charge of all Chthonian spirits, and using his superior knowledge and identification as the God, he says,

"Calm them all and give me strength, form (add the usual), and let them give me gold and silver and every sustenance which will never fail."

So in this spell, just one of many, the magician uses the God and the God's power, the secret magical knowledge and superiority he holds over the dead spirits, to control them. And with control comes protection from them also.

A Stone for Each of the Dead

What role do the stones in the spirit expedition play? This feature of the curse seems almost tacked on at the end of the rite, yet it is a vital part of the magic. First, the stones are left overnight in the cemetery at the site of the spirit expedition's burned cross. Then they are placed on the property of the target of the expedition, or at a crossroads if the location of the victim is unknown to the sorcerer.

The first possibility of purpose is that the stones – one for every dead spirit – provide a temporary home in which the spirits can live until they are taken to the location in which they must do the work they have been given. There are many superstitions and beliefs in many traditions about ghosts and the spirits of the dead being tied to one place, unable to move far away from it. Indeed, even the infamous Dracula – not a ghost, but a supernatural being of death – cannot go far away from the earth in which his body originally lay. Even Plato commented that the spirits of the dead were to be found in the vicinity of their own graves, attached to their earthly remains:

"One must imagine this corporeal element to be burdensome, heavy, earthy, and visible. The sort of soul that has it is weighed down and drawn back to the realm of the visible, in fear of the unseen [aïdous] and of Hades [Haïdou], as it is said, and rolls [kulindoumenê] around gravestones and tombs, around which in fact some shadowy manifestations of souls are seen, such as are the ghosts that souls of this kind produce, souls that have not been purely released, but still participate in the realm of the visible, and for that reason are seen." [59]

It seems possible that the stones used in the spirit expedition have a similar role to graveyard dirt – portable homes for the spirits of the dead from which they can perform the magic required of them. It is also conceivable that, since these stones have been present for the spirit expedition and therefore connected with death, they carry with them the infectiousness of death to the victim – just as the graveyard dirt above in *envoi mort* practices carries with it the power to bring about a death upon the victim that originally plagued the person from whose grave the dirt came. However, there are other examples of items being left by the home or threshold of the victim's doorway for a curse, which may provide clues to the function of these stones.

The Graeco-Roman sources are teeming with items deposited in the walkway or vicinity of the victim of a malefic spell. Usually such items are placed in doorways or beneath the threshold of the doorway to the victim's home; often they are buried where the victim will walk, and sometimes left in a bath-house that the victim frequents. The idea is that the victim will pass over the item in their everyday business. For instance, a "Charm for causing separation" in the Greek Magical Papyri prescribes:

"On a pot for smoked fish inscribe a spell with a bronze stylus and recite it afterwards and put it where they [i.e., your victims] are, where they usually return, repeating at the same time this spell…"[60]

A spell for a similar result advises the magician to take the dung of a creature (the text is fragmented and thus we do not know which creature), put it in a document, and to write upon the document the names of Gods together with the names of those he/she wishes to separate, and then to bury this under the doorsill of the house they live in. [61] From the same source text comes a spell that chooses to deposit a curse item not in the vicinity of the victim but rather in the vicinity of the magician himself. In this case, the spell is to "give favour to a man before a woman and vice versa…" It seems that whereas the previous two spells focus the magical effects upon the victim or passive recipient(s) in the spell, this one focuses the effects upon the magician, who instead of controlling the victim's mind in some way changes the natural attractiveness he possesses. In this spell, a "…black Nile fish nine fingers long" is sacrificed, has various things done to it over a number of days from which some sort of anointing oil is created. This oil is smeared upon the face of the magician when he lies with a woman, and the fish is then embalmed and buried in the magician's house.[62]

The use of dead animals in this way is common in the Graeco-Roman sources. The teacher Libanius writes in his Orations that, although usually an eloquent and verbose speaker, he suffered a sudden inability to speak or teach at all. He complained to his students, and later one of them made a grisly discovery in the walls of the schoolroom:

"However, a chameleon, of uncertain origin, was discovered in the classroom. It had been there a long time, and had been dead for many months. We saw that its head had been placed between its hind feet. Of its forefeet, one was nowhere to be seen, and the other was closing the mouth to keep it silent."[63]

Upon the discovery of this item and its removal from the schoolroom – and therefore from the vicinity of Libanius – the teacher regains his ability to speak and debate once more. The proximity of a curse item to the victim seems to be directly proportional to the control or effectiveness of the magician and spell over the victim.

One spell in particular gives us an idea of the purpose of the stones from the spirit expedition:

"A prescription for making a [woman] love you: An image of Osiris [made] of wax – you should… your bringing hair (?) and [wool] of a donkey together with a bone of a lizard. / You should [bury them under the] doorsill of her house. If stubbornness occurs, you should bring it… the image of Osiris with (?) ram's wool; you should put the lizard bone…; / You should bury it again under the doorsill of her house; and you should recite… before Isis in the evening when the moon has risen. Listen before you bury…

'O secret image of Osiris [made] of wax, O powerful one, O protection of..., O lord of praise, love, and respect, may you go to every house which so-and-so is [in and send so-and-so] to every house which so-and-so is in; the tips of her feet follow after her heels... / while her eyes are crying, while her heart longs (?) her... which she will do. O image of Osiris [made] of wax, if you will be stubborn [and not send so-and-so] after so-and-so, I shall go to the chest which... and I shall come... black, I shall gather it with a tooth... black, and I shall cause [Isis] to receive... after Osiris her husband and [brother...]. / Hail to you, O lord of time, the one whom I caused [...] who is in the House of the Obelisk. Come [to me...].' [64]

Here the waxen doll of Osiris is given some semblance of life to enable it to search out the whereabouts of the victim of the spell and send her to the person who she is meant to go to (this indicates that the spell may not have been performed on behalf of the magician, but rather performed by him at the request – and payment – of another.) Like the spirits of the dead from the spirit expedition, the spirit of Osiris is sent after the woman. Earlier examples of fetching spells discussed above made use of the "stuff" (*ousia*) of the victim to allow the spirits to locate her so that the effects of the spell might be wrought upon her, but in this case the magician knows the location of the victim, so needs to employ a far less time-consuming and hit-and-miss method. Placing the curse object containing the spirit that enacts the spell effects in the vicinity of the victim allows the spirit to go about its work upon the victim almost instantly. The hoodoo tradition gives us a number of spells that require placing a magical item in proximity to, or upon the person, of the target of the spell. In hoodoo, it is very common to carry mojo bags upon your person for various reasons: a gambler may carry his mojo "hand" with him at all times, but particularly at the card table for extra luck; somebody who wants prosperity might carry certain herbs in a small bag in their purse or wallet; a woman wanting to keep her lover faithful might put together an item which invariably uses her lover's "stuff" or *ousia*, and place it beneath their bed, or may even put something of herself – her own *ousia* – in his foodstuff so that he may consume it. In hoodoo it's just good common sense to put the magical items in question as close as possible to the person upon whom the magic needs to work, whether it is yourself or somebody else.

In the great tradition of human figurines used in malefic magic, Greek sources give us an intriguingly large number of surviving "voodoo dolls" found in the walls of buildings or buried in doorways, in a similar way to the waxen image of Osiris. From Hellenistic Delos we have a cache of four male figurines discovered together in a house near the agora, that have had their hands bound behind them.[65] Also from Delos in the first century CE come another four figurines, deposited in the retaining wall in the sanctuary of Zeus Hypsistos, which have been bound and had nails pierced through their eyes, ears, and mouths.[66] Later, Jerome writes of a Virgin of God who is sent into a love madness when a curse tablet is deposited beneath her threshold:

"He inscribed some verbal monstrosities and monstrous forms on plates of Cyprian bronze and buried them under the threshold of the girl's house. At once the virgin went mad. She cast off her veil, she swung her hair around, she gnashed her teeth, she shouted out the young man's name. The enormity of her love had transformed itself into frenzy."[67]

There is a striking similarity here between the waxen image of Osiris, the "voodoo dolls" from Delos, and the stones from the Spirit Expedition: all are items of raw material somehow sanctified, deified, or given magical properties. On this note, one could conceivably use anything or any item for such a purpose; however, a bunch of stones placed upon somebody's lawn may look less conspicuous to the victim than a waxen image or pink flamingo. Note that the items discussed here are all buried beneath the ground or otherwise out of sight – hidden, in other words, from the sight of the victim.

Many people have suggested that the deposition of curse items upon the homeland of the victim is to make the victim keenly aware that a curse has been performed against them, so that the effects will begin to occur through psychosomatic power rather than magical power. This type of argument is often perpetuated by those who would rather view the existence of magic as a primitive misunderstanding of the power of the human mind and the control of superstition over the pre-modern man. However, since most, if not all, of the curse items in question are buried out of sight or placed in an inconspicuous manner, this possibility falls away rapidly. Here, it seems that the purpose of deposition near the victim is to have the contagious effects of the curse items rub off on the victim quickly and efficiently, rather than to play upon superstition and fear.

Of course, the magician performing the spirit expedition may not know the location of the victim's home or place of work, and in this instance the technique prescribes that the sorcerer deposit the stones at a crossroads. The crossroads is a prevalent symbol in the Vodou, hoodoo, and Graeco-Roman traditions, yet this is where the traditions separate also. The deposition of curse items in the Graeco-Roman practices at crossroads seems to be particularly focused on three-way crossroads, sacred to the matron Goddess of magic and the dead, Hekate. To bury something at the crossroads could be seen as giving it to Hekate, or putting the magical working under her special protection. It is Hekate, after all, who allows the entrance and exit of the spirits of the dead from the Underworld. However, Vodou and hoodoo much prefer four-way crossroads, these being not only sacred to several lwa but also symbolic of the intersection between the worlds.

In particular the four-way crossroad can be found in the *veves* (sacred symbols) of the lwa Papa Legba, the Marassa, Maman Brigitte, Met Kalfou and Simbo Andezo. Papa Legba has many "stars" or "roads" (aspects or faces) and is found in every rite of Vodou. He is the opener of the way, and allows for communication between human and divine. He stands at every threshold, and is honoured near the beginning of every Vodou ritual. Without him, the relationship between humans and the lwa just could not manifest. Some say he stands at the crossroads too, but in the house I am initiated in we say it is Papa Legba that stands at the threshold, and his counterpart Met Kalfou who stands at the crossroads. Met Kalfou is, like Legba, often viewed as a trickster, but his actions can often be more malevolent than benevolent, and he is not usually served except by those he walks with and usually as a cursory nod to ensure he does not cause trouble during a service. However, the crossroads appears, nevertheless, upon Papa Legba's veve also:

Fig 1. Veve for Papa Legba.

Note that this is one version out of two commonly seen versions of the veve. Both feature the crossroads prominently.

On the right of the crossroads above we can see Papa Legba's walking stick – also symbolic of the *poteau mitan*, the *axis mundi* of Vodou, a giant pole that features centrally in a *peristyle* (temple), that allows the spirits to travel up and down it to our world. Papa Legba's walking stick, therefore, holds up the universe at its most basic and essential levels. On the left of the crossroads is what looks like a bow: this could be a reference to one of the possible origins of Legba in Africa, where he may have been a solar warrior deity.

The Marassa are the sacred twins of Vodou, containing within them very important aspects of Vodou cosmology and understanding of the role duality plays in the Vodou universe. They are also usually seen as children, served as twins would be – what one gets, the other must get equally. They are also essential parts of every Vodou ritual, and can be found in most rites.[68]

FIG 2. VEVE FOR THE MARASSA.

Note that this is one version amongst a few commonly used versions of their veve.

The veve for the Marassa is particularly interesting as we see not just a single crossroad, but three of them. The Marassa, despite being twins, are often depicted as triplets, and they represent the cosmic principle of creation – when one thing and another thing unite, a third is created. More importantly perhaps, each crossroads in the veve of the Marassa is contained within its own circle.

Simbi Andezo is part of the Congo nation and the Simbi family. Usually seen as a serpent, this Simbi (one of many) lives in the waters that are created when fresh water and saltwater mixes. The Congo nation bridge the divide between the Petro and Rada (hot and cool) rites, and Simbi Andezo is the one that opens the way (like Legba) between the rites. He is thus seen as a messenger – although he does not always walk with somebody or other lwa, he can bring messages from any of the lwa to any human. In this sense he could be seen as the Mercury or Hermes of Vodou. His veve is simple and similar to Legba's:

FIG 3. VEVE FOR SIMBI ANDEZO.

Here, the crossroads features centrally to the figure, surrounded by a circle, set upon a larger crossroads. Simbi Andezo seems, therefore, to be a figure that not only opens the way for the Congo rite, but also for communication between the different nations, families, and rites of lwa.

Finally, the veve of Maman Brigitte has a crossroads beneath a heart (the heart is often found on the veves of female lwa), surrounded by stars, accented with what I can only see as rib bones, ribbons, and a three-headed candlestick. Her veve points to the fact that she walks at night – she is the mother of the dead, of the Ghede lwa, and of the ancestors.

She and Bawon choose from the ancestral waters which souls will become lwa, and she also presides over death rites and cemeteries.

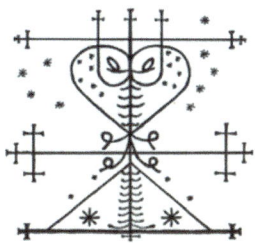

FIG 4. VEVE FOR MAMAN BRIGITTE.

These lwa all share the crossroads symbol upon their sacred image. In the case of Maman Brigitte, this links the crossroad to the spirits of the dead very clearly, but also presents her as the doorway through which new lwa are born, and through which the dead must pass on their way to the ancestral waters. For the other lwa, the crossroads in their veve indicates that it is given to messenger lwa, and to lwa that in some way open the road between the divine realm and human realm, or between the different families of spirits. From the centre of the crossroads the lwa can go anywhere.

Herein lies our clue. Although some traditions hold the crossroads to be a place of confusion (in medieval times, suicides, executed criminals, and suspected witches were often buried at crossroads so they could not find their way back to cause trouble for the living), in Vodou it is a gateway to any part of the universe. You can step into the crossroads through one door, and exit from it through another. And every crossroad is linked to the Great Crossroad. There are crossroads everywhere around us – every intersection or connection in physical and non-physical reality is a crossroads. Thus, when the stones from a Spirit Expedition are placed at a crossroad, they are able to move to any other point in the world, and thus effectively seek out the victim of the spell.

CONCLUSION

Our sorcerer from the beginning of this paper seemed a shady character initially; now, he seems decidedly malevolent! Perhaps we may have been happier with the simple, external view of these necromantic practices? After all, such a simple technique as sending the dead after a victim to send them into madness, or love-madness, or sickness, or even death, on the surface seems almost too simple. The truth is that the spirit expedition, *envoi mort*, and related practices demonstrate a remarkable amount of understanding of the dead, the Underworld/Afterlife, the deities and spirits that rule over them, the nature of suffering, and an idea of the interconnectedness of the universe. Where the Vodou and hoodoo traditions remain quiet on such things, they claim them as their own by their very use of such practices; and the Graeco-Roman sorcerers instead can supply us with the information and context we need to understand the underpinnings of these rites.

Further questions are raised by this examination however, which are best studied separately. These magical rites all use the spirits of the dead – what place do ancestors and our beloved dead hold here? Could they be used for such practices? What makes the difference between angry ghost and benevolent ancestors? It is clear that all the traditions discussed above have within their universe both the existence of ghosts to be used in necromancy, and spirits of our beloved forefathers.

This study is of interest to anybody looking at these practices from an academic perspective; however it is also useful for those wishing to use the techniques themselves: if one does not understand the full extent of the rite one is performing, it can leave one considerably open to error and danger. Thus, forewarned is forearmed, and for those venturing into the cemetery to send out the dead, remember: take coins with you to pay the guardian of the gate; bring some seasonal flowers to lay at the grave; arm yourself with funerary prayers; pack plenty of rum and Florida Water, but don't forget the matches; and for added precaution don't forget to take something with which you can chop bits off a corpse.

Notes

[1] Yronwode, Catherine. *Hoodoo Herb and Root Magic*, pp. 51.

[2] "Ticket Agent" by Curley Weaver. Can be found on the album, "Blind Willie McTell and Curley Weaver, The Post-War Years 1949-1950." BDCD-6014

[3] Ovid, *Metamophoses* VII. 245-251.

[4] A brief study of this is given in d'Este and Rankine, *Hekate: Liminal Rites*, pp. 154-6.

[5] PDM xii. 76-107.

[6] Homer, *Odyssey*, 10.488–540.

[7] Horace, *Satires*, 1.8.

[8] PDM xiv. 428-50. Emphasis mine.

[9] PGM IV. 1390-1495.

[10] Lucan, *Pharsalia* 642.

[11] Lucan, *Pharsalia*, 719.

[12] In PGM LXX. 4-25 the magician is supplied with a list of features of Hekate that if he recites will send away dead spirits that come too close.

[13] PGM IV. 1390-1495.

[14] Lucan, *Pharsalia*, 6.719. Although Lucan's account of this witch is thoroughly bowdlerised and sensationalised, his work yet retains references to several actual magical practices.

[15] Ogden, *Magic, Witchcraft and Ghosts in the Greek and Roman Worlds: A Source Book*, pp. 179.

[16] PGM IV. 296-466, "Wondrous Spell for Binding a Lover."

[17] Homer, *Odyssey* 10.503.

[18] Pinckney, *Blue Roots: African-American Folk Magic of the Gullah People*, pp. 68.

[19] Virgil, *Aeneid* 6.325

[20] Pausanias 1.32.4–5

[21] See C. Faraone, "*Binding and Burying the Forces of Evil: The Defensive Use of 'Voodoo Dolls' in Ancient Greece.*" In Classical Antiquity, Vol. 10, No. 2 (Oct. 1991).

[22] Pinckney, pp. 77.

[23] Pickney, pp. 83.

[24] Taylor, *The Mother of the Lares,* pp. 300-1.

[25] Flaccus, *Censorinus* 3.2. In Hushke, 1889.

[26] Apuleius, *De Deo Socratis*, 15.

[27] Pinckney, pp.95.

[28] PGM IV. 1390-1400.

[29] Psalm 23, King James Bible.

[30] Plato, Phaedo 81c-d.

[31] Hurston, *Tell My Horse*, pp.237-8.

[32] Ibid.

[33] G. Meier. *Die assyrische Beschwörungs Sammlung Maqlû*. Archiv für Orientforschung, Maqlu IV, 29-30.

[34] Originally recorded in Trumpf, J. "*Fluchtafel und Rachepuppe.*" *Mitteilungen des deutschn archäologischen Instituts.* <u>Athenische Abteilung</u>, 73, pp. 94 –102. The inside of the coffin lid simply reads: "*Barburtides, Xophugos, Nicomachos, Oenocles, Mnesimachos, Chamaios, Tesonides, Charisander, Democles, and any other advocate or witness they have on their side.*" Clearly these are names of advocates and witnesses, yet it is Mnesimachos only whose name is found on the accompanying doll. Also found in C. Faraone's survey, "*Binding and Burying the Forces of Evil: The Defensive Use of 'Voodoo Dolls' in Ancient Greece.*" In <u>Classical Antiquity</u>, Vol. 10, No. 2 (Oct. 1991), pp. 201: no. 5. There is also a possibility that the coffin-lead tablet was pierced with nails, since there are two holes in the lid, adding to the symbolism of the victims being bound and stuck down, unable to take action against the magician.

[35] Filan, *The Haitian Vodou Handbook*, pp.186.

[36] PGM XIXa. 1-54.

[37] Apuleius, *Metamorphoses*, 9.30.

[38] PGM XIXb. 4-18.

[39] PDM xiv. 636-69.

[40] Lucan, *Pharsalia* 6.507.

[41] *Keilschrifttexte aus Assur religiosen Inhalts*, no.80, lines 30-3, quoted in M. Thomsen and F. Cryer eds. *Witchcraft and Magic in Europe: Vol. 1 - Biblical and Pagan Societies*, pp. 38.

[42] Trans. R.I. Caplice "*Namburbi Texts in the British Museum IV*", <u>Orientalia</u> 39 (1970) 134-41 no. 40, II. rev 1-4.

[43] R. Daniel and F. Maltomini eds. *Supplementum Magicum*, 49.

[44] Sophocles, *Electra* 4426.

[45] "Spell of Attraction of King Pitys over any skull cup. PGM IV. 1928-2005.

[46] Though it is likely that the practice of burning figurines made to represent somebody was also used by the sorcerer/esses themselves. In a Maqlu inscription we read: "*You have given figurines of me to the Fire god.*" (Maqlu IV, 47, see Meier 1937, 29-30.) This suggests that the method of cursing in some cases (alongside the many other methods described in the same inscription) was to burn the figurine made to represent the victim; and thus the method of burning figurines of the sorcerer/esses to destroy their magic was, literally, "fighting fire with fire"!

[47] Quoted in Daniel Ogden, *Magic, Witchcraft, and Ghosts in the Greek and Roman Worlds: A Source Book*, pp.246.

[48] From Theocritus' "*The Witch*", *Idyll 2*. Quoted in D. Ogden, *Magic, Witchcraft, and Ghosts in the Greek and Roman Worlds: A Source Book,* pp. 109.

[49] *Ibid.*

[50] C. Faraone, *Ancient Greek Love Magic*, pp. 38- 39.

[51] Virgil *Eclogue* 8.64–109, quoted in D. Ogden, *Magic, Witchcraft, and Ghosts in the Greek and Roman Worlds: A Source Book*, pp. 113.

[52] Horace, *Satires* 1.8.

[53] *Ibid.*

[54] C. Faraone, *Ancient Greek Love Magic*, pp. 43-55.

[55] Note here the prescription of a "magnetic stone" that breathes. Lodestones and magnetic filings are a well-known ingredient in many Hoodoo Conjure spells and mojos, particularly to attract something to the magician – usually money or love.

[56] PGM IV. 1416-1419.

[57] R. Daniel and F. Maltomini, *Supplementum Magicum*, 47. Interestingly, in this spell it is a

long-term relationship as well as a sexual one that is envisaged, whereas a lot of erotic-attraction spells focus merely on the short term slaking of lust.

[58] PGM VIII.64-110.

[59] Plato, *Phaedo*, 81c-d.

[60] PGM XII. 365-8.

[61] PDM xii. 50-61.

[62] PDM xiv. 355-65.

[63] Libanius, *Oratio* 1.243-250. Quoted in D. Ogden, *"Magic, Witchcraft, and Ghosts in the Greek and Roman Worlds: A Source Book"* pp. 259.

[64] PDM lxi. 112-27.

[65] In Faraone, "Binding and Burying the Forces of Evil: The Defensive Use of 'Voodoo Dolls' in Ancient Greece." In Classical Antiquity, Vol. 10, No. 2 (Oct. 1991), pp. 202: no. 11.

[66] *Ibid*, no. 12. No. 32 in the survey, an example from Palestine from no later than the first century BCE, is a cache of sixteen figurines that were discovered near a sanctuary to an unknown deity. It is likely they were placed there for similar reasons to those found in the sanctuary of Zeus Hypsistos.

[67] Jerome, *The Life of Saint Hilarion the Hermit*, 21.

[68] For more information on the Marassa, see Huggens, *"Marassa Dossou-Dosa"* in Vs. Duality and Conflict in Magick, Mythology and Paganism. Avalonia Books, 2010.

Bibliography

Apuleius, ed. Lütjohann, Christian. *Apulei Platonici Madaurensis De Deo Socratis Liber.* Nabu Press, 2010.

Apuleius, *Metamorphoses,* trans., Walsh, P.G. Oxford World Classics, 2008.

Betz, Hans Dieter, ed. *The Greek Magical Papyri in Translation, Including the Demotic Spells, vol. 1: Texts.* University of Chigao Press, 1997.

Bonner, Campbell, *"Witchcraft in the Lecture Room of Libanius",* Transactions of the American Philological Association, 63, (1932), pp. 34-44.

Burriss, Eli, Burriss, *Taboo, Magic, Spirits: A Study of Primitive Elements in Roman Religion.* Kessinger Publishing, 2003.

Caplice, R.I. trans., *"Namburbi Texts in the British Museum IV",* Orientalia 39 (1970)

Daniel, R.W., and Maltomini, F., eds. 1990–92. *Supplementum Magicum.* Papyrologica Coloniensia. Vols. 16.1 and 16.2. 2 vols. Cologne.

d'Este, Sorita and Rankine, David. *Hekate: Liminal Rites.* Avalonia Books, 2009.

Dickie, Matthew W., *Magic and Magicians in the Graeco-Roman World.* Routledge, 2001.

Faraone, Christopher A., *"An Accusation of Magic in Classical Athens,"* Transactions of the American Philological Association (1974), Vol. 119. (1989), pp. 146-160.

Faraone, C. *"Binding and Burying the Forces of Evil: The Defensive Use of 'Voodoo Dolls' in Ancient Greece."* In Classical Antiquity, Vol. 10, No. 2 (Oct. 1991).

Faraone, Christoper A., and Obbink, Dirk, eds. *Magika Hiera: Ancient Greek Magic and Religion.* New York: Oxford University Press, 1991.

Faraone, Christopher A., *"The Agonistic Context of Early Greek Binding Spells"* in *Magika Hiera: Ancient Greek Magic and Religion.* Faraone, Christopher A. and Obbink, Dirk, ed., Oxford University Press, 1991, pp. 3-32.

Graf, Fritz, *Magic in the Ancient World*, trans. Phillip, Franklin. Harvard University Press, 1999.
Homer, *Odyssey*, trans. Rieu, E.V. Penguin Classics, 2003.
Horace, *Satires and Epistles*, trans. Jacob Fuchs. W. W. Norton and Co., 1977.
Huggens, Kim., ed. *Vs.: Duality and Conflict in Magick, Mythology and Paganism*. Avalonia Books, 2010.
Huschke, Phillip Edward. *Iurisprudentiae anteiustinianae quae supersunt*. Leipzig, 1889. 4th Ed. (Collection of the fragments of Granius Flaccus.)
Jordan, D.R., H. Montgomery, and E. Thomassen, eds. "*The world of ancient magic.*" Papers from the Norwegian Institute at Athens 4. Bergen, 1999.
Lucan, *Pharsalia (Civil War)*, trans., Braund, Susan H. Oxford Paperbacks, 2008.
Meier, G. *Die assyrische Beschwörungs Sammlung Maqlû*. Archiv für Orientforschung, beiheft 2. Berlin, 1937.
Luck, Georg, *Ancient Pathways and Hidden Pursuits: Religion, Morals, and Magic in the Ancient World*. Ann Arbor: The University of Michigan Press, 2003.
Luck, Georg, *Arcana Mundi*. John Hopkins University Press, 1985.
Meiggs, R., and Lewis D., eds., *A selection of Greek historical inscriptions to the end of the fifth century B.C.* Oxford, 1969.
Ogden, Daniel. *Magic, Witchcraft and Ghosts in the Greek and Roman Worlds: A Source Book*. Oxford University Press, 2002.
Ovid, *Metamorphoses*, trans. Melville, A.D. Oxford University Press, 1996.
Pinckney, Roger. Blue Roots: African-American Folk Magic of the Gullah People. Llewellyn Publications, 1998.
Plassart, A., "*Les sanctuaries et les cultes du mont Cyrene*", Exploration Archéologique de Délos 11. Paris, 1928.
Plato, *The Laws*, trans. Saunders, Trevor J. London: Penguin Classics, 2005.
Plato, *Phaedo*. Oxford World Classics, 2009.
Sophocles, *Electra and Other Plays*, trans., Raeburn, David. Penguin Classics, 2008.
Taylor, Lilly Ross, *The Mother of the Lares*, American Journal of Archaeology, Vol. 29, 3, (July - Sept. 1925), 299 - 313.
Strubbe, J.H.M. "Cursed be he that moves my bones" in Faraone, C. and Obbink, Dirk, eds. *Magika Hiera: Ancient Greek magic and religion*, pp. 33-59. New York: Oxford University Press, 1991.
Thomsen, Marie-Louise, and Cryer, Frederik eds., *Witchcraft and Magic in Europe: Vol. 1 - Biblical and Pagan Societies*. London: Athlone Press, 2001.
Trumpf, J. "Fluchtafel und Rachepuppe." Mitteilungen des deutschn archäologischen Instituts. Athenische Abteiliung, 73, pp. 94 –102.
 Yronwode, Catherine. *Hoodoo Herb and Root Magic*. Lucky Mojo Curio Company, 2002.

IO AGIOS HEKATE

ADVERTISEMENTS

GUIDES TO THE UNDERWORLD

Hadean's collection of pamphlets for the discerning reader, including the Spirit Work Series, an introduction to working with spirits, particularly those of the True Grimoire.

WWW.HADEANPRESS.COM

THE SAINT MARTHA BOTANICA

HOME TO THE OCCULT CONSULTANCY

TRADITIONAL HOODOO AND CONJURE, TAROT READINGS AND MAGICAL SERVICES

WWW.THEOCCULTCONSULTANCY.COM

UNDERWORLD APOTHECARY

The Underworld Apothecary makes available materials for magical praxis through a combination of New and Old World formulary skills and traditional magical experience. Herbs are gathered and prepared in accord with traditional timing and using the best available materials and all incense is graded.

Jake Stratton-Kent and Madame Misha have united their talents and vision to produce a unique formulary, emphasising quality, tradition and magical power.

WWW.UNDERWORLD-APOTHECARY.COM

SCARLET IMPRINT
TALISMANIC PUBLISHERS

THE TRUE GRIMOIRE
by Jake Stratton-Kent

The True Grimoire is a major contribution to the practice and study of Goetic magic. The neglected Grimorium Verum has been restored to its rightful place as a potent and coherent system of Goetic magic. As a practicing Necromancer with 37 years of experience Jake Stratton-Kent's *True Grimoire* is a clear exposition of how to contact and build a relationship with the spirits. Copiously illustrated with characters, sigils, magic squares, diagrams and pontos riscados.

www.scarletimprint.com

WWW.SCARLETIMPRINT.COM

Midian Books

Rare, secondhand and selected new books on occult subjects.

Midian Books
112 Hartshorne Road, Woodville
Swadlincote, Derbyshire
DE11 7HY
England

www.midianbooks.co.uk
j.davies@midianbooks.co.uk

Witchcraft Paganism & Folklore

The Cauldron is a non-profit-making, independent, privately published magazine featuring serious and in-depth articles on Traditional Witchcraft, Wicca, Ancient and Modern Paganism, Magic and Folklore. Published quarterly in February, May, August and November since 1976 and is written for adults.
Visit www.the-cauldron.org.uk for more information and subscription rates.

KEEP BRITAIN PAGAN!

www.ingramcontent.com/pod-product-compliance
Lightning Source LLC
Chambersburg PA
CBHW041514220426

43668CB00002B/19